The Line of Forts

The Line of Forts

*Historical Archaeology on the
Colonial Frontier of Massachusetts*

ε◖ *Michael D. Coe*

University Press of New England   •   HANOVER AND LONDON

Published by University Press of New England,
One Court Street, Lebanon, NH 03766
www.upne.com
© 2006 by University Press of New England
Printed in the United States of America

5   4   3   2   1

Library of Congress Cataloging-in-Publication Data
Coe, Michael D.
The line of forts : historical archaeology on the colonial frontier of Massachusetts / Michael D. Coe.
   p.   cm.
Includes bibliographical references and index.
ISBN-10: 1–58465–542–9 (paperback : alk. paper)
ISBN-13: 978–58465–542–8 (paperback : alk. paper)
1. Massachusetts—Antiquities. 2. Fortification—Massachusetts. 3. Historic sites—Massachusetts. 4. Archaeology and history—Massachusetts. 5. Massachusetts—History, Military—18th century. 6. Massachusetts—History—Colonial period, ca. 1600–1775. 7. Frontier and pioneer life—Massachusetts. 8. Massachusetts—Ethnic relations. 9. British—Massachusetts—History—18th century. 10. Indians of North America—Massachusetts—History—18th century. I. Title.
F66.C64   2006
974.4′01—dc22   2006000144

Contents

Preface

During the mid–eighteenth century, a Line of Forts was constructed along the northwest boundary of Massachusetts as a defense against the French and their Indian allies. Of the three major forts in the line, one, Fort Massachusetts, is irremediably buried beneath a parking lot in the town of North Adams and is lost forever to history and archaeology. The present study reports excavations that were undertaken at two of these garrisons, Fort Shirley in the town of Heath, and Fort Pelham in Rowe.

I am a culture historian, and my hope is that this report will be a contribution both to the knowledge of British America during the mid-eighteenth century and to the history of the northeast Berkshires where these forts were built. My own interest in the area began in 1970 when my late wife, Sophie, and I purchased a hilltop farm in Heath. I soon learned that the local people took great pride in Fort Shirley; while hardly any traces remained of the structure itself, the site had been donated at the beginning of the last century to the newly formed Heath Historical Society, and timbers said to be from the fort had been lovingly preserved in several houses and barns.

Although I am primarily a Mesoamericanist, I have long been interested in historical archaeology and had taught a senior seminar in the subject at Yale that further whetted my taste for research that combined digging with documents. In Heath, our friend the late Reverend William Wolf was the leading local enthusiast for Fort Shirley, and he agreed with my wish to dig Shirley. Permission to carry out an archaeological project there was granted in 1972 by the Heath Historical Society, but it was not until the summer of 1974 that the project actually got under way.

Meanwhile, to my considerable surprise, I learned in 1972 that Dr. Daniel Ingersoll, then of the University of Massachusetts, had been excavating the site of Fort Pelham, only five miles west in the neighboring town of Rowe, during that summer and in the previous year. I visited his team several times, and carried on fruitful discussions with him. When Dr. Ingersoll subsequently resigned from the university, he and the Rowe Historical Society kindly turned over to me all of his notes, plans, and artifacts for publication.

I am painfully aware that I was then a neophyte in the field of military archaeology. A lifetime spent as an anthropological archaeologist in Latin America will not train one to recognize important features of a fortification, features that any practiced military historian could pick out at a glance, or at any rate predict accurately. I had to learn as I went along. I am also aware that while perhaps as much as 80 percent of the main part of Fort Pelham was exposed, we only managed to dig about 20 to 30 percent of Fort Shirley during one summer's work (of course, we could have done more had we not been so hampered by rains and waterlogged soil conditions). Thus, what is said in this report about the site of Pelham is considerably more reliable than what is said about Shirley.

Two circumstances combine to make these two forts more important to the study of eighteenth-century life in the American colonies than their very modest size would warrant. First, their period of occupation was extremely short, having been built in 1744 and abandoned in 1754; there never was any subsequent occupation, nor was there an earlier one. Like shipwrecks, they are single component sites, and those components are of very brief duration—a mere blinking of an eye in archaeological terms. The artifact inventory of the forts should thus serve as a chronological datum line in the analysis of the material culture of British America. In this respect, Pelham and Shirley are comparable to the British fort at Frederica, on Saint Rimons Island, Georgia, which was occupied from 1735 to 1749,[1] and to the somewhat later Fort Ligonier in Pennsylvania.[2]

Second, the Line of Forts is abundantly documented. The Williams family of western Massachusetts virtually controlled most of the colony from the Connecticut River valley west to the New York line, and it was they who provided the leading officers of the forts and ran the commissary system that supplied them. Important Williams archives are in the Massachusetts Historical Society, in the Memorial Libraries of Deerfield, and in Williams College (founded by a legacy left by Ephraim Williams, Jr., onetime commanding officer of the Line of Forts). Many of the most important data were gathered by Arthur Latham Perry and published by him in 1904 in his *Origins in Williamstown*. Among the surviving letters, receipts, orders, and so forth are fairly complete muster rolls for the militia who manned the forts.

A few years after the dig at Fort Shirley, David Proper of the Pocumtuck Valley Memorial Association (PVMA) drew my attention to some remarkable eighteenth-century account books in the PVMA's collections. These belonged to Elijah Williams, commissary to the forts and longtime storekeeper in Deerfield, and to Joseph Barnard, who also owned a store in that frontier town. One other "day book" was located in the Smith College Library. Almost every soldier in the Line of Forts could be found making purchases from these merchants, and the total number of transactions for the ten-year period amounted in the thousands: these books were, in fact, a wonderful window into the material culture and mass consumerism that characterized British America at this time. I began a large-scale computer analysis of these twelve ledgers that extended over five years, but that was never completed. Perhaps some day it will be.

I am deeply indebted to the officers and membership of the Heath Historical Society and of the Rowe Historical Society for making this study possible. In particular, the late Helen McCarthy of the latter group expedited all phases of the work. Arthur P. Silvester, then the superintendent of schools for Franklin County, kindly allowed me use of a room in the Rowe Elementary School as a field laboratory.

Jack Kloppenburg, then a student at Yale and now professor of rural sociology at the University of Wisconsin–Madison, acted as field supervisor during the 1974 season at Fort Shirley, and William K. MacDonald of the University of Massachusetts acted in the same capacity at Fort Pelham in 1970 and 1971. The excavators at Pelham were all students enrolled in a summer field course; those at Shirley were all volunteers, including students from Yale, Brown, and the University of Massachusetts, along with archaeological enthusiasts from Heath and nearby towns in Franklin County. My thanks to all.

I must acknowledge the important contribution of Dr. Joanne Bowen, now of the College of William and Mary, who provided the in-depth analyses of faunal remains from Fort Pelham and military foodways; these analyses are included as appendix 1. Dr. David Starbuck not only identified the seeds recovered by flotation from both sites, but has also acted for a number of years as my cicerone and friend through the world of colonial American military archaeology. The late Dr. B. Francis Kukachka of the U.S. Department of Agriculture's Forest Products Laboratory, in Madison, Wisconsin, identified wood and charcoal specimens: and Dr. Margaret B. Davis of the University of Minnesota, pollen and spores.

Dr. Kevin M. Sweeney, now professor of history and American studies at Amherst College, gave much appreciated information and advice on the River Gods of western Massachusetts, on whom he is the acknowledged authority.

Artifact drawings are by Diane G. Peck; all other drawings and plans are by David Peck or myself. Mrs. Cornelia Marsh graciously allowed me to publish the portrait of her distinguished ancestor Governor William Shirley, who plays such an important role in these pages.

On the documentary side, I am grateful to Stephen T. Riley, librarian of the Massachusetts Historical Society, for granting me access to the Israel Williams Papers; to the personnel of the Berkshire Athenaeum in Pittsfield, Massachusetts, for searching in the William Williams Collection for papers relating to the Line of Forts; and above all, to the PVMA's Dr. David Proper for allowing me to microfilm all of the Williams and Barnard account books. These are now housed in the PVMA Library in Deerfield.

NOTES

1. Mauncy 1962.
2. Grimm 1970.

The Line of Forts

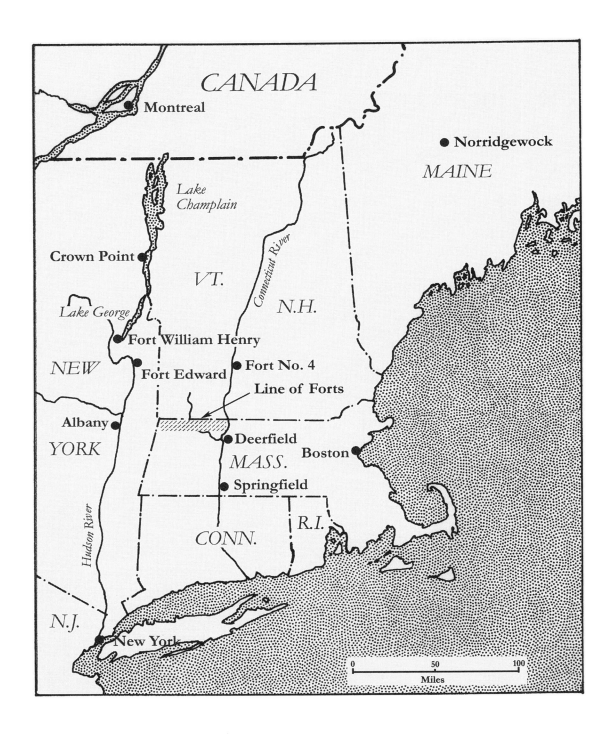

Chapter 1

Introduction

*T*HIS BOOK IS an account of how the English-speaking inhabitants of a remote part of New England, itself but a part of a larger British America, reacted to a very large threat to their very existence. Our story is laid geographically in the northwest frontier of Massachusetts, and is confined in time largely to the years between 1744 and 1763. On this small stage was enacted a scene of far wider drama, namely, the struggle between England and France for North America. But there were other parts to the play, such as the final standoff between New England's English settlers and the Indians, the ideological conflict between Calvinistic Protestantism and Roman Catholicism, and even the occasional frictions between colonial militia and the British regular army (a situation dramatized in Fenimore Cooper's *Last of the Mohicans*).

In many respects, this struggle was but one aspect of what can arguably be thought of as the planet's first world war, a vast enterprise that involved not only the English and French, but also the Prussians, Austrians, Spanish, and Native Americans, and that was carried on in both Americas, in Europe, and in India. The initial phase of the conflict in North America is sometimes called King George's War, and lasted from 1744 to the Treaty of Aix-la-Chapelle in 1748. The second phase is known to Europeans as the Seven Years' War, extending from 1755 to the Treaty of Paris in 1763, when all of French Canada save two tiny islands was ceded to the British. Both phases are sometimes confusingly grouped in American minds as the French and Indian Wars. Like World War I and World War II, this enterprise was essentially a single war, divided by a period of unstable peace.

This conflict and the Korean War of 1950–1953 are unjustly dismissed in the public conscience as America's "forgotten wars" (even though they were far more significant than, say, the Spanish-American War or even the Vietnam War); the first assured that the future United States would be English-speaking under the rule of the common law, while the second essentially saved Europe and Asia from Stalin's imperial schemes.

Most of my story concerns Fort Shirley and Fort Pelham, two modestly sized strongholds in a Line of Forts that extended from the Connecticut

FIG. 1-1. Portrait by Thomas Hudson of Massachusetts Governor William Shirley, the most able administrator in colonial America. It was he who ordered the building of the Line of Forts.
Courtesy National Portrait Gallery, Smithsonian Institution.

Valley on the east, westerly in a line just south of the Massachusetts border (then with New Hampshire), and over to the Dutch settlements east of the Hudson River. It was a scheme of defense against the French and Indian enemy planned by the royal governor, William Shirley (fig. 1-1), in conjunction with his political allies.

Governor Shirley was an unusual man. During his term of office, he was the channel for the flow of patronage and support from Parliament and from the duke of Newcastle, his patron in London; from Shirley to the powerful elite; and from these latter down the chain of command and influence to the "gentlemen" and yeomen farmers of the frontier. As Fred Anderson summed up the position and role of Shirley:

> While Shirley, like all royal governors, enjoyed enormous formal powers within the province, his real power to govern depended instead on his ability to distribute patronage among his followers in the provincial legislature. In

times of peace his patronage resources were simply too slender to ensure him anything like a majority in the Massachusetts General Court. War, however, brought a rich harvest of military commissions, supply and clothing contracts, credit, and hard cash. With these assets and the sense of common purpose war engendered, Shirley could create a truly effective network of supporters in the political and commercial elites of the province. Thus it was in his own interest as much as the king's that the governor became the most accomplished projector of schemes in eighteenth-century North America. Although he had been trained as a lawyer and possessed no formal military background, Shirley proved to be as adept and resourceful a strategist as he was a politician.[1]

No less a person than George Washington said this about him in 1755: "I have had the honor to be introduced to ... Mr. Shirley, whose character and appearance has perfectly charmed me, as I think every word and every action discovers the gentleman and great politician."[2]

The River Gods

During the mid–eighteenth century, the entire province west of the Connecticut River was in the hands of six elite families (fig. 1-2), collectively known to their detractors in Boston as "the River Gods."[3] These great landowners effectively controlled all political, mercantile, religious, juridical, medical, and military affairs of their domain. Consider the powerful and ubiquitous Williams family, the very creators and maintainers of the Line of Forts. Colonel Israel Williams of Hatfield was in overall charge of military matters in western Massachusetts. If you were stationed in any one of these forts, his nephew Ephraim Williams, Jr., or Ephraim's cousin William Williams was your commander. If you needed to buy something in Deerfield, the item in question was sold to you by the leading storekeeper, Elijah Williams; if you ended up in court, this same Elijah was the justice of the peace. When you attended Sabbath in Deerfield's meetinghouse, the Reverend Jonathan Ashley (a Williams brother-in-law) was the minister. If you needed a nostrum or a bleeding, Ephraim, Jr.'s brother Thomas was your medical man, either in the Line of Forts or in Deerfield. Writing a century ago, the historian Arthur L. Perry summed them up: "The Williams family, as such, were aristocratic in their tendencies, in their intermarriages with other families, in their political opinion strongly inclined to monarchy, and in their social instincts and practices haughty, even if not positively unjust towards the masses of man."[4] A more recent observer says of them: "Wealthy, proud, headstrong, they were as likely a collection of political oligarchs as were to be found in Massachusetts."[5]

The River Gods virtually amounted to a caste rather than a mere upper class; they were bound to one another with marriage alliances and seldom

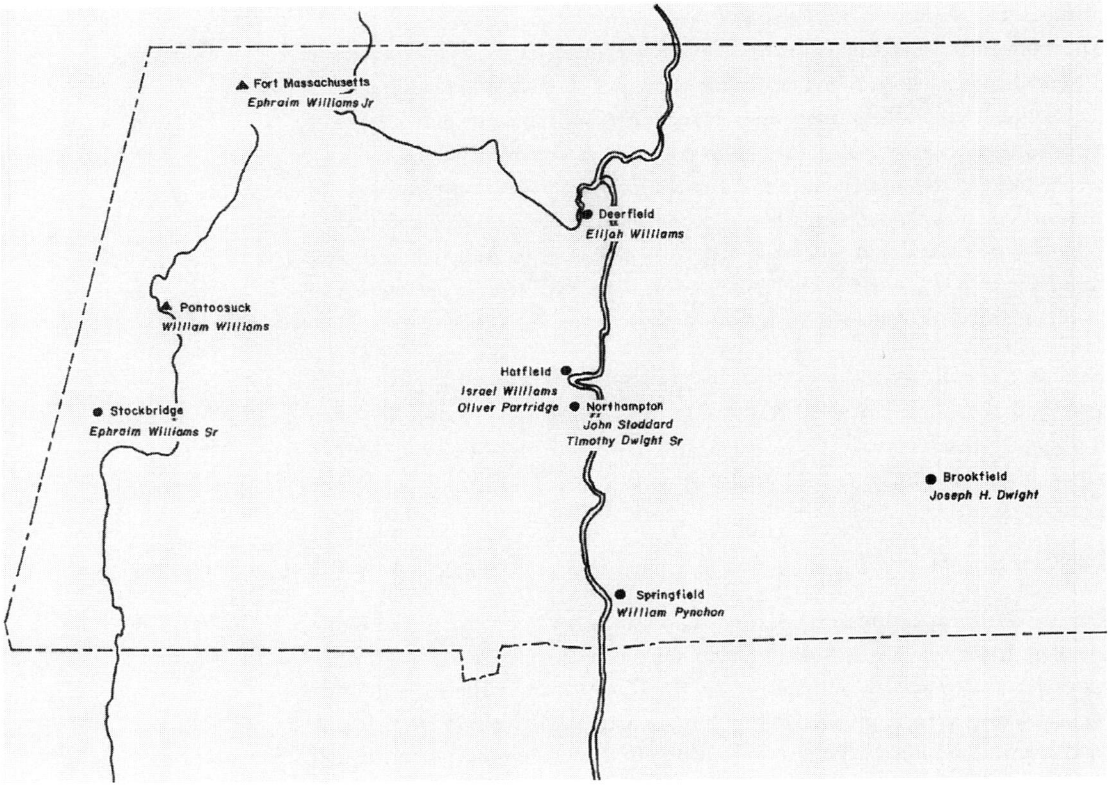

FIG. 1-2. Map of western Massachusetts, with the location of the principal "River Gods" who controlled the destiny of this part of New England. These include the powerful Williams family.

if ever married out of their class. Their sons went to Harvard and Yale, and were always listed in the top third of their respective classes in an age when the listing was not on the basis of academic performance but on that of perceived social rank. Like many other wealthy families in Massachusetts (until the institution lost its legal standing in 1781), they were owners of black slaves. As an example, one surviving bill of sale reads:

> For and in consideration of the sum of two hundred and twenty-five pounds Old Tenor to me Ephraim Williams Jr. well and truly paid, by Israel Williams Esq., of Hatfield, I do hereby assign, sell & convey to him a certain negro boy named Prince, aged about 9 years a servant for life, to hold to him, his heirs, ag^t ye Claims of any person whatsoever, as witness my hand this 25th day of September Anno Domi 1750

> Ephraim Williams Jr.[6]

Lest it be thought that the Puritan religion was any obstacle to slave-holding, the Reverend Ashley owned three slaves, whom he set to work (for a price) in the fields of his trading partners; Ashley also took it upon himself to preach in favor of the institution.[7]

There can be no question that the Williamses and other River Gods had real aptitude in military matters, and that Shirley was wise to place frontier defense in their hands. They were generally liked by the officers and militiamen under their command, far more so than were the strict, often brutal, British regular army officers in whose hands they found themselves during the 1755–1762 campaigns in New York and Canada. Elitist they may have been, but they were also democratic in a way that was absolutely unknown to the aristocracy of the old country.

The Forts

The Line of Forts (see appendix 3 and fig. 3-4) began in the east among settlements in the Connecticut Valley (Northfield and Fall Town), and ran west to West Hoosuck (now Williamstown), a straight-line distance of about 38 miles, but over the extremely rough terrain of the northern Berkshires. Beyond West Hoosuck were the fortified farmhouses and settlements of the Hudson Valley Dutch. Most of the Massachusetts forts were between three and six miles south of the northern border of the province.

The exact number of forts in the line is difficult to ascertain, as many of the structures so designated in the documents and histories were little more than fortified houses, usually palisaded, while others were more formal blockhouses built by provincial soldiers; in the latter category were Fort Shirley (in modern Heath), the first headquarters for the Line; Fort Pelham (in Rowe); Fort Massachusetts in East Hoosuck (now North Adams), the next headquarters; and the fort in West Hoosuck (now Williamstown). All construction in them was timber, with no masonry beyond chimneys and chimney bases, and no earthworks.

Only two of these forts—Shirley and Pelham—have ever been formally excavated, and it is these excavations that are presented in this report. Sadly, Fort Massachusetts is now lost to archaeological science, having been buried some decades ago by the buildings and parking lot of a Price Chopper supermarket.

The Documents

The sheer volume of documents relating to the Line of Forts, to the northwestern frontier of the colony, and to the principal figures involved in its defense is staggering. As will be seen, there are fairly complete muster rolls for the forts, numerous military orders from River Gods such as Israel

Williams, correspondence, and a vital set of account books maintained by a Williams storekeeper in Deerfield who was also subcommissary for the Line. The main reason why we have these papers today is that the powerful Williams family that produced them managed to survive the vicissitudes of the American Revolution and the early republic, although their influence was much diminished.

These documents provide a unique window into the mid-eighteenth century on the Massachusetts frontier, and a means of interpreting what we found on the ground in the remains of the forts. This was an age of consumerism, not of self-sufficiency, and the British colonial system was there to ensure that little was produced at home, but much bought from the mother country. As Baugher and Venables have said in their study of eighteenth-century ceramics: "The colonial ties to England were not just cultural and spiritual—they were also economic. British goods were not just fashion, they were often "the only." The British empire was organized so that the 2.6 million colonists supplied raw materials to, and consumed the finished products of, the 8 million who lived in the British Isles."[8] We shall see how true this statement was, even for the occupants of two small, palisaded blockhouses in the remote New England wilderness.

NOTES

1. Anderson 1984:8.
2. Schutz 1961:196.
3. See Zemsky 1971 and Sweeney 1982 for a full coverage of this subject.
4. Perry 1904:485.
5. Zemsky 1969:509.
6. Sheldon 1893:58.
7. Sheldon 1893:57–58. See Jonathan Ashley's account book, at http://memorialhall.mass.edu/collection.
8. Baugher and Venables 1987:35.

Chapter 2

The Natural Setting

Geology and Landscape

*T*HE STRUGGLE between the English settlers and their French and Indian foes was in part determined by the nature of the landscape of New England and eastern New York. An inescapable fact is that the mountain systems of westernmost New England were a natural barrier to east-west travel, and that the great river systems (such as the Connecticut) and their valleys run in a north to south direction. Thus, the New Englanders faced great impediments in extending their influence and populations westward into the Berkshires, and beyond. On the other hand, it was relatively easy for the hostile Indians, led by their French officers, to carry out raids from their Canadian bases against the English settlements in the Connecticut and Hudson valleys.

Geologically speaking, the Berkshire Hills of western Massachusetts are closely related to the Green Mountains of Vermont.[1] Both are part of a large upfold extending from central Pennsylvania, through southern New York and western New England, well into Canada. Although the mountains are less spectacular, the Berkshires are only slightly lower than the Green Mountains, and actually present a more formidable obstacle to east-west travel. The reason is that the Berkshires represent a profoundly dissected upland plain, with deeply cut valleys and precipitous slopes. For example, along the Mohawk Trail (present-day Route 2) there is a drop of about 1,000 feet (about 300 meters) from the western escarpment of the Berkshires down to North Adams and the Hoosic River valley.

The rocks of the Berkshires and the Green Mountains are very ancient, consisting of Precambrian metamorphics between 700 and 1,000 million years old, and metamorphic schists and gneisses ranging from 250 to 600 million years old. In Rowe, Fort Pelham is underlain by schists of Ordovician date (the Hopetown Formation), and Fort Shirley in Heath by somewhat younger Silurian schists (the Goshen Formation); folding generally runs from northeast to southwest.[2]

Like the rest of New England, the Berkshires were subject to intensive glaciation during the Pleistocene, and the entire area is overlain by glacial till, except on eroded surfaces where natural outcrops (locally called "ledge") protrude. On this till have developed acid to highly acid soils, often full of rock, derived from schists, gneisses, or siliceous limestone.[3] The profusion of field walls in every part of the Berkshires—often in deep, second-growth forests—is ample testimony to the backbreaking struggle of the pioneer settlers to clear this land of unwanted field stones and "ledge" rock. In the region of Fort Shirley and Fort Pelham, the soil is loamy and probably fairly fertile, but bedrock lies within 18 inches (45 cm) of the surface at the latter site. Fort Shirley is cursed with an almost impermeable, clay hardpan at generally less than 2.5 feet (91 cm) from the surface, with the result that seepage from higher areas flows on top of the hardpan, causing waterlogged conditions during the spring and for much of the summer.

After dropping down from the Berkshire escarpment, an early traveler heading west to the valley of the Hudson would have had to face one more barrier: the Taconic Range. In contrast to the unbroken mass of the Berkshires, the Taconics (which contain Massachusetts's highest mountain, Mount Greylock) are cut into peaks and valleys, and there is easy passage through several river systems. One such access route is the Hoosic River, which flows by the now desecrated site of the most important stronghold in the Line of Forts, Fort Massachusetts.

On the east, the northern Berkshires descend relatively gently through rolling foothills into the broad Connecticut Valley (fig. 2-1). In those foothills, elevations are generally less than 600 feet, and winter conditions are not so severe as they are in the higher townships like Heath, Rowe, Hawley, or Florida. The valley itself is another world, with a totally different geology, climate, biota, and perhaps even cultural outlook than the Berkshire uplands. Produced over red Triassic sandstone, the valley's soils are rich enough for highly successful corn and tobacco agriculture, carried out today on a large scale.[4] It is small wonder that Indians once contended with Indians, and Englishmen with Indians, for control over these fertile lands.

Thus, the history of the Line of Forts has unfolded in not one, but four landscapes: the Connecticut Valley, the Berkshire uplands, the Hoosic River valley, and the Taconics.

Climate

Summers in the northern Berkshires are all too brief, and winters are severe and long. Because the last killing frost in Heath and Rowe can occur as late as the end of May (and, rarely, even in the first week of June), and the first frost as early as 15 September, the growing season is relatively short: 105 to

110 days. In low-lying areas, where nighttime frosts tend to settle, the season may be even shorter.

There is no alternation of dry and rainy seasons here. Precipitation records kept in Heath show that total annual rainfall averages 50 inches (1,270 mm), evenly distributed through all twelve months.[5] With this kind of pattern, wells seldom dry up in summertime, and crop failure due to drought is unknown.

The winters can only be described as rigorous, with temperatures that can go as low as −18°F (−7.8°C) in Heath, and much lower at higher elevations, such as in the town with the unlikely name of Florida. The winter weather fronts generally come in from the west and Great Lakes regions, with a steady pattern of lows followed by highs at weekly intervals. Snowfall is heavy, usually beginning in November and persisting through March; major snowstorms are not unknown for early April and even May. In Heath, the average annual snowfall is 80.3 inches (2,040 mm), and there is an average of 25 days in the year with a snowfall of one inch or more.[6] Strong winds often pile up this snow in great drifts, blocking roads and trails; in early days, they must have been a significant impediment to foot travel, unless snowshoes were employed. When the surveyor Richard Hazen (or Hazzen) crossed these hills in early April 1741, his party had to force their way through snow three feet deep, and on 2 April 1757 Lieutenant John Hawks

FIG. 2-1. View of the northern Berkshires, looking north toward the Deerfield Valley from Florida, Massachusetts.

and two companions measured snow 4 feet 8 inches deep in Colrain (see appendix 5).[7]

Summer sees a different weather pattern, when long periods of relatively high temperatures and afternoon thunderstorms result from stalled high pressure systems (Bermuda Highs) off the New England coast; these systems draw warm, moist air off the Atlantic and the Gulf of Mexico. Although generally cooler than southern or eastern New England, temperatures in the northern Berkshires have been known to go as high as 97°F (36°C). Hurricanes occasionally have wrought great destruction in the forests, particularly the great one of 1938. However, the only hurricanes known for earlier times in New England occurred in 1638 and 1815; massive tropical storms on this scale were apparently unknown during the eighteenth century.

Flora

Today, the landscape of the northern Berkshires looks more like that seen by the first English settlers than at any time since the beginning of the nineteenth century, when broad-scale clearing of woodlands began. From 1800 until the first decade of this century, much of this region, now largely covered with second-growth forest, was farmland and sheep pasture; but now, much of it looks like wilderness, only the stone walls buried in the forest standing as mute testimony to another way of life.

The varied assemblages of trees characterizing the Berkshires are classified as "northern hardwood forest."[8] There is every reason to believe from wood and pollen samples collected in the Shirley and Pelham excavations (appendix 2) that this was the prevalent forest type during the French and Indian War. Most prominent among the hardwoods in this association are American beech (*Fagus grandifolia*), sugar maple (*Acer saccharum*), red oak (*Quercus rubra*), white ash (*Fraxinus americana*), American white birch (*Betula papyrifera*), gray birch (*Betula populifolia*), and yellow birch (*Betula lutea*). The eastern hemlock (*Tsuga canadensis*) occurs almost everywhere, and there are large stands of white pine (*Pinus strobus*), valuable to early settlers as a source of building material. Having fallen victim to the great blight that began about 1900, the once common American chestnut (*Castanea dentata*) has disappeared from these hills.

Of course, this is now all secondary forest, the last tract of primeval, hardwood forest in New England having been destroyed by the 1938 hurricane. What did the forest look like to the New Englanders of the mid–eighteenth century, and to their Native American predecessors? Some idea of the immense size of the primeval forest can be gained from a tract in Colebrook, Connecticut, that was cut to the ground in 1913.[9] This tract had trees up to 110 feet (33.5 m) in height, with trunks more than 3 feet (91 cm) in diameter, some of which were more than 350 years old. More than half the trees were eastern hemlock and American beech, with smaller percentages of yellow birch, sugar maple, red oak, and other species. On the forest floor grew shade-tolerant shrubs like mountain laurel (*Kalmia latifolia*), as well as ferns. Another tract that has been studied was the one on Mount Pisgah, in southwestern New Hampshire, prior to its destruction in 1938. It had white pine up to 150 feet (45.7 m) in height, with trunks up to 4 feet (122 cm) in diameter; this was the most common species in the stand, along with eastern hemlock. In colonial days, such pines were reserved for the masts and spars of the Royal Navy. The hardwoods on Mount Pisgah included red oak, American beech, black birch (*Betula lenta*), American white birch, and maple, in that order of abundance. Some of the hemlocks were 450 years old, and the white pines and hardwoods about 250 years old.

This, then, was something like the forest cover that had to be tackled by the men in the Line of Forts. Once cleared for cultivation or pasture and then abandoned, the northern Berkshires offer a fairly uniform succession. Old pastureland often goes into conifers and yews. In Heath, among the first plants to pioneer old fields (whether farmland or pasture) are prickly brambles (*Rubus* spp.), which provide much-prized berries, and hawthorns (*Crataegus* spp.); soon appear white pine, cherries (*Prunus* spp.), sugar maple, various birches, and poplars (*Populus* spp.). By the time two or three decades have passed, it is difficult to realize that this had once been cleared land; the forest now provides a canopy of shade, beneath which grow ferns, club mosses (*Lycopodium* spp.), and other shade-loving plants such as Indian pipe (*Monotropa uniflora*) and various orchids.

The most valuable tree in the northern Berkshires and adjacent Vermont is undoubtedly the sugar maple. From early March on, when daytime thaws alternate with nighttime freezing, the maple sap starts to flow. The 1756–57 journal of John Hawks (appendix 5) shows that the men in the Line of Forts went "a shugerin" at that time, as the local farmers do today.

Fauna

Many of the larger and more conspicuous game animals in the Connecticut Valley must have been exterminated at an early date by the English settlers. In the Berkshire Hills to the west, during the great land clearance of the first half of the nineteenth century, a similar devastation of the fauna took place; however, with the return of the forest to the hills, game is now abundant, and must have been similarly plentiful in the mid–eighteenth century, at least prior to the peace of 1763. Seasoned hunters like Aaron Denio were able to supply quantities of wild meat and pelts to the stores in Deerfield (and presumably to the forts, as well).

During the period of conflict that we know of as the French and Indian War (or Wars), the entire area of northwest Massachusetts and what is now southern Vermont was truly a war zone, a highly dangerous frontier between hostile forces—the English settlers to the south and the French and Indians to the north—bent on killing as many of their foes as possible. Harvard anthropologist Richard Wrangham has recently argued that such zones—like the Demilitarized Zone (DMZ) between the two Koreas—are usually extraordinarily high in game species, as they are entered never at all or with great trepidation even by seasoned warriors.[10] He calls such regions "game sinks." It is thus no surprise to find wolf skins and marten pelts often being offered for credit in Elijah Williams's Deerfield store.

The most common of the larger game animals in the northern Berkshires is now the white-tailed deer (*Odocoileus virginianus*), and it was probably prevalent in the area of the forts during the period that the Line of Forts was occupied. Equally conspicuous among the local fauna is the black bear (*Ursus americanus*), now no longer a rarity and considered a delicacy by local hunters. Other mammals locally shot and/or trapped for food are the raccoon (*Procyon lotor*), a serious threat to plantings of sweet corn; the red squirrel (*Tamasciurus hudsonicus*); the eastern gray squirrel (*Sciurus carolinensis*); and the woodchuck (*Marmota monax*), another garden pest. Identifiable by its eery nocturnal screaming, the bobcat (*Felis rufa*) is trapped for its valuable pelt, as is the red fox (*Vulpes fulva*), a familiar animal of open pastures. Although now protected, certain other species would have been sought for their furs, such as the beaver (*Castor canadensis*, from an ecological viewpoint probably the most important mammal of the area through its alteration of streamside forests into water meadows and swamps); and the river otter (*Lutra canadensis*), still to be seen along some of the larger streams and rivers of the hill country.

Before its extermination by the New England settlers, the gray wolf would have roamed these hills, but it has been extinct in all but northernmost New England since the mid–nineteenth century. When still prevalent in Vermont, it was said to have been a savage predator on sheep, calves, dogs, and other domestic animals; in the forest, however, it preyed upon deer, foxes, and other wild creatures.[11] The account book of Elijah Williams, Deerfield storekeeper and commissary to the Line of Forts, has a number of entries showing credit given for wolf pelts, as well as those of bobcats.[12] Within the past quarter-century, the eastern coyote (*Canis latrans*) has built up large populations in the northern Berkshires, but it is still unclear whether this area was part of its original range, or whether there has been a recent incursion from the west or from Canada.

Tradition has it that there were more than a few puma (*Felis concolor*), locally called "catamounts," in this area during the early days of settlement. There is a Catamount Hill lying four miles (6.6 km) southeast of Fort Shirley, in the town of Colrain; and two men are reported to have killed a "cata-mount" on Mount Massaemet, just east of Shelburne Falls, in October 1849. The moose (*Alces alces*) is another animal that had been wiped out in most of New England by 1850, but it was probably present a century earlier in the Berkshire forests; like the coyote, it has been expanding its range south-ward in recent decades, and frequent sightings have been made in Heath and other towns of northwestern Massachusetts. One mammal now found nowhere south of far northern New England is the marten (*Martes ameri-cana*), yet it was surely in the area of the Line of Forts: its bones have been unearthed at Fort Pelham (appendix 1), and Elijah Williams gave credit at his store for marten furs.

Of the approximately 110 species of birds that have been identified in the northern Berkshires, only a few are of concern to humans. The ruffed grouse (*Bonasa umbellus*), a year-round resident, abounds in second-growth thickets; Berkshire natives know it as "partridge," and prize it as a game spe-cies. Also valued is woodcock (*Philohela minor*), but as this is a shy, largely nocturnal bird that leaves for the south in winter, it is seen and known by few. The Canada goose (*Branta canadensis*) passes to the north from April until June in great, V-shaped, honking formations, and returns south in late September and the first two weeks of October. On these migrations, flocks often alight in large numbers in open fields to eat grass, a habit probably appreciated by a hungry pioneer with a fowling piece.

Totally extinct since 1914, the passenger pigeon (*Ectopistes migratorius*) existed in almost unbelievable numbers in early North America. In the mid–nineteenth century, during the breeding season in Vermont, trees might be loaded with nests over an area of several hundred acres, with 25 nests fre-quently seen on a single tree; the ground beneath would be thick with their dung.[13] When Richard Hazen made his survey for the northern boundary of Massachusetts in the spring of 1741, as he crossed through the northern-most part of Heath, he found pigeons' nests so thick upon the beech trees that 500 could be counted at one time.[14] It is little wonder that passenger pigeon bones are found in the faunal inventory of Fort Pelham.

Many of the small, neotropical birds that arrive from the south in the spring are insect-eaters—a blessing, as a fact of life with which the Indians and the intrusive New Englanders had to cope was the presence through-out the spring and summer of numerous biting insects. The worst of these breed in ponds and streams, and include black flies (Simuliidae); mosquitos (Culicidae); and horse and deer flies (Tabanidae). These must have caused considerable torment to the inhabitants of the forts, bereft of such modern luxuries as window screens, repellants, and insecticides. If one adds to these houseflies, which would have followed the English settlers and their domes-tic animals into the region, the insect world would have been all too pres-ent for comfort.

FIG. 2-2. The Deerfield River in Rowe, Massachusetts. This river was a major route for parties of French and Indian raiders coming down from Canada.

Finally, one should mention fish. In the United States east of the Rocky Mountains, the native trout is the brook trout (*Salvelinus fontanalis*), ubiquitous in even the smallest streams as long as they are cool and totally unpolluted. During the eighteenth century, before the building of dams on the Connecticut River by commercial interests, the American shad (*Alosa sapidissima*) and Atlantic salmon (*Salmo salar*) came far up the Deerfield into the Berkshires (fig. 2-2). In fact, Shelburne Falls (located in the towns of Buckland and Shelburne, about 8 miles or 12.9 km southeast of Fort Shirley) was originally called Salmon Falls "because the salmon and shad came up the river in the spring of the year to spawn."[15] Before the French and Indian War, this fishery was said to have been exploited by both Englishmen from Deerfield and by the Indians; the whites used nets to catch the salmon as they jumped the falls, while the Indians employed spears. A land grant of 1743 to the proprietors of Huntstown (now called Ashfield) specified that these falls "be reserved to the use of the publick with Twenty Acres of Land Around them."[16]

Less "noble" fish certainly would have provided food both to native Americans and to the soldiers in the Line of Forts. These would have included the white sucker (*Catostomus commersoni*), the chain pickerel (*Esox niger*, a denizen of warm-water ponds), and yellow perch (*Perca flavescens*). The sucker is easily taken from streams by spearing, while the perch is caught in largest numbers by ice fishing on ponds and lakes.

NOTES

1. Jorgensen 1971:26–31.
2. Hatch and Hartshorn 1968.
3. Mott and Fuller 1967.
4. Jorgensen 1971:48.
5. Mott and Fuller 1967:table 15.
6. Ibid.
7. Hazzen 1879:8.
8. Jorgensen 1971:179.
9. Jorgensen 1971:184–90.
10. Wrangham 2005.
11. Thompson 1853:34.
12. PVMA 5380. See comments about this account book in chapter 7.
13. Thompson 1853:100.
14. Hazzen 1879:8.
15. Kendrick 1937:9.
16. Kendrick 1937:10.

Chapter 3

General History of the Conflict

As I HAVE SAID, the conflict that resulted in the construction of the Line of Forts in a remote frontier of colonial America was global in scope. The two great enemies were England and France, but in their ancient struggle they embroiled other European nations, and the war spread into Asia and the New World. The eventual outcome, confirmed by the Treaty of Paris in 1763, was the downfall of New France and the overwhelming triumph of English power. But it was not only France that lost; wherever they were involved in the war, the Native Americans were almost totally crushed. The Algonkian-speaking peoples of northeastern North America never again were to be a threat to the settlers of British stock. Even those Iroquoians who had allied themselves with the British were to meet eventual disaster when they remained loyal to the Crown in the subsequent American Revolution.

The Indian Background

To understand the bitter enmity the Native Americans felt toward the settlers on the New England frontier (a feeling that was mutual), and their willingness to carry out hostilities against them on French orders, one must go far back into New England history. All of the New England natives were speakers of Algonkian languages, and it was they who suffered from the Puritan policy of what can only be called genocide. Cotton Mather's famous diatribe against John Eliot for his kindly motivated attempts to convert the Indians makes this policy very clear. The result was a large-scale native uprising in the 1670s that almost wiped out the English altogether. Placed in the greatest peril were the English towns on the Connecticut River.

The trouble began among the Wampanoag of eastern Massachusetts. Their chief sachem was Metacomet, called by the English "King Philip." Unlike his father Massasoit, who was a warm friend and ally of the English at Plymouth, Philip had deep (and apparently justifiable) suspicions. In 1671, the authorities at Plymouth demanded that the Wampanoag surrender their arms, which they did reluctantly under Philip's urging. The execution of three Wampanoag at Plymouth in 1674, however, touched off a mass uprising among almost all the tribes of New England. Only the colony of Connecticut acted swiftly enough to defend its settlements, while Massachusetts and Rhode Island suffered severely at the hands of Philip's Indians.

Among the tribes to become involved in the conflict was one that had once been the major power in the Connecticut Valley north of Hatfield: the Pocumtuck.[1] These were the hereditary enemies of the Mohegan and especially of their chief, the English ally Uncas. At times they were friends, then the last mortal enemies of the Mohawk. Pocumtuck territory centered upon the west bank of the Connecticut River near what became the town of Deerfield, but they controlled much of the northern Berkshires to the west and the hill country to the east of the river. So powerful and numerous were the Pocumtuck, that in 1638 they could send fifty canoes laden with corn downriver to relieve the starving English at Hartford, Windsor, and Weathersfield. In 1646, a fleet of Pocumtuck warriors went down the Connecticut and crossed the sound to make war on the Indians of Long Island. The English found them intractable and troublesome, especially in the 1650s when they became involved in the battles of the New England Indians against the pro-English Uncas.

Disaster first came to the Pocumtuck in 1664, when their bitter enemies the Mohawk came from the west, down the trail that has ever since borne their name, and besieged the Pocumtuck in their stronghold called Fort Hill. The Mohawk were victorious and most of the Pocumtuck were massacred. The result was a political vacuum of which the English were quick to take advantage: the next year the English in Dedham (eastern Massachusetts), acting through their agent Thomas Pynchon of Springfield, bought from the surviving Pocumtuck leaders an eight thousand–acre grant that became the settlement of Deerfield.

Demoralized and living a degraded existence around the English settlements, the Pocumtuck nevertheless nurtured such a bitter dislike of the whites that they were led to participate in Philip's uprising in 1675. On 1 September of that year, they attacked and burned houses in Deerfield, which caused great consternation in the towns further down the river, such as Hadley.[2] A second attack, less successful than the first, took place eleven days later. On 18 September, Captain Thomas Lothrop and his men marched out of Deerfield into an ambush by several Indian groups, which included not only the Pocumtuck but even the so-called Praying Indians of eastern Massachusetts; the slaughter is still known as the Bloody Brook Massacre. Hatfield, Springfield, and Northampton came under subsequent attacks and it was clear that the Indians intended to remove the English entirely from the Connecticut Valley north of Hartford. Notwithstanding their massive defeat at Turner's Falls at the hands of the English, the Indians attacked Hatfield in force in May 1676, and Hadley in June of that year.

Nevertheless, their end was soon to come. The death of Philip at Mount Hope, Rhode Island, left them confused and demoralized. The Wampanoag and Narragansett drifted toward Maine and Canada, while the Nipmuck and Pocumtuck went westward, seeking refuge with the Mahican of Hudson Valley.[3] However, some of the Indians came back to wreak further havoc. In 1677, a party consisting of one Narragansett and twenty-five Pocumtuck attacked houses in Hatfield and carried off their prisoners to Canada. This was the first indication that New France was sheltering or perhaps even encouraging Indian raids in New England; however, when a delegation from New England reached a probably dissimulating Governor Frontenac, he received them kindly and helped with the ransom payment to claim the captives back from the Indians. This support was an important reversal of policy: until the end of King Philip's War the Indians had always fought the English on their own, without French intervention. It boded ill for the future. And in fact, in July 1688 Governor Denonville sent a war party from Canada against Northfield in time of peace.[4] If this was France's policy when there were no hostilities with England, what would it do in time of war?

In spite of this ominous development, it was a time of general peace in New England, and the English once again returned as permanent settlers in the frontier towns of the Connecticut Valley.

King William's War (1690–1697)

The abdication of James II in 1689 and the ascent of William and Mary to the throne changed all this. William III brought England into the League of Augsburg; and a general war with religious overtones soon began between that country and the France of Louis XIV that spread to their New World possessions, "and a scene of blood and slaughter was again to open."[5] Governor Frontenac was now free to carry out his policies openly against the New Englanders, using Indians expelled from New England at the close of King Philip's War. An unsuccessful attempt in 1690 by New York and New England to end the menace by capturing Quebec only served to rouse Frontenac's ire, and he responded by loosing his Indians in every quarter of the English colonies, with special attention paid to western Massachusetts. Brookfield, west of Worcester, was assaulted in 1692, and Deerfield the next year. On 15 September 1694, Deerfield was again attacked by the enemy, this time under French officers, but they were repulsed. In fact, during the whole of this war there were constant depredations by roaming bands of Indians on the settlers of the Connecticut Valley, with numerous incidents of English being cut down or taken captive in their fields while farming, or tending cattle. Not surprisingly, the Indians who raided Hatfield in 1697 were recognized as Pocumtuck.

The peace between France and England that was signed at Ryswick in September 1697 brought a temporary respite to the frontier settlements, but this was to be short-lived.

Queen Anne's War (1702–1713)

King William died in 1702 and was succeeded on the throne by Queen Anne. The European war began again. As General Hoyt put it: "England and France were now to measure swords to decide some misunderstanding between crowned heads, and the frontiers of the English colonies in America, again to suffer devastation, the bloody tomahawk, and all the horrors of an Indian War."[6] As the French had now made peace with the Five Nations (the Iroquois Confederation minus the Mohawk), which they had crushed during King William's War, they were free to turn their full forces, including their Indian wards, against New England.

The situation on the frontier was again desperate. Northfield had been abandoned during King William's War and remained so, making Deerfield the principal English outpost and a focus for French intentions. Because it had no English neighbors to the north, east, and west, the town's place on the frontier for the first half-century of its existence was tenuous indeed. It was simply an "easy mark."[7] On the evening of 29 February 1704, a force of 200 French and 142 Indians, led by Major Hertel de Rouville, fell upon a snowbound Deerfield, which was plundered and burned, houses and barns alike.[8] About 100 men, women, and children were marched off in the bitter cold and snow to Canada, an appalling trek that was recorded by the Reverend John Williams, pastor at Deerfield and one of the captives.[9] During the journey, twenty of the prisoners were murdered by the Indians, and it is clear that if the French had not been there to protect them, most or all would have been slaughtered.

The Williams journal has several items of interest, besides its chronicle of amazing fortitude in the face of terrible sufferings. First, it describes the routes taken to the Saint Lawrence, which must have been among the trails used throughout the wars, including the period of the Line of Forts. The main trail led up the Connecticut to the mouth of the White River (at White River Junction, Vermont). There the trail split into two. One fork ascended the White, passed over the Northfield Mountains, then descended the Winooski or Onion River to Lake Champlain; the march continued along the lake to Missisquoi Bay, then to the Richelieu (or Sorel) River, where canoes carried them via Chambly to the village of Sorel on the Saint

FIG. 3-1. Distant view of the Fortress of Louisbourg, Cape Breton, from the north. This fortification was the most powerful north of Mexico, and guarded the Gulf of Saint Lawrence. It was the base of operations against the English settlements in New England and Nova Scotia.

Lawrence. The other route went far up the Connecticut to the "Coos meadows" (Near Coos Junction, New Hampshire), but Williams, who took the other fork, is vague on the way from there to the Saint Lawrence.

The other item of note is that the Reverend Williams was taken through the Indian village of Saint Francis (St. François-du-Lac), about a third of the way down the Saint Lawrence from Montreal to Quebec. This was an "Indian village" only in the sense that here were gathered a diversity of anti-English and nominally Catholic Indians who had fled the New England provinces; their Jesuit mentors were continually instigating them against the New England heretics, and Saint Francis remained a thorn in the English side until it was totally destroyed by Colonel Robert Rogers's Rangers in 1759. The Society of Jesus had received the enthusiastic patronage of Louis XIV, and in Canada enjoyed great success among the Indians (excepting the Iroquois). When the captives arrived in Jesuit territory, they were continually besieged by Jesuit proselytism, and it is clear that this was a war on the spiritual as well as the sociopolitical front.

There were many depredations along the frontier during this war. Deerfield itself was assaulted again in 1709, but this time the enemy was repulsed, as many of the inhabitants were returnees from Canadian captivity and had urged proper safeguards. It was again clear to the colonial authorities that Canada had to be taken by force to ensure a lasting peace. In 1711 an effort was made to take Quebec, but this failed. In that year, however, the English seized Nova Scotia. When the Treaty of Utrecht was signed in 1713, France was forced to admit the alienation of Nova Scotia, but retained the shores of the Saint Lawrence. She also kept Cape Breton Island, where the Fortress of Louisbourg was quickly raised to reassert French supremacy in that part of North America (figs. 3-1 and 3-2). The shadow hanging over the New England pioneers had again not been lifted by peace.

The False Peace (1713–1744)

The Treaty of Utrecht encouraged the settlement of lands in which it was too dangerous to live during the time of open hostilities between the two great powers. Such, for instance, were the grants of land made by the Massachusetts legislature along the upper Housatonic River, including parts of present Sheffield, Great Barrington, and Stockbridge.[10] Stockbridge, bought from the Indians, was to be an important base for the Williams family that controlled the Line of Forts. Northfield was again settled, and the village of Green River (Greenfield) was founded in 1718, so that Deerfield was no longer the critical northern outpost it had previously been. The signing of the

FIG. 3-2. The King's Bastion, Fortress of Louisbourg, following its reconstruction through archaeological and documentary research. This supposedly impregnable fort was captured by New England militiamen in 1745, following a strategy devised by Shirley.

peace also permitted attempts to "redeem" captives taken to Canada, and on 13 November 1713, a party led by the Reverend John Williams and Captain John Stoddard (to figure prominently in these pages) set out for Quebec; their mission was only partly successful as many of the children and younger people who had been carried off to Canada had gone "native" and had no desire to return. This state of affairs led Williams to exclaim that the captives were "rather worse than the Indians."[11]

The Indian threat suddenly increased on the eastern frontier of New England. When "Acadia" was finally ceded to England, the latter claimed much of the coast of Maine as well; this claim was disputed by the French and by the hostile Abenaki. According to the English, the principal instigator of trouble against them was the remarkable Sebastian Rasle (or Rale), a Jesuit missionary who had established headquarters at Norridgewock, Maine—and they were probably right. In July 1722, war was declared by the English on the Eastern Indians, a conflict that became known as "Father Rasle's War." The Abenaki depredations were strongly supported by Governor de Vaudreuil of Canada, which prompted the English to make preparations all along the frontier of New England.

To protect Massachusetts and New Hampshire, in 1723 the Indians of the Six Nations were encouraged to neutralize their brethren further east, and to make war on the Abenaki. At the same time, an important defensive work was begun up the Connecticut River where it was to form the boundary between New Hampshire and the future Vermont. This was Fort Dummer, below the present town of Brattleboro, Vermont, erected in 1724 by Captain Timothy Dwight, Sr., of Northampton (the grandfather of the future Yale president by that name), and a party of soldiers and carpenters. A second fort was built upriver in 1743 in what was known as Township No. 4, one of the Massachusetts land grants in New Hampshire; the fort, ordered by Colonel John Stoddard, was surrounded by a stockade, according to a plan conserved in the Yale College Library, and it acted as the most advanced post in that part of New England in the subsequent war between France and England.

In addition to these preparations, the pressure on the settlers was considerably relieved by a successful English attack on Rasle's village in 1724. Eighty of the enemy were killed, in addition to Rasle himself.[12] Rasle had been an unusual person. Besides his obvious military capabilities, he was a scholar of Indian affairs and a capable linguist, having compiled an important dictionary of the Norridgewock language that after his death found its way to the Harvard College Library. The pressure was kept up on the enemy, helped by a bounty set by the government of Massachusetts of one hundred pounds for each Indian scalp brought in by scouts (a practice that was to continue until the conquest of Canada).

Be that as it may, a kind of uneasy truce prevailed at times between the

Indians and the whites on the frontier. Into outposts such as Fort Dummer came groups of Indians to trade and to obtain rum. The disorder and menacing behavior of the drunken natives so disturbed Colonel Oliver Partridge that he wrote a letter to Governor Belcher in June 1727 suggesting that either such trading be altogether prohibited, or that it be closely regulated by the General Court. At the same time, he cautioned that certain whites were acting like "disorderly spirited men," and mentioned one soldier stationed at Fort Dummer, Daniel Severance (see appendix 4), who was loudly threatening to kill the Indian that scalped his father.[13] Quite obviously in the twilight zone between the two races, there was a tremendous amount of latent hostility that could explode into violence at any time. It is small wonder that when true war came again, the trading Indians were once more to disappear to the north. It also probably helped that Philippe de Rigaud, marquis de Vaudreuil and governor of Canada, died in 1725; he had been "the mainspring and spur of the war" according to Sheldon.[14]

Nonetheless, it remained clear that if Europe should flare up into war, the position of the frontier settlers would again become precarious. Distant and complex events in the Old World began to make this flare-up seem inevitable, precipitated by the age-old rivalry between France and Britain. The War of the Austrian Succession was triggered by the invasion of Silesia by Frederick II of Prussia in 1740, and lasted for eight years. George II, as a Hanoverian prince, was drawn into the war on the side of the Austrians through jealousy of the Prussian monarchy, and Holland joined them as a neutral ally; on the other side, allied with Frederick II, were France and Spain. King George led an Anglo-allied army on the Rhine, and in 1743 scored the great victory of Dettingen over his enemies, the last time a reigning monarch was to stand at the head of an English army in battle.

News traveled slowly to New England, but it must have been increasingly clear to the English in the New World that peace, never fully established for them in any case, was near an end, and that the wolf would again descend into the fold.

King George's War (1744–1748)

Although hostilities had been going on for years, France formally declared war against England on 15 March 1744, opening a struggle (variously known in New England as King George's War or Governor Shirley's War) that was to last until 1748. England reciprocated, and declared *its* war fourteen days later. However, ocean travel being what it was in those days, the news did not reach Boston until the third week in May. In the meantime, a French force from the Fortress of Louisbourg, the great stronghold on the southeastern corner of Cape Breton Island, had descended on the English trading and fishing station of Canso, in the straits between Cape Breton and the mainland of Nova Scotia. The province of Massachusetts Bay was able to respond quickly enough to prevent the same fate from overtaking the English settlement of Annapolis.

Massachusetts was extremely fortunate in those dark days to have as its governor William Shirley (see fig. 1-1; appendix 4), perhaps the most able, forceful, and popular administrator ever appointed by the Crown in its American colonies. Shirley was born in England and trained in the law there, but had emigrated to Massachusetts in 1731; after being appointed advocate general for all of New England (except Connecticut), in 1741 he was made governor of Massachusetts, succeeding Jonathan Belcher, and remained in that post for fifteen years. Shirley's first reaction was to strengthen the western frontier of the province; history had taught that New England would receive most pressure on that front. For this, he appointed a committee of three all-powerful men in western Massachusetts to oversee the construction of a Line of Forts just south of the Massachusetts line. These men were John Stoddard of Northampton (appendix 4), Oliver Partridge of Hatfield (appendix 4), and John Leonard of Springfield. Stoddard was one of the so-called River Gods of the region, virtually the ruler of Hampshire County, and related to the ubiquitous and important Williams family. We shall examine the social, political, economic, and religious network in which the Line of Forts was placed in chapter 8.

There had been some dispute in previous years as to the location of the northern boundary of Massachusetts. In 1741, to resolve the argument between that colony and New Hampshire, Governor Belcher sent out Richard Hazen (or Hazzen) with a small party to run a line due west; due to administrative mix-ups, however, the line was run not from the head or mouth of the Merrimac River, as it should have been, but from its southernmost bend at what is now Lowell. Accordingly, ill will sprang up between the two colonies: Massachusetts rightly felt that it had been cheated; and Belcher, who had governed both provinces, was recalled. Hazen began his survey on 21 March, crossing the northern Berkshires in deep snow and passing only two miles north of the future sites of Forts Shirley and Pelham, finally reaching the New York border. It was a feat of incredible endurance and some danger, but Hazen's border has remained unchanged until today.

The Building of Fort Shirley and Fort Pelham

Events moved fast along the frontier, and a table of organization was soon organized. Colonel John Stoddard, as commanding officer of the Hampshire County Militia, was placed by Governor Shirley in overall charge of the defense of western Massachusetts. Major Israel Williams, Stoddard's nephew, was second in command, and made commissary, while Captain Elijah Williams, a distant cousin of Israel, had charge of the scouting parties from Deerfield to cover the frontier on the north and west.[15] One of these parties set out on 8 June 1744 for Hoosac Mountain near the New York border; three days later they returned with a report of having seen the trail of about forty Indians, at the head of the West Branch of the North River (about a mile north of the future Fort Shirley). Another scout sent out on 10 June found the tracks of three parties of the enemy between the North and Green Rivers. A scout sent out on 13 June discovered traces of a hostile camp on the Deerfield River, about eight miles above Moses Rice's fort (of which more later), and Indians were seen in the south part of Deerfield and on the Green River on 15 June. Stoddard himself was then in Albany attending a conference with the Indians, and there received intelligence that a large party from Canada was being raised against the New England frontier.

On 20 July 1744, Colonel Stoddard wrote a letter from Northampton to his nephew Captain William Williams of Deerfield, acting under the authority of Shirley and the General Court, headed by the following memorandum: "The fort 60 feet Square Houses 11 feet wide Mounts 12 feet Square 7 feet High the fort roof of the Houses to be shingled the Soldiers Employed to be allowed the Carpenter nine shillings others six shillings a day Old Tenor."[16] The letter itself deserves quoting in full and reads:

> Sir you are hereby Directed as soon as may be to Erect a fort of the Dimensions above mentioned, and you are to employ the soldiers under your Command, viz such of them as are effective men and to allow them by the day in manner as above expressed and in cases your soldiers chuze rather to undertake to build sd fort for a sum in Gross or by the Gret you may promise them Two Hundred pounds old Tenor Exclusive of the Nails that may be necessary the fort is to be erected about five miles and a half from Hugh Morrison's house in Colrain in or near the line run last week Under the Direction of Col° Tim° Dwight by our order and you are hereby further directed as you may have Opportunity to Search out some Convenient places where two or three other forts may be Erected Each to be about five miles and a Half Distance upon the line run Last week as above mentioned or the pricked line on the platt made by Col° Dwight you will have with you.
>
> and further you are to order a sufficient Guard out of the men under your Command to guard such persons as may be Employed in erecting sd fort and further you have liberty to Exchange of the men under your command for those that are undr the Command of Capt. Elijah in case there be any such that will be proper to be Employed in Building sd fort you will take care that the men be faithful in their business, they must be watchful and prudent for their own safety.

there must be good account kept of the various Services in case men work by the day.[17]

A few words should be said about some of the persons named in this letter, although a fuller account will be given in appendix 4. Captain William Williams, Stoddard's sister's son, was head of the militia company based at Deerfield. Colonel Timothy Dwight, Sr., was a native of Northampton and had been in charge many years before of the building of Fort Dummer; he was a professional surveyor, and had established the line, running due west just two miles south of Hazen's border, that was to be the Line of Forts. "Capt. Elijah" is Elijah Williams, Deerfield storekeeper and commander of the Deerfield scouts. We are to meet other Williamses in this chapter, for the Line of Forts came to be their territory.

Hugh Morrison's was the largest of three forts in Colrain during King George's War, all built by local citizens. The village had been settled by courageous Scotch-Irish pioneers from Londonderry and its environs in northern Ireland. They came to Colrain in 1736, with Hugh Morrison as their most prominent leader; he organized their defense in the face of repeated Indian ambushes and sniping, and his fortified house was a key point in the Line of Forts planned by Governor Shirley. In spite of prejudice suffered by them at the hands of the English Congregationalists of New England, the Scotch-Irish of Colrain were a bastion of strength against the French and Indians until the end of the war in 1763.

Some time in late July or early August 1744, construction began on the first of the new forts, to be named Fort Shirley (fig. 3-3) in honor of the governor, under the supervision of Captain William Williams; he was to be its first commander. Because this was new land, to be cleared for the first time, all provisions for the men had to be sent in from Deerfield by Elijah Williams. It is fortunate that the detailed accounting of expenses for the fort is still extant; it gives a fair picture of a site for which no plan has yet been discovered (see chapter 4). The total expenses were £300 11s 9d, Old Tenor, as against the estimate of £114 16s that appeared on Stoddard's original letter.[18] Fort Shirley had been finished by 30 October, for on that date William Williams commenced to billet himself within it.

The next spring Colonel Stoddard penned another letter to Captain William Williams, then at Fort Shirley, as follows:

Northampton, March 6, 1745
Sir you are hereby fully authorized and Impowered In ten days after this Date to employ so many of the soldiers under your command as you Judge necessary In finishing a fort in the place where the Com[itt]ee for Building a Line of Block Houses &c agreed with Capt. Moses Rice to Build one and employ for that purpose the Timbers the sd Rice has drawn together (the sd

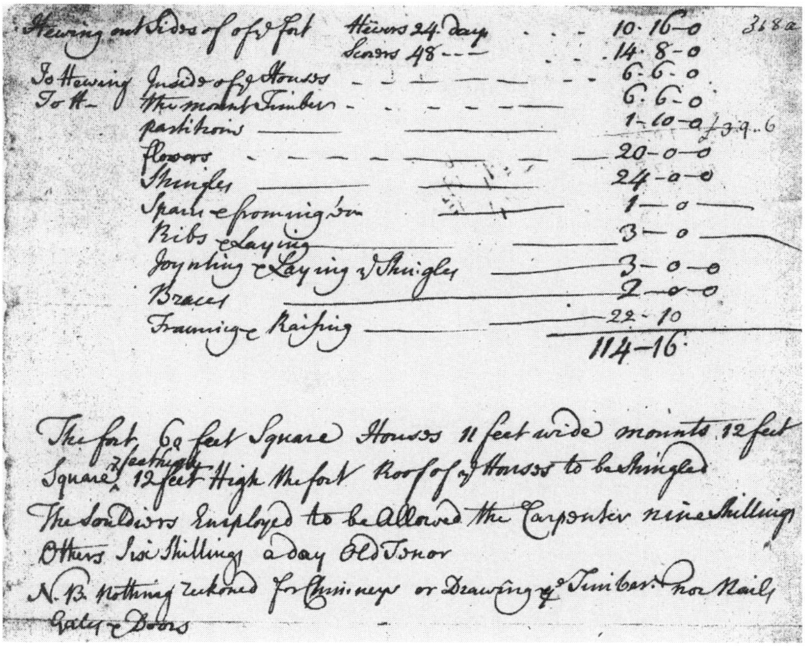

Hewing out Sides of ye fort Hewers 24 day . . . 10-16-0 318a
Scorers 48 - - - . . . 14-8-0
To Hewing Inside of ye Houses - - - - - - - 6-6-0
To H— the mount Timber - - - - - - - 6-6-0
partitions ——— ——— 1-10-0 £39-6
flowers - - - - - - 20-0-0
Shingles ——— ——— 24-0-0
Spars & framing — — 1—0 ——
Ribs & Laying ——— ——— 3—0 ——
Joynting & Laying ye Shingles ——— 3-0-0
Braces ——— 2-0-0
Framing & Raising ——— ——— 22-10
114-16

The fort 60 feet Square Houses 11 feet wide mounts 12 feet Square 7 feet high 12 feet High the fort Roofs of ye Houses to be Shingled
The Souldiers Employed to be Allowed the Carpenter nine Shillings Others Six Shillings a day Old Tenor
N.B. Nothing reckoned for Chimneys or Drawing ye Timber nor Nails Gates & Doors

FIG. 3-3. Facsimile of the written orders for the construction of Fort Shirley, dated 20 July 1744 and signed by John Stoddard.

> Rice having Desired sd Timber may be employed for that purpose) you are to allow to a Carpenter Nine Shillings and other Effective men Six Shillings a Day Old Tenor you are to finish sd fort with all convenient speed provided the sd Rice do not within sd ten days take effectual care to your Satisfaction that he will finish it.[19]

The letter was signed by Stoddard and by the two other members of the committee, Oliver Partridge and Thomas Ingersole.

Captain Moses Rice, who according to the above had been contracted to build a new fort on a hill in what is now Rowe, had arrived in Charlemont as its first settler in 1742, probably with his elder sons. This being extremely dangerous territory (he himself was tomahawked and scalped by Indians in 1755), the house that he built was really a fort; for many years it was an important stopping-off place for militiamen passing east and west along the Line of Forts. Rice was apparently a somewhat cantankerous individual, as Stoddard's letter suggests. Whether or not he carried out his end of the contract, the new strongpoint in the Line of Forts was actually completed at this time. It was located according to Dwight's survey, five and a half miles west of Fort Shirley and two miles south of Hazen's line. Stoddard's letter suggests that perhaps Rice had begun it in the preceding year, but had not finished it, and he was apparently urged to carry out his agreement. Certainly ten days would not have been sufficient to have built the fort from scratch.

In a politically astute move, the new fort was named (probably by Governor Shirley) after Henry Pelham (1696–1754), prime minister under George II from 1743 until his (Pelham's) death, and brother of Shirley's great patron the Duke of Newcastle. In a way this was ironic: Pelham had been strongly in favor of peace with the French in opposition to the wishes of the king, and carried on the war "with languor and indifferent success."[20] At any rate, the honor could not but be appreciated by the British government, although I doubt whether the great Pelham would have felt favorably disposed had he actually seen the tiny, palisaded post christened after him in the depths of the Berkshire wilderness.

The Siege and Capture of Louisbourg

The greatest fortress in North America was Louisbourg, located on the cold, foggy coast of Isle Royale or Cape Breton Island. Founded in 1713 after the Treaty of Utrecht, by which France kept Isle Royale but lost Nova Scotia, Louisbourg became not only a bastion of the French defense of the mouth of the Saint Lawrence, but an important mercantile and cod-fishing station. Believed by the French and most New Englanders to be virtually impregnable, with fortifications designed by some of France's top military engineers, the fortress became and remained a thorn in the side of New England.[21] The successful attack on Canso from Louisbourg made it more of a threat than ever.

William Shirley began to have doubts about Louisbourg's defensibility, however, when a returned English prisoner gave him valuable intelligence about the poor design and workmanship of the fortress. He had also learned that the French garrison was near mutiny—weakened, resentful, and dispirited.[22] In January 1745, Shirley began planning for an attack, and gave orders for recruitment from the four New England provinces. Included were the Hampshire County militia from the Line of Forts, and there are several extant documents listing those men and officers who marched to Boston. Among those who left was Captain William Williams; he was replaced as commander at Fort Shirley by Ephraim Williams, Jr., his cousin. Seth Pomroy (or Pomeroy), the famous gunsmith and blacksmith of Hampshire County and commander of a snowshoe company of scouts operating from Deerfield, was on the expedition and left the most valuable eyewitness account of its progress.[23] Under the command of William Pepperell, and armed with instructions from Shirley, the force of about 4,300 New Englanders, most of them without much idea of military discipline, left Boston with transport provided by the British Navy. On their arrival at Louisbourg, they took advantage of the fatal flaw that Shirley had seen: the outer walls of the Fortress did not include the nearby hills that overlooked it. During the siege, the New Englanders dragged their artillery through the swamps up to these hills and inflicted a merciless bombardment on Louisbourg. The French, under very bad advice, had abandoned the Royal Battery to the northeast of the Fortress; the English forces drilled out the sealed up touch-holes of the guns left there, and bombarded the enemy from a new direction. At the end of 46 days, the French gave up. The New England "farm boys" had scored one of the greatest military victories of all time.

The triumph was celebrated not only in Boston, where a principal square was named for the victory, but in the home country. Pepperell was made a knight for his services, but Shirley, who had conceived and carried out the plan, was not so honored. Eventually, those members of the Hampshire County Militia who had served at Louisbourg returned to their former posts. William Williams, on the other hand, went to look after his interests at Pontoosuck (the future Pittsfield), leaving Ephraim Jr. at Fort Shirley.

The Building of Fort Massachusetts

It will be remembered that Stoddard's original orders for the Line of Forts specified that in addition to Shirley, there were to be "two or three other forts" each about five and one half miles apart from each other. Pelham had already been built as so directed; unfortunately, however, Stoddard at the time of his letter had only a vague knowledge of the topography further west. Two and one half miles west from Pelham is the deep gorge of the Deerfield River (see figs. 2-1 and 2-2), while beyond the gorge rise Hoosac Mountain and its foothills. Obviously, to place a fort here would have been impossible. However, following the Mohawk Trail up the Cold River and down the other side of Hoosac Mountain, one enters the valley of the Hoosac River, which turns west at the present town of North Adams and continues along the flat bottomlands until it reaches Williamstown.[24]

The Williams family, already well entrenched in Stockbridge to the south, and in the Line of Forts to the east, must have been well aware of the possibilities of this part of the Hoosac Valley, both for settlement and for the line of defense against the French and Indian foe. There was also the opportunity, if any fort should be built there, of supplying it more directly from Albany than over the arduous roads and trails leading from Deerfield. The exact date of construction of the new fort, to be named "Massachusetts" in defiance of New York's pretensions to that part of the province, is not known exactly, but it was probably carried out under the supervision of Lieutenant John Catlin with men from the Line of Forts some time before August 1745: there are letters written by Catlin to Major Israel Williams from Fort Massachusetts, describing his attempts to buy provisions from the Dutch settlers in the Albany area. The fort itself was placed on a broad terrace to the

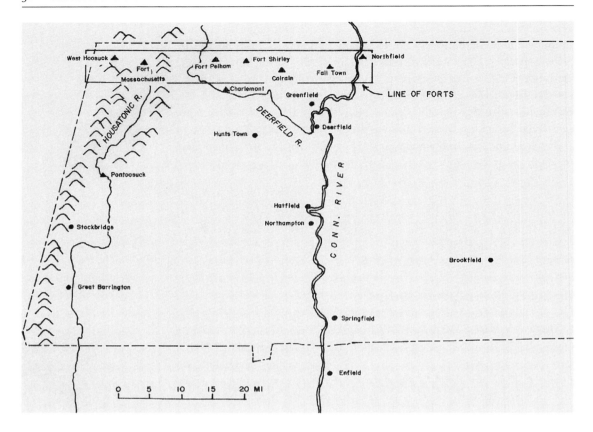

FIG. 3-4. Map of western
Massachusetts, with the
Line of Forts.

north of the Hoosac River and just west of what would some day be North
Adams.

Fort Massachusetts, then, became the westernmost bastion in the Line
of Forts (fig. 3-4) and was soon to outstrip in importance its sister forts to
the east. It was also soon to prove to be in an extremely dangerous position.
Existing muster rolls show that 43 men garrisoned the fort during the following winter, during which time Captain Ephraim Williams, Jr., remained
at Fort Shirley with 47 men.[25] By June 1746, however, Williams had moved
his headquarters to Fort Massachusetts, taking some Shirley men with him.
While some of his motivation could have been the damp and uncomfortable
situation of Fort Shirley, subsequent events prove that Williams had every
intention of making his Hoosac Valley bastion the center for a large and
successful real estate operation, something that would not have been con-
templated for the rugged and rocky hills of Heath and Rowe.

The success of the Louisbourg operation inspired Shirley to present the
British government with a grand plan for the reduction of Canada, one that
might well have achieved its end had it ever been carried out. Approval
came from London, and the summer of 1746 saw feverish preparations in

New England for the new campaign. In Massachusetts, Seth Pomroy was commissioned captain in a regiment raised by Colonel Joseph Dwight. But fresh events, stemming from the intention of France to crush New England once and for all, resulted in the cancellation of Shirley's plan. Although the colonists had been expecting a British fleet to join and support them, that fleet never came, due to the vacillating policies in the home country. In its stead appeared a French armada of 40 ships, under the command of D'Anville, with 3,000 veteran troops aboard, and it was believed that Boston was its target.[26] The Canada expedition was called off. In spite of the fact that D'Anville's armada perished off Halifax in September gales, the French moves toward New England and the withdrawal of troops for the Canada campaign had left its frontiers in great peril.

The Fall of Fort Massachusetts in 1746

In revenge for the loss of Louisbourg, Governor Beauharnois of Canada sent three or four war parties each week during that spring and summer against the frontier.[27] At this time, according to a statement of expenses in the William Williams Papers in the Berkshire Athenaeum, Captain Ephraim Williams had 350 men under his command in the Line of Forts, which included forts in the Northfield (Shattuck's Fort), "Falltown" (that is, Bernardston), Fort Shirley, Fort Pelham, and Fort Massachusetts.[28]

Most of these enemy attacks were directed not against the forts themselves, but against local settlers working in their fields under the protection of the Line of Forts. However, an attempt on Sheldon's Fort at Fall Town on 9 May was defeated, although John Burke, the local commander, was wounded in the affair.[29] Hostile intentions against Fort Massachusetts were revealed the same day, when Sergeant John Hawks of Deerfield and one John Mighills were crossing the Hoosac River on one horse. They were ambushed by two Indians; Mighills escaped to the fort, but Hawks was shot in the left arm. Hawks nevertheless held them off with his gun, and the two enemy fled. On 11 June, a party of Indians fell upon a group of soldiers working near Fort Massachusetts (probably planting corn), killed and scalped Elisha Nims who had just come from Fort Shirley with Captain Williams, wounded Gershom Hawks, and took Benjamin Taintor captive.[30]

The ensuing events were strikingly narrated by the Reverend John Norton, chaplain of the Line of Forts, a graduate of Yale in the class of 1737 and 32 years of age in 1746.[31] He had been living in Fort Shirley since the preceding February with his wife Eunice, and children Elizabeth, John Jr., and Anna. On Thursday, 14 August, he left Fort Shirley with Dr. Thomas Williams, Ephraim Jr.'s brother and surgeon on the Line of Forts, along with fourteen soldiers. Passing through Fort Pelham, they traveled down to Rice's

Fort on the Deerfield, where they spent the night. The following day, they went over Hoosac Mountain to Fort Massachusetts, with the intention of spending a month. On Saturday, Dr. Williams departed for Deerfield along with fourteen soldiers (apparently those who had been replaced), carrying a letter from Sergeant Hawks to the absent Captain Ephraim Williams, Jr., at Deerfield asking for stores, especially ammunition, which was running low; this request was particularly urgent, as signs of the enemy had been discovered. Unknown to Hawks, however, the doctor's party had left under the very eyes of the encircling but concealed enemy, who had let them pass in peace as they so reduced the number of the fort's defenders.

The force at Fort Massachusetts was seriously depleted; eleven men were seriously sick with dysentery, and just about everyone else was afflicted with "griping and flux"—this out of a total complement of twenty-two men, along with three women and five children.

Between eight and nine o'clock in the morning of Tuesday, 19 August, the enemy struck. There suddenly appeared an army of 440 French and 300 "French" Mohawks and Abenakis led by General François-Pierre Rigaud de Vaudreuil, brother of the French governor of New France. With "hideous acclamations" the enemy force rushed forward upon the fort, while firing continually. The intrepid Hawks, who had been left in command, ordered that they should not be fired on until they had approached to within a suitable distance. At 20 rods (330 feet or 100 meters) the defenders opened fire, at which the enemy darted behind trees, stumps, and logs. Eventually the English sharpshooters learned how to hit their mark, and the chief of the Saint Francis Indians fell dead from a shot in the chest by Hawks. Rigaud himself almost lost his life when he approached his ensign, who stood some 30 rods (495 feet or 151 meters) from the fort displaying the standard; on being discovered, the general was winged in the arm by a shot, at which both retreated to their camp. With ammunition running low, Sergeant Hawks set the sick men to casting bullets and shot, and forbade unnecesary firing.

By the end of that day, two of the English had been wounded. Toward evening the enemy could be seen using their axes and hatchets, and it became clear that they intended to set fire to the fort. To counter this move, Hawks gave orders that every tub, pail, or vessel of any sort be filled with water, that the doors be made fast, and that passages be cut between rooms. All that night the French and Indians kept up their firing, and the English retaliated with buckshot, as they were unable to see their targets. Between eight and nine o'clock, there was another outcry from the enemy; the defenders thought this was the sign for a general attack, but such failed to materialize.

The next morning (Wednesday, 20 August), the enemy began to fire again; particularly disturbing was that some of them had mounted the hill north of the fort and started firing into the parade, a grave state of affairs because Fort Massachusetts had been poorly sited. Many of them could be seen making further preparations for burning the fort. Around 11 o'clock, Thomas Knowlton was shot through the head in the mount, where his body remained.

About noontime, the enemy indicating that they wished to parley, Sergeant Hawks and the Reverend Norton went to talk to the French general, who told them that unless they surrendered, Fort Massachusetts would be taken by storm. On their return to the fort, Hawks judged the place indefensible: there were not more than three or four pounds of powder left, and the same amount of lead, with most of the soldiers ill. If the fort were to be taken by violence, all—men, women, children, and the sick—would surely be killed at the hands of the Indians. Eventually terms were agreed upon with Rigaud, specifying that they should all be prisoners of the French, and not of the Indians; that the children would stay with their parents throughout the period of captivity; and that they should all be exchanged or ransomed at the first opportunity. Rigaud also promised that those too ill to walk to Canada would be carried.

Accordingly, Rigaud entered the fort with his officers and set up his standard. The restless Indians, having to remain outside, began to undermine the fort and opened the gates, so that the parade was soon full of Indians. On seeing Knowlton's bleeding corpse in the mount, they let out a great shout, and dragged down the body, scalping it and cutting off the legs and arms. The English were all taken off to the enemy camp, but Norton was allowed to return briefly to leave a note on the well-sweep crotch, describing to their friends what had happened.

Then began the long journey to Montreal and Quebec. The great fear of the prisoners was that they would be put into the hands of the Indians, from whom they expected little mercy. In spite of his earlier promises, Rigaud was forced to turn some of them over; incredibly, however, the English were treated by the "savages" with unwonted kindness. On 10 September they arrived in Montreal, and on the fifteenth they came to Quebec, where they were imprisoned with other English and Dutch taken at sea or along the frontier with New England and New York.

They were not to be exchanged until 27 July of the following year (1747), by which time many of the prisoners had died. John Norton, John Hawks, and the other survivors arrived at Boston on 16 August. Norton had not seen his family for almost one year, and must have soon after journeyed to Fort Shirley, where he was met with distressing news. In his absence, his youngest child Anna had fallen ill, and had died at the fort. The soldiers buried her outside the walls of the fort (see fig. 4-2) and placed on her grave a simple, schist headstone that is still there, and that reads:

HEAR • Lyes
ye: body of Anna
Nort[on] D[aughte]r of ye Rev
Mr John Norton She Died
in ye 7th ye[a]r of H[e]r Ag[e] 1747

Soon after, Norton and his family removed to East Hampton, Connecticut, where he remained pastor of the First Congregational Church until his death in 1778.

It was ten days before the news of the fall of Fort Massachusetts reached Deerfield and Hatfield. A party was immediately sent to the fort under the leadership of Captain Oliver Partridge, where they found the fort burned to the ground and Norton's letter fixed to a post on the well. Knowlton's body was discovered and buried. The clearing where the fort stood was mysteriously white as with new fallen snow; the Indians, in search of plunder, had ripped open the feather beds of the garrison and scattered the contents over the ground.[32] But the consequences of the Indians' disappointment at not finding the expected loot and a large number of prisoners were severe. Following the surrender of the fort, a party of 60 Indians separated from the French and came down the Deerfield River via the Mohawk Trail, with the intent of securing captives to sell to the French in Canada.[33] On 25 August they reached Deerfield Meadows, where a group of men and children was making hay. The haymakers were ambushed; four of them were killed, and one small boy, Samuel Allen, was taken prisoner and carried off to Saint Francis. The Indians once more returned to Canada.

The Rebuilding of Fort Massachusetts

While the captives languished in their unhealthy Quebec prison, Governor Shirley made haste to see that the Line of Forts was again intact. On 10 April 1747, he appointed John Stoddard, Eleazar Porter, and Oliver Partridge as a committee to oversee the construction of a "good commodious blockhouse" at the site of Fort Massachusetts; he also called for "another blockhouse at some convenient place west of Fort Pelham," but of course this would have been anything but "convenient" thanks to the precipitous topography.[34] On 21 April, two companies from the regiment raised by Colonel Joseph Dwight of Brookfield for the Canada campaign were assigned to Lieutenant Colonel William Williams for the purpose of rebuilding Fort Massachusetts. The total workforce and guard was 370 men.

It was the belief of Perry that Ephraim Williams, Jr., had probably spent the preceding winter at Fort Shirley, and was still in command of the Line of Forts.[35] However, his cousin William Williams, who outranked him following his service at Louisbourg, was clearly in charge at the rejuvenated Massachusetts, where the second in command was Ephraim's father, Major Ephraim Williams, Sr., the River God at Stockbridge. On its completion, the elder Williams would for a time remain at Massachusetts, with his son responsible for the forts to the east.

With the previous disaster before their eyes, the authorities decided to provide sufficient artillery for Fort Massachusetts. Three 4-pounders were sent from Boston, via New York and Albany, and a "great gun" by way of Colrain. The account of Ephraim Williams, Jr., for the last operation reads as follows:

> May 9, 1747 To 1 gallon of rum expended for transporting the great gun by hand between Colrain and Taylor's farm.
>
> May 10 Ditto to 5 gallons expended in transporting the gun & part of the baggage by hand to the Great Mountain [the Hoosac Range]. Ditto 3 gallons more in gitting the gun down the mountain & also gitting it over several bad places.
>
> May 12 To 12 gallons for the benefit of the workman to grease the wheels.[36]

It has usually been assumed that the "great gun" was taken from Fort Shirley, but the mention of Colrain as the starting point of the itinerary suggests that the gun was for a while at Hugh Morrison's Fort. The bringing of the new guns and other supplies from Albany was not without incident. Major Ephraim Williams, Sr., was in charge of the party. On its return to Fort Massachusetts, the party had been observed by Indian scouts from the French stronghold at Crown Point, and were ambushed west of the fort. Fortunately, the garrison had heard the noise of firing and came to their support, routing the attackers with the loss of one Stockbridge Indian.

When Lieutenant Colonel William Williams left Fort Massachusetts on 2 June 1747, he gave detailed instructions to Ephraim, Sr., for building the barracks:

> Sir, —Intending by the leave of Providence to depart this fort to-morrow, which, through the goodness of God towards us is now finished, I must desire you to take the charge of it; and shall, for the present, leave you with eighty men, which I would have you detain here till the barracks are erected, which I would have you build in the following manner, viz., seventy feet in length, thirty in breadth, seven-feet post, with a low roof. Let it be placed within five feet of the north side of the fort, and at equal distances from the east and west ends.
>
> Let it be divided in the middle with a tier of timber; place a chimney in the centre of the east part, with two fire-places to accommodate those rooms. In

part, as if the house was but twenty feet wide from the south; making a partition of plank, ten feet distance from the north side of the barrack, for a storeroom for the provisions, &c.

This letter, in the William Williams Papers at Pittsfield, is extremely important: it throws light on the probable appearance of the barracks at Shirley and Pelham, as they were both designed by the same man, although very much smaller in scale. Presumably, in the interim, the eighty men left at the fort would have been sleeping in tents or other temporary shelter.

Early in 1748, Sergeant John Hawks, the hero of Fort Massachusetts, made an incredible wintertime journey.[37] He had been commissioned by Governor Shirley to take a young French captive, the cadet Pierre Raimbault St. Blein, to Canada and exchange him for two English captives. One of these was Hawks's nephew Samuel Allen, who had been taken in the meadows south of Deerfield following the capture of Fort Massachusetts. Hawks, the French officer, and two other militiamen were fitted out by William Williams, and left Deerfield on snowshoes on 8 February 1748, reaching Montreal on 27 February. They found young Allen with the Indians, but he virtually had to be removed by force as he had gone completely native, refusing to speak English and barely acknowledging his own uncle; to the end of his days in Deerfield, Allen maintained that the Indian way of life was the best. On their return home, Hawks's party was continually dogged by Indians who were on their trail, but they managed to elude their pursuers.

The Second Attack on Fort Massachusetts

The French and Indian pressure on the Line of Forts was not to abate until the autumn of 1748. Perhaps the death in this year of Colonel John Stoddard, who had been a bulwark for the frontier during the war, encouraged new ventures; he was succeeded by Colonel Israel Williams as the chief defense officer for western Massachusetts.

In June, Captain Humphrey Hobbs, with forty men, was ordered from Fort No. 4 (in the present Charlestown, New Hampshire, on the upper Connecticut River) on a scout to Fort Shirley.[38] Hobbs had his men halt for rest at what is now Marlborough, Vermont, about 15 km north of the Massachusetts border. While there, they were discovered and attacked by a large body of Indians led by Chief Sackett, said to have been a half-blood descended from a captive taken at Westfield, Massachusetts. Hobbs, however, had wisely posted a guard on his trail who gave sufficient warning for the men to take action. Although Sackett had four times the number of men as the English, the latter held them off for four hours, after which the Indians withdrew with their dead. Hobbs then marched east to Fort Dummer; it is not known whether he got to Shirley. This incident points out that scouting militiamen on the frontier passed regularly between forts; these even included the forts on the upper Connecticut that, because New Hampshire could not afford it, were staffed and supplied by Massachusetts. According to Perry, that summer and fall Israel Williams, with the rank of major, had supposedly established his own headquarters at Fort Shirley, from which he took personal command of the Line of Forts from Pelham east (however, he must have been much of the time at Hatfield); while his cousin Ephraim Jr. ruled over Fort Massachusetts and the militia from there south-southwest to Stockbridge.[39]

Although there had been a cessation of arms in Europe for several months, the war continued unabated for the men on the frontier. On 23 July 1748, a scout sent out from Fort Massachusetts was discovered by the enemy and followed in.[40] For the next eight days the fort was watched day and night by Indians. To the considerable joy of Ephraim Jr., at 2 P.M. on 1 August, Lieutenants Elisha Hawley and Daniel Severance arrived with 40 relief troops from Deerfield. Two hours later, however, the dogs outside the fort began to bark loudly, a sure sign that the enemy had followed these men and were nearby. The following morning the dogs were again restless; Williams determined that the enemy lay in ambush and resolved to go out against them with 50 men, supported by the "great cannon." But several of his troops had sallied out prematurely and were caught by enemy fire. To save them, Williams was forced to go out with about 35 men; after engaging the enemy ten minutes, the English drove them off their ground. No sooner had they done this than they were ambushed on their right by about 50 of the enemy, who partly blocked their way between them and the fort. Williams and his men managed to get back into the fort, and "played away with our cannon & small arms" for about an hour and three quarters, after which the enemy withdrew.

Captain Williams, in a letter to his cousin Israel, estimated that the enemy force had consisted of 200 to 300 men, mostly Indians but with about 30 French, and a French commander. Because they carried off their dead, there was no way of knowing how many had been killed. On the English side, none were killed, but three were wounded, including Lieutenant Hawley who was hit in the calf by a large buckshot. As Wright comments,

> This minor engagement presents surprising likenesses in detail to the "Bloody Morning Scout" of the Battle of Lake George, in which Ephraim Williams lost his life. There is the same initial lack of discipline characteristic of militia operations, the same lack of caution, the same personal bravery in the commander in leading his men directly at the enemy, the same retreat, and the same success in repulsing the enemy when attacked in the fort.[41]

The skirmish also demonstrates that Fort Massachusetts, whatever its tactical failings from the viewpoint of military design, served an important strategic role in attracting the attention of the French and their Indian allies, and keeping them away from the settled areas to the south and east.

Another Peace (1748–1754)

The long-awaited peace finally came. With the signing of the Treaty of Aix-la-Chapelle on 18 October, the War of the Austrian Succession was finished, and the two great powers, Great Britain and France, once more laid down their arms. The peace, which like all its predecessors was only to be a respite, brought a degree of tranquillity to New England's frontiers, but to most of its citizens it brought a major loss and the growing sense that the mother country had betrayed them: by the terms of the treaty, Great Britain traded Cape Breton and the hard-won Fortress of Louisbourg for Madras in far-off India. The people of Massachusetts were never to forget this, and nurtured a smoldering resentment that was to burst into flame during the succeeding quarter-century.

This time was a period of retrenchment for the Line of Forts, and Shirley and Pelham were to dwindle to nothing, as they had proved to have little strategic importance. Nevertheless, Fort Massachusetts remained a center of activities; it was to be a pivotal location for the permanent settlement of the northern Berkshires.

That autumn, there was a severe sickness among the men at Fort Massachusetts. The muster roll from 11 September of that year to 11 March 1749 shows 56 men stationed there under Ephraim Williams, Jr., and another one from 1 November 1748 to 3 April 1749 lists 53 men at Shirley, Pelham, and Colrain under Israel Williams. On 15 July 1749, however, acting Governor Spencer Phipps (with William Shirley absent in England from that year until 1753) sent the following letter to Israel Williams:

> Sir
>
> You are hereby directed to give imediate orders that the forts within ye County of Hampshire be reduced to the number of fifteen men only, including officers and these to be posted at the fort called Massachusetts Fort and to be continued in pay till the first of May next, the rest of the men to be forthwith discharged.
>
> Phips[42]

This order could never have been carried out in its entirety, as the muster roll of Lieutenant William Lyman, June 1749 to January 1750, shows that there were still 26 men in the Line of Forts from Shirley to the Connecticut River;

and there exists an account from Ephraim Williams, Jr., dated 3 June 1750, for billeting 11 men at Shirley and Pelham.[43] Perhaps Israel Williams had convinced Phipps that it would be premature to abandon any of the forts, and that 15 men could never have held off an attack on Massachusetts.

Nevertheless, there was considerable reduction of the forces. From 11 December 1749, to 3 June 1750, there were 31 militia posted at Fort Massachusetts,[44] while the next muster roll, to 13 January 1751, shows only 16 men stationed there.[45] As for Forts Shirley and Pelham, the decline was even more abrupt. On the muster roll of 11 December 1749 to 3 June 1750, Lieutenant William Lyman has four men with him at Shirley, and Sergeant Joseph Allen has an equal number at Pelham.[46] From June 1751, until the renewal of hostilities in 1754, there is but one man each in these two forts! Although they were accompanied by their families, life must have been very lonely for Archibald Pannell at Shirley and George Hall at Pelham.

The Williams family turned the peace to good account for themselves as well as for the province. During these years Ephraim, Jr. was far more often in Boston or elsewhere than at his command on the banks of the Hoosac. The years from 1749 to 1753 show him as a real estate entrepreneur and developer on the modern scale. Petitions to the General Court made after the return of the captives taken at Fort Massachusetts in 1746 indicate that some of them have been already established as "proprietors" of land with their own houses and lots. In April 1749 the General Court directed Colonel Timothy Dwight, Sr. (a recognized surveyor), Colonel Choate, and Oliver Partridge to act as a committee to see to the laying out of two townships in "Hoosuck," the eastern one near the fort, and the western in what was to become Williamstown. Their report and surveys were submitted on 10 November 1749.

On 17 January 1750, Ephraim Jr. presented a petition to a committee appointed the same day to lay out 63 house lots in West Hoosuck: he claimed that if land in the northwesterly part of East Hoosuck could be improved, it would supply most of the provisions for the fort, and that if he were granted 200 acres, he would agree to build a grist and sawmill to so provide.[47] At the same time, he was wheeling and dealing with his cousin Colonel William Williams and Governor Wentworth of New Hampshire to get land around the future Bennington, Vermont, as well as consolidating his holdings in Stockbridge. On 4 February 1751, he was in Boston trying to get the province to pay his soldiers speedily so that they could purchase the Hoosuck lots they had been promised; eight days later, the General Court in fact granted to him 190 acres of land near the fort under the conditions he had laid down.

The work of laying out the new town of West Hoosuck, the future Williamstown, was completed by September 1752; the original plan is in the hand of Ephraim Williams, Jr. He had disposed of his grant from the General

Court the previous March to Moses Graves and the unfortunate Elisha Chapin (of whom more later), but retained the prime land around Fort Massachusetts as well as land he had purchased in West Hoosuck. Some anxiety had been created the previous September when a group of Scatticook Indians (pro-French natives from Canada who had been dispossessed from the Connecticut River during King Philip's War) arrived at the fort to present their claims to all these lands, but they were turned off by threats and court action. Ephraim Jr. and his aging and difficult father, along with William Williams, remained the River Gods of the western Berkshires.

The absence of an active enemy, and the obviously self-serving behavior of the Williams family and their allies, led to rancor that had not been apparent in King George's War. Much of the trouble was at Fort Massachusetts, not surprisingly. The fort itself had actually been physically strengthened, although it was weak in personnel. The "proprietors" at Fort Massachusetts had petitioned the General Court on 18 August 1751, that with financial support from the province, they would "picket" (that is, palisade) the fort— a blockhouse on the order of Fort Shirley—with 3,000 stakes with fire-hardened bottoms, a proposal that was agreed to, as few in New England had illusions about future intentions of the Indians and French.

The problems at Fort Massachusetts probably began with the resignation of his command by Ephraim Williams, Jr., in the spring of 1752; he removed to his holdings in Stockbridge where his father and sister Abigail were engaged in a bitter feud with Jonathan Edwards, recently appointed missionary to the Indians there.[48] Edwards, although a distant relative, was a bête noire of long standing for the Williams family, had been ousted by them from Northampton, and continued to be their target in such an exposed situation as Stockbridge afforded. The new commander of Fort Massachusetts was Lieutenant Elisha Chapin; while he stood high in the estimation of Governor Shirley, he stood correspondingly low in that of the Williamses. Under him were 13 men, plus the ever-faithful Archibald Pannell at Shirley and George Hall at Pelham.[49] Chapin's rule was difficult, and at times the men were near mutiny and often intolerably drunk. This potential for insurrection was to weigh heavily in the decision to replace him in 1754.

The French and Indian War (1754–1763) Begins

History began repeating itself in 1754. During the past three years various events had indicated that the Indian foe once again had hostile designs on New England: a number of Penobscot from Maine had joined the Saint Francis Indians with intentions of attacking the frontiers, and the latter carried this out in 1752 with a raid on New Hampshire. On 28 May 1754, about 100 Scatticook Indians descended on "Dutch Hoosack" (now Hoosac Falls), about 10 miles (16.1 km) west of and downstream from Fort Massachusetts, killing one man and destroying the settlement.[50] This hostile conduct on the part of the Indians and the encroachments of the French on the Ohio led to the convening of an extraordinary congress in Albany on 14 June of that year. Present were delegates from the New England provinces, Pennsylvania, and Maryland, under the wise aegis of Governor Shirley. A treaty was signed with the Indians, and the delegates proposed adoption of a plan of union among the colonies that was largely authored by Benjamin Franklin. In a way, this was the first American congress. Unhappily, when the plan was sent to the provinces and to the Crown, both parties rejected it; each province was thus left to its own devices in the face of the common enemy.

Governor Shirley, recently returned from England, was already taking steps to protect the western frontier. On 13 June, he acceded to the request of Elisha Chapin, commanding Fort Massachusetts, that an additional five men be sent to Chapin's exposed fort. In his letter to the House of Representatives, Shirley also observes:

> Upon this occasion I must put you in mind of the hazardous Condition Fort Pelham and Fort Shirley are now in, if there should be any sudden Assault from the Indians on that Frontier; we must expect that the thing they will do would be to burn those forts, which they might easily do in their present Circumstances.
>
> Therefore I must recommend it to you, that provision be made that some better care may be taken for preserving them.[51]

Considering that there was only one soldier each at these forts, Shirley was hardly exaggerating the situation.

In August 1754, the governor placed his old ally Colonel Israel Williams in command of all forces raised or to be raised for Hampshire County. The Line of Forts was strengthened under Elijah Williams, commissary, who was commissioned major; Deerfield was made the depot for military stores for the northwest frontier. John Hawks was commissioned lieutenant and put in command of the garrisons to the east of Fort Massachusetts by Israel Williams; his headquarters were at Morrison's Fort in Colrain.[52]

About the first of the following month, Ephraim Williams, Jr., returned to the command of Fort Massachusetts, thereby causing the demotion of Captain Elisha Chapin, a turn of events that was to embitter Chapin and lead to a near schism among the westernmost garrisons on the Line of Forts. Meanwhile, William Williams had completed the fortification of his house in Pontoosuck to the south, and christened it Fort Anson. He thought this vastly superior to such fortified houses as Taylor's in Charlemont; in a letter to Ephraim Jr., he asks what Taylor had done "but built two mounts and picket. And what are all the forts that are built about houses but scare crows that they pull down as soon as ever the war is over."[53] Further south, the ruler of Stockbridge, the cantankerous and unscrupulous Ephraim Williams, Sr., had died on 11 August while in Deerfield. In spite of this loss in the family, their distant relative and sometime enemy Joseph Hawley saw that the Williamses had once more gotten all frontier matters in their hands by scheming among themselves and with Governor Shirley; he vowed to block them in the House of Representatives but never seems to have been able to carry out his plan.

On 12 September 1754 (the day after a raid on Stockbridge by the Scatticook Indians, in which one man and two children were killed), Israel Williams sent to Governor Shirley an extended letter outlining the full seriousness of the situation and detailing steps to be taken in the defense of the western frontier.[54] He proposed that augmented garrisons be maintained at Fall Town, Colrain (Morrison's), Charlemont (two garrisons), Fort Massachusetts, and Pontoosuck. He suggested at least 50 men to be posted at Massachusetts and 30 at Fort Anson; these were to maintain a constant scout extending from Stockbridge north to the top of Hoosac Mountain. There were to be 12 men at each of the Charlemont forts (Rice's and Taylor's), 20 at Morrison's, and 12 or 14 at Fall Town (Burk's); these were to scout from Northfield west to the top of Hoosac Mountain. Scouting parties were also to be sent from Fort Massachusetts toward the French and Indian stronghold of Crown Point on Lake Champlain. Israel suggested two additional forts between Fort Massachusetts and the Hudson, but this wise counsel seems to have fallen on deaf ears as they were never built. The death knell for two of our forts was rung by these observations in Israel's letter:

> The reason why I would neglect Shirley and Pelham is because the Indians were scarce ever known the last war to come down Deerfield river, and that road is almost impassable. Shirley is rotten, and if maintained must be rebuilt—and I think that at Morrison's will answer all intents full as well, & be much easier supply'd.

The governor replied to Israel Williams on 26 September, fully approving of his plan with the intention of submitting it to the General Court. As far as can be determined, Shirley and Pelham were thereupon abandoned and the swivel guns removed. George Hall at Pelham and whoever had replaced Archibald Pannell at Shirley (Pannell had died the previous February) were presumably sent home.

Both of these forts must soon have begun collapsing and rotting away as soon as they were decommissioned. As a structure, the deserted Pelham may have lasted longer than Shirley; according to John Hawks's journal (appendix 5), he lay over there on 27 May 1756 while returning on a scout between Colrain and Charlemont.

Fort Massachusetts and Crown Point

Although Ephraim Williams, Jr., had been placed in command of Fort Massachusetts, he seems seldom to have been there from the fall of 1754 through the following spring. Much of the time he appears to have been in Boston on personal, family, and province business. The acting commander was Lieutenant Isaac Wyman, in whom the Williams family had great confidence. The disappointed Elisha Chapin, however, must have been currying favor with Governor Shirley, in spite of the fact that the Williamses considered him an imprudent failure. On 21 November 1754, Ephraim Jr. wrote to his cousin Israel that the governor had promised to restore Chapin to his command if and when a new fort (presumably West Hoosuck) would be built to the west, which Shirley would offer to Ephraim. But on the following 16 December, Israel answered his cousin in Boston that he was "determined never to restore Capt. C[hapin] to his butlership. He has almost ruined the garrison as I am sufficiently informed—the soldiers were debauched &c." Israel said that Wyman "behaves well—has restored good order & government."[55] Israel must later have received news of a near mutiny that month under Wyman's command, however, for he wrote a strong letter of reprimand to him on 31 December 1754, complaining of the "clamorous, mutinous behavior of many if not most of the men under your com'and" and suggests that it was due to drunken men demanding more rum; he told Wyman to threaten the delinquents that if their behavior continued, they will suffer death "or other such punishment as by a Court Marshal shall be inflicted."[56] The unfortunate Chapin was probably right when he told Ephraim Jr., in a letter of 29 January 1755, that if he (Chapin) had not been there, the "late disturbance" would have been carried further than it was, for Chapin seems to have been more popular in the westernmost forts than Wyman. The real problem was probably the prolonged absence of Ephraim Williams, Jr., who was both liked and respected by his men.

The undeclared war between France and Britain in North America proceeded apace. In February 1755, General Edward Braddock arrived in Virginia from England as commander in chief of British forces in America. At a conference called by him in Alexandria, it was decided that there would be four great military operations against the enemy, as follows:

1. Braddock would proceed against Fort Duquesne on the Ohio, using his own regulars and southern militia.

2. Governor Shirley, as second in command to Braddock, was to attack Niagara in order to cut French communications with the Ohio, using two Royal regiments raised in New England and militia from New Jersey.

3. William Johnson, the virtual baron of the Mohawk Valley and
   the keystone of the British alliance with the Six Nations, was to
   lead an expedition to take Crown Point on Lake Champlain, with
   troops from all the northern colonies.

4. Troops from Massachusetts and Nova Scotia were to take Fort
   Beauséjour, on the neck of land between Nova Scotia and New
   Brunswick.[57]

It was destined that only the fourth objective (the capture of Beauséjour
under Lieutenant Colonel Monckton) would be met; the three failures were
a disaster for the British colonies.

That spring, Ephraim Williams, Jr., was busy recruiting and organizing a
regiment for the Crown Point expedition, for which he was commissioned
colonel by Shirley. On 31 May 1755, the governor ordered him to proceed
with his regiment to the General Rendezvous at Albany to join the forces of
Johnson. Under him were old colleagues and relatives: Seth Pomroy, the former armorer of the Line of Forts, as lieutenant colonel, his brother Thomas
Williams as surgeon, his cousin Stephen Williams of Longmeadow as chaplain, Perez Marsh, who was betrothed to Israel Williams's daughter Sarah,
as surgeon's mate, and Elisha Hawley as captain.

While these preparations were being made, the Indians were busy as usual
in harassing the western frontier. They were thick around forts on the upper
Connecticut, Bridgman's Fort in Hinsdale being attacked in June, while in
July 1755, frequent signs of Indians were seen around Fall Town, Colrain,
Charlemont, and Fort Massachusetts. On 11 June, a party of six Indians
attacked Captain Moses Rice while he was hoeing corn in the meadows
near his fort in west Charlemont, together with his son Artemas, grandson Asa Rice, and several others. One of the laborers was killed, and Captain Rice was wounded and taken prisoner with his grandson and one other.
After a struggle with his captor, the sixty-year-old Moses was tomahawked
and scalped, dying after some hours.[58] It would appear that the abandonment of Forts Shirley and Pelham had not been a wise move. But the major
factor was surely that the Crown Point expedition had drained the Line of
Forts and other exposed garrisons, leaving the settlers in a very precarious
position when tending their fields and livestock.

Some very bad news reached the expedition in Albany. On 9 July, Braddock, leaving a picked column of troops in which George Washington was
serving as a volunteer officer, was ambushed on the road to Fort Duquesne
by a large force of French and Indians. Braddock, who had little knowledge
of American-style warfare, was killed and his men routed; only the intelligence and bravery of Washington saved the remnant of his force. This terrible defeat left Shirley as commander in chief for North America, but New
England was badly disheartened. So were Johnson's Indians, who failed to

give the full support to the expedition against Crown Point. All of Braddock's papers fell into the hands of the enemy, which gave them ample warning of the full British strategy against the French.

This brings us to the affair of the "Bloody Morning Scout," in which Colonel Ephraim Williams, Jr., so much concerned with the story of the Line of
Forts, lost his life. William Johnson and Shirley had been bickering on and
off in the Albany camp, in spite of the goodwill effused during their dinners
together as documented in Seth Pomroy's journal of the expedition.[59] On
8 September 1755, Johnson, who by this time probably had little love of the
New Englanders, ordered Williams to lead his force, along with Chief Hendrick and his Mohawk allies, against the rear guard of a strong army brought
into the field by the French enemy commander, the German mercenary
Baron Dieskau. Williams and Hendrick, who should have known better,
failed to send scouts in front of them. As in the affair of 1748, Williams
showed great bravery but little sense. He walked into an ambush; Williams
and Hendrick were shot and killed, and the troops retreated in confusion.
However, in the action, the French commander in chief, Dieskau, was captured (his wounds were dressed by Dr. Thomas Williams). The French and
their Indian allies lost their momentum, and what could have been defeat
was turned into victory by Johnson. Captain Elisha Hawley was mortally
wounded in this "Battle of Lake George;" so was Sergeant Caleb Chapin,
Sr., of Fall Town, who was found dead and scalped after he had insisted that
his sons Joel and Hezekiah leave him to his fate.

There can be little doubt that the death of Ephraim Williams, Jr., can be
laid at the feet of Johnson, who while in many ways to be admired was not a
wholly admirable man. For the victory of the Battle of Lake George, he was
knighted; one of the best allies England had among the Six Nations died;
and New England lost one of its finest officers in the Line of Forts.

Because of lack of support from the old country, and through a lack of
unity among the participating colonies, Shirley bogged down after storms
and torrential rains in winter quarters at Oswego, and the Niagara campaign
failed to materialize.

The Dark Days

The years 1756 and 1757 were the darkest period of the French and Indian War.
Early in 1756, the Seven Years' War broke out in Europe. A coalition among
Austria, France, Russia, Sweden, and Saxony had formed against the power
of Frederick the Great of Prussia; France's traditional foe, England, naturally
joined the Prussians, and the ancient maritime and colonial war was resumed
on a formal basis. To make matters worse, a cabal headed by William Johnson had Governor Shirley recalled to England in this year, to face ridiculous

charges of treason (of which he was subsequently absolved). But his wise counsel and aid on the side of New England was removed forever, a circumstance that probably led to the development of the American Revolution.

Shirley was superseded by the indolent Earl of Loudon, who took his time in assuming his duties in America. While he dallied, he sent the even more incompetent General Abercrombie to take his place. Abercrombie arrived in Albany on 25 June, but did little but wait for the appearance of Loudon, an event that finally transpired on 29 July. On 4 August, while Loudon was celebrating his arrival and that of his staff and mistress, the great French commander in chief, the Marquis de Montcalm, took Fort Oswego, with great English loss of supplies and men.

These events stimulated the hostile Indians. Within half a mile of Fort Massachusetts, two soldiers were shot on 7 June. The "poor, distressed, and imprudent Captain Elisha Chapin" (who had been so named in the generous will of Ephraim Williams, Jr., under which he was given 100 pounds), had taken a kind of refuge in the West Hoosuck fort from Capt. Isaac Wyman's animosity. There he had been protected by William Chidester of Connecticut and his son. On 11 July 1756, Chapin and the two Chidesters were killed by Indians when hunting their cows near the western fort, thus removing some old-time antagonists to the Williamses and to their client, Isaac Wyman of Fort Massachusetts.

The course of events took an even worse turn in 1757, both for New England and for British America in general. As a sign of the times, one might point to the continued lethargy of Loudon, who in this year sent 1200 men against the Fortress of Louisbourg, but returned without having struck a blow.[60] On 9 August, General Montcalm captured Fort William Henry on Lake George; the English garrison surrendered honorably, but were shamefully massacred by the Indians, under the eyes of the French officers. A number of the garrison were from the Line of Forts; among those who escaped the holocaust was John Burk of Fall Town, who reached Fort Edward with only his breeches and a watch.

During this year, it seemed certain that the French would end in capturing New England and retain the land beyond the Alleghenies. The Line of Forts and the western frontier were in grave jeopardy. That June, John Taylor had written from Colrain to his brother, Sergeant Othniel Taylor, that Indians "are Discovered very thick between North River and Deerfield River"; six days later a party of Indians came to Charlemont, killing a man and a horse.[61] They had certainly come through the gap created by the demise of Forts Pelham and Shirley. The downfall of Fort William Henry created general alarm on this frontier, and the capture of Fort Edward followed by the invasion of New York and New England was shortly expected. All militia in western Massachusetts were mobilized, but by the end of August the attack had failed to materialize.

The infighting between the settlers of West Hoosuck, and attached to the blockhouse there, and the powers in Fort Massachusetts continued unabated in these gloomy days. On 11 January 1757, some 21 householders of West Hoosuck presented a petition to Lieutenant Governor Phips and to the General Court complaining of Captain Isaac Wyman that among other matters he would only allow them 14 days' provisions for 10 men at a time from the storehouse in Fort Massachusetts. The continuing friction was most evident between natives of Connecticut, who were in the ascendancy at West Hoosuck, and the "Bay" natives at Fort Massachusetts. After some temporizing, the General Court appointed Timothy Woodbridge to head a committee of investigation. Woodbridge took extensive testimony, and decided in favor of the West Hoosuck settlers. Among other observations, he reported that this fort was more strategically located than was Fort Massachusetts, and as the whole idea of these forts was to stimulate settlement of the region, it would be more logical to strengthen West Hoosuck.[62] One of three 4-pounders and two swivel guns were ordered taken there from Fort Massachusetts, so that Isaac Wyman must have felt himself increasingly isolated in his eastern stronghold. That September, in the general alarm, John Catlin and three officers plus 49 men were sent to reinforce West Hoosuck, which they found rotting; they returned to Deerfield on 1 December.

Turn of the Tide and the Close of the War

Luckily for English America, there were other forces running counter to this current. William Pitt, the Earl of Chatham, had succeeded the incompetent Duke of Newcastle (William Shirley's inconstant protector) as prime minister, and he proved to be an exceptionally able administrator. For the first time in the history of the hostilities with the French and Indians, sufficient men and funds were made available by the homeland to counter the enemy in two hemispheres. On 30 December 1757, Loudon was recalled by Pitt to England, but Loudon was unhappily replaced as commander in chief by the even more inept Major General Abercrombie. Historian Fred Anderson tells us that he was a corpulent man and an indifferent officer, who wanted to undertake nothing for which he might later be blamed."[63] Nevertheless, Pitt did back up his promises to America by authorizing the arming and payment of provincial troops by the home government, by ordering that the rank of provincial officers be recognized by regular army officers, and by ordering thousands of regulars to be sent to America.

Abercrombie moved against Fort Ticonderoga with 7,000 men in July 1758, and was beaten by Montcalm with terrible losses of both regulars and provincials. But this great reverse was turned around 18 days later, when General Jeffrey Amherst, supported by the fleet of Admiral Boscawen, took the Fortress of Louisbourg with the total surrender of its troops, supplies, and the whole of Cape Breton Island. Britain now controlled the entrance of the Saint Lawrence River, and threatened Quebec and Montreal. The following 27 August, Fort Frontenac was captured by General Bradstreet, and on 24 November, Fort Duquesne fell to General James Forbes. In the face of these successes, Amherst succeeded the useless Abercrombie as commander in chief.

On March 21, 1758, about 50 Indians appeared at Morrison's Fort in Colrain, wounding two men, burning Captain Hugh Morrison's house and barn (which were apparently outside the fort), and killing several cattle and sheep. The Indians settled down nearby and (in the words of Jonathan Ashley) "after they had roasted, and fed themselves, came and fired at the fort and went off and lodged within a mile and a half of the fort."[64] The valiant John Hawks must have been absent on a scout, for he would never have countenanced the failure of the soldiers to go after the Indians; Ashley was furious when he heard of the incident, and preached a sermon against inactivity in the face of such provocation.

Although John Catlin had written from Colrain to Sergeant John Taylor at Charlemont on 30 May of that year that a scout "had made some discovery of an Enemy not far from the Pelham fort," it was evident that Indian raids on the New England frontiers had virtually ceased by that month, and that the die had been cast against its original inhabitants when French power began to weaken.[65] The last Indian incursion on the frontiers of Massachusetts took place on 21 March 1759, when between 10 and 12 Indians captured a resident of Colrain, along with his wife and child. The Line of Forts was still extant, however, and the following 4 June, Captain Samuel Wells took command of its eastern garrisons following the departure of Major John Hawks for active service in the reduction of Canada.

The final revenge of the New Englanders against the Indian foe transpired in the autumn of that year. On 13 September, Major Robert Rogers, under secret orders from Amherst, took a party of 200 of his Rangers into Canada, with the goal of destroying the village of Saint Francis, source of so many guerrilla-type attacks on the frontier settlers. He accomplished this by a surprise raid on 5 October, his troops discovering 600 or 700 English scalps waving from poles in the village. Out of the estimated 300 defenders, 200 were killed. Rogers's return from this foray is one of the sagas of the French and Indian War.[66] The Indians had found and destroyed their boats and provisions; on arrival at Coos Meadows, where Amherst had ordered supplies to be sent for them, the Rogers party found that the relief party had just left for the south and in a cowardly gesture had refused to be detained by shouts or the sound of gunshots. Only through Rogers's superb woodsmanship did any of the starving survivors reach Crown Point.

The Battle of Quebec took place in September 1759, when Generals Wolfe and Montcalm both fell on the Plains of Abraham. With Quebec in English hands, it was a foregone conclusion that the French power was finished in North America. In September 1760, Governor Vaudreuil (brother of that Vaudreuil who had captured Fort Massachusetts in 1746), surrendered the whole province of Canada to Great Britain. Signed in 1763, the Treaty of Paris forced France to cede to her foe all of North America east of the Mississippi, except the tiny islands of Saint Pierre and Miquelon.

The End of the Line of Forts

I have been unable to discover any reports of muster rolls for the Line of Forts later than 1758. Certainly by the fall of Quebec in 1759, most of Israel Williams's militia had been dismissed, to follow their own fates as civilians in the momentous years leading up to the American Revolution. By that time, Shirley and Pelham were moldy, worm-eaten ruins, surrounded and infested with second-growth brush and young trees. After 1759, Captain Isaac Wyman continued to farm the ten acres surrounding the Fort Massachusetts stockade (acreage that had originally been set aside for the use of the fort), but on 13 November 1761, he sold all his West Hoosuck property and moved to Keene, New Hampshire. A few of the homeless soldiers hung around the fort for the next few years, but by 1766, it was in total ruin, the stockade leveled by decay and farmed over.

The fate of the other forts to the east was probably similar. As early as 1758, the inhabitants of Deerfield, feeling secure from invasion, voted to sell the timbers provided during the panic year of 1756 for building garrisons, and to dispose of the remains of the old garrisons that they judged unfit for use. Perhaps some found a practical purpose for these now obsolete structures; John Burk moved his house in Burk's Fort to a new site in Fall Town (now Bernardston) and remodeled it into a flourishing tavern.

NOTES

1. Sheldon 1898.
2. Sheldon 1972, 1:93.
3. Sheldon 1972, 1:175.
4. Sheldon 1972, 1:213–14.
5. Hoyt 1824:151.
6. Hoyt 1824:183.
7. Melvoin 1989:285.

8. Hoyt 1824:188. Haefeli and Sweeney 2003 present a comprehensive history and analysis of the 1704 raid on Deerfield.
9. Williams 1969.
10. Hoyt 1824:209.
11. Sheldon 1972, 1:388.
12. Hoyt 1824:2, 3.
13. Sheldon 1972, 1:517.
14. Sheldon 1972, 1:452.
15. Sheldon 1972, 1:533.
16. Perry 1904:80.
17. Ibid.
18. Perry 1904:81–88.
19. Perry 1904:96.
20. *Encyclopedia Britannica* 1911, 21:67.
21. See Fry 1984 for a comprehensive history of Louisbourg, its fortifications, and its inherent weaknesses.
22. Chet 2003:103.
23. De Forest 1926:14–72.
24. Costello 1975.
25. Perry 1904:117.
26. Perry 1904:123.
27. Sheldon 1972, 1:541.
28. Wright 1970:18.
29. Sheldon 1972, 1:541.
30. Perry 1904:119.
31. Norton 1870. There is also an important account of these events from the French point of view in Parkman 1892, 2:245–70, based upon Rigaud de Vaudreuil's journal.
32. Aiken 1912:340.
33. Sheldon 1972, 1:545–49.
34. Wright 1970:22–23.
35. Perry 1904:195.
36. Wright 1970:23.
37. Hoyt 1824:256–58; Sheldon 1972, 1:554–61.
38. Hoyt 1824:249–50.
39. Perry 1904:226.
40. Wright 1970:30–32.
41. Wright 1970:32.
42. Israel Williams Papers.
43. Ibid.
44. Ibid.
45. Perry 1904:236.
46. Israel Williams Papers.
47. Wright 1970:36.
48. Wright 1970:55.
49. Perry 1904:249.

50. Hoyt 1824:262–63.
51. Perry 1904:254–55.
52. Sheldon 1972, 1:630.
53. Wright 1970:81.
54. Perry 1904:289–91.
55. Wright 1970:84.
56. Perry 1904:271.
57. Wright 1970:94–95.
58. Perry 1904:273 and Healy 1965:28–30.
59. De Forest 1926:100–127.
60. A completely different reassessment of Loudon can be found in Guy Chet's *Conquering the American Wilderness* (2003), where he is praised for his concentration on logistics (communication and supplies) that eventually led to the French collapse in North America.
61. Sheldon 1972, 1:658.
62. Perry 1904:416.
63. Anderson 2000:141.
64. Sheldon 1972, 1:655.
65. Sheldon 1972, 1:657.
66. See Starbuck 2004:16–18 for a history of this controversial and colorful figure.

Chapter 4

Fort Shirley

T HE SITE OF Fort Shirley (72°48'W, 42°40'N) is located in the town of Heath, Massachusetts, at an altitude of between 1610 and 1650 feet (491 to 503 m). It is to be found in a wooded area just west of Hosmer Road (also known as the Oxbow Road), on the northeastern slope of a hill that drops abruptly more than 600 feet (183 m) to the West Branch Brook. This stream flows in a generally eastern direction to meet the East Branch Brook in the town of Colrain, both brooks joining to form the North River, which flows south into the Deerfield River (fig. 4-1).

Construction and Occupation of the Fort

The letter of 20 July 1744 from Colonel John Stoddard of Northhampton, ordering his nephew Captain William Williams to construct Fort Shirley has already been given in chapter 2. It was to be a blockhouse 60 feet on a side, with 11-foot-high walls and 11-foot-wide barracks (certainly no more than two because of the modest size of the fort). A total of 54 men worked on it over a period of about three months, but not all at the same time.

According to the surviving account of the expenses, the major work was clearly the cutting down, hewing, and scoring the timbers that were to be laid horizontally to form the walls of the blockhouse; and making the flooring for the houses and the parade.[1] Altogether, 4,774 feet of timber went into the construction. Stones had to be hauled for the chimney foundations, these stones laid, and the chimneys built up of clay and nine "horseloads" of straw. Professor Perry surmised from this account and from foundations that were still visible in his day that there were four chimneys, two for each house, a conclusion that we were able to confirm archaeologically. The roofing for the barracks required 12,000 shingles and 16,000 shingle nails; the rest of the construction used up 2,000 board nails, and five hundredweight of 20 penny nails. Hardware that went into the houses and possibly also the gate or gates were five pairs of hooks and hinges; five hasps and staples; three padlocks; and two pairs of small door hinges (if, as seems

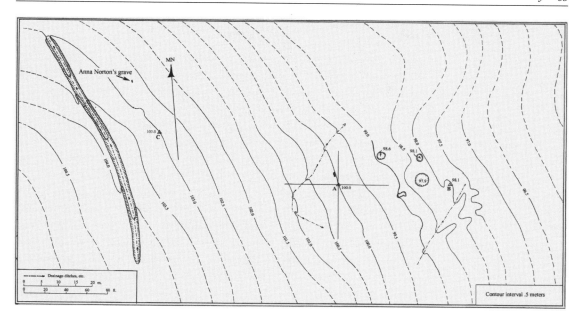

likely, there were only two barracks, this would mean only one door for each house).

Post-abandonment History of Fort Shirley

How long it took the fort to disappear after it was decommissioned in 1754, and the site returned to forest, is unknown. Colonel Asaph White (1747–1828), who settled as early as 1769 in what would be Heath, and lived there until his removal to Erving, Massachusetts, in 1800, took out six timbers from Fort Shirley and incorporated them in his barn, so some of the wooden structure was still standing then.[2] Fragments of three of these timbers are still extant in the town, and will be described in this chapter.

To understand the trajectory of the fort site after the death of its last known occupant, Archibald Pannell, one must consider the land speculation that was rife in Massachusetts during the eighteenth century. About 1725, there had come about a change in the practice of certain New England colonies, including Massachusetts Bay, in the making of town grants. The prudent policy of distributing new land purely for the sake of settlement was abandoned; instead, both Massachusetts and Connecticut sold whole townships to grantees who intended not to settle but to resell at a profit.[3] There followed a period (1730–40) of speculation in "wild lands," speculation that, although in the end proving disastrous to those who had bought large tracts, nevertheless did stimulate pioneering on the part of others. Thus, long

FIG. 4-1. Contour map of the general area of Fort Shirley, with the location of Anna Norton's grave, and the deep drainage ditch dug by the soldiers to keep groundwater from flowing into the fort. Regardless of this precaution, the fort eventually rotted out. Elevations are taken from Station A, given the arbitrary value of 100.0 meters.

before this part of the frontier was inhabitable, the General Court of Massachusetts granted to Boston, in June 1735, a township that comprised the larger part of the present towns of Heath and Charlemont, and a smaller fraction of Buckland; this was named Boston Plantation No. 1.[4] One would hardly think that lands that were hardly defensible could have been subject to speculation, but such was indeed the case.

The rest of the story is told by land transactions kept in the Registry of Deeds of Hampshire and Franklin Counties. From these, it is clear that wheeling and dealing in frontier lands did not cease in 1740. Before 1742, John Green of Boston had bought 8,575 acres of Boston Plantation No. 1, lands comprising the northern half of Heath and an adjacent part of Rowe. This property was said to have been surveyed by Richard Hazen (who had established the northern line of Massachusetts in the previous year) and Nathan Kellogg. In 1742, these lands—to be known for more than five decades as the Green and Walker Tract—were passed to the Boston merchants Joseph Green and Isaac Walker, to Byfield Lyde, and to their respective heirs and assigns.

Joseph Green and his colleague Walker were prominent storekeepers; in the early 1760s, they were selling goods from their establishment at the north corner of Queen Street in Boston. Most important for our story, Green and Walker were principal wholesalers to Elijah Williams of Deerfield, who in turn was retailing to the officers and men in the Line of Forts. In February 1743, they became sole owners of their tract when Lyde and his spouse sold their part of the acreage to them; the Lydes sold another portion to Dr. Thomas Bulfinch of Boston, father of the renowned architect of the Massachusetts State House. By 1767, both Green and Walker were deceased; in that year Messrs. Cox and Berry had opened a new store at the same Queen Street address, and announced themselves as the successors to their late predecessors.[5] In November 1768, the two widows disposed of the Green and Walker tract to two English speculators resident in London: Thomas Lane and Benjamin Booth.

By that time, the tract had already been subdivided into 100-acre lots; the deeds say that this was done on 18 December 1764—probably for a considerable fee—by Oliver Partridge (a River God and Williams relative), Moses Graves (formerly a lieutenant at Fort Massachusetts, one of the original proprietors of West Hoosuck, and now a merchant), and Elijah Williams. The stone walls running through the fields and woods of northern Heath yet conform to this subdivision, which was made possible by the peace treaty of 1763. As always on the New England frontier, real estate speculation and development were the camp followers of military defense.

Astonishingly, the Lane and Booth title survived the American Revolution, and it must have been during their absentee ownership of the tract that Colonel White removed the fort's timbers. Surely, the fort clearing was by now second-growth forest. In 1796, their heirs John Lane and Thomas Fraser appointed a Boston attorney to unload their overseas territories, and in July these were passed for $17,100 to a Yankee speculator, Nathan Rice of Hingham, Massachusetts. Rice shortly began selling off his lots to land-hungry young men residing in the overpopulated region between Boston and Worcester in the eastern half of the state. It was this region that supplied most of the pioneers who were to settle the hill towns of the northern Berkshires in the decades between 1790 and 1830.

In 1814, Samuel Higgins of Heath bought Lot No. 8, "commonly called the fort lot" (according to the deed), consisting of 103 acres. Higgins was not exactly affluent; he did not finish paying Hunt for the land until 1824, by which time he had disposed of 25½ acres to a third party. Sheep farming was the economic mainstay of early nineteenth-century Heath, and it was almost certainly Higgins who cleared the "fort lot" for pasture, and he who built the house—now represented only by an imposing cellar hole—on the east side of Hosmer Road. The foundations of this structure as well as the base of a large central chimney are made entirely of local schist and gneiss, as are the various field walls in the vicinity. It is not difficult to envision Higgins, with the aid of a team of oxen and a "stone boat" or sledge dismantling the four stone chimney bases of Fort Shirley, and incorporating these materials in his new homestead.

Higgins and his family and heirs probably pastured their sheep and cattle in the "fort lot" until the close of the Civil War. At some later date, the property passed to Philip S. Gale, and then in 1872 to William L. Cook. For the next three decades mortgages passed back and forth between the improvident Cook (who at one time was declared bankrupt) and others, but the site continued to be open pastureland. Finally, in 1909, Mrs. Felicia Emerson Welch, daughter of one of Heath's most distinguished doctors, bought 20 acres around Fort Shirley and presented them to the Heath Historical Society.

This brings us to the documentary and archaeological activities of Arthur Latham Perry, professor of economics at Williams College during the latter half of the nineteenth century; he and George Sheldon of Deerfield were the finest local historians of the period. Perry had boundless admiration for the founder of Williams, Colonel Ephraim Williams, Jr., and for the men who had manned the Line of Forts under his command. Armed with documentary and oral information on Fort Shirley, he visited the site a number of times, and carried out rough-and-ready excavations that were more or less typical of the times. Unlike our own project, he did have the advantage that the site was then open and free of trees, so surface features were more visible than they were to us. In 1886, Perry dug a depression that proved to be one of the wooden wells of Shirley, and I believe that it was he who was responsible for some of the small pothunter's pits that dot the surface 5 to 10 m southwest of this well.[6] What may be a token of the professor's presence at Shirley is a surface find of our project, a wine bottle that seems to date to the 1880–90 decade.

During his activities at the site, Perry removed the small schist headstone commemorating the death and burial of the little Anna Norton (fig. 4-2), daughter of the fort's chaplain, and carried it off to his museum in Williams College. This aroused great local ire, and two of Heath's leading citizens, the sisters Mary Abby White and Flora White, forced its return to its original location. The stone was reset during an imposing ceremony (fig. 4-3), complete with Heath children in "colonial" costume, probably during a Heath Fair celebrated between 1901 and 1909.[7] The stone is still there.

There is some uncertainty about the exact date on which the large stone marker, incised with the words "Fort Shirley, 1744–1754," was placed on the site, but it was probably around 1901, when the Heath Historical Society was founded by the White sisters. Following the site's transfer to the society in 1909, all but the immediate area around the stone—which was to be kept

FIG. 4-2. The schist headstone of Anna Norton's grave, carved and erected by Fort Shirley's soldiers after the little girl's death in 1747.

FIG. 4-3. Rededication of the Norton grave site c. 1901–9, after Professor Perry of Williams College was forced to return it from his museum. Some of the young girls and boys of Heath have donned colonial costume. The portly orator is unidentified. At that time, the site was open pasture-land. Heath Historical Society.

in grass according to the terms of Mrs. Welch's deed—began to revert to brush and then to second-growth forest.

Between the days of Perry and our own excavations, only one attempt was made to investigate the site of Fort Shirley. During two summer days in the 1960s, the Reverend William Wolf of Heath and Edward DeRose of Greenfield probed the well depression left by Perry; they recovered some of the very few bricks ever found at Shirley, anomalous pieces of cut wood, and a fragment of brown-glazed earthenware.

From this history, it is quite clear that there has never been any significant occupation of the Fort Shirley site subsequent to its abandonment in 1754. Because there was no settlement here, either Indian or white, prior to 1744, it may be concluded that all artifacts and archaeological features here can be assigned to a single decade.

Surface Features

The most striking feature of the Fort Shirley site is its extreme wetness in all seasons, above all in late spring and early summer. A clay hardpan underlies

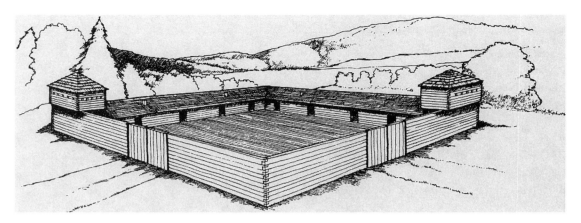

FIG. 4-4. Hypothetical reconstruction of Fort Shirley, based largely on the 1744 order. The Yale excavations indicate that the barracks were on opposite (west and east), not adjacent sides. The chimneys are probably much too small for the period.

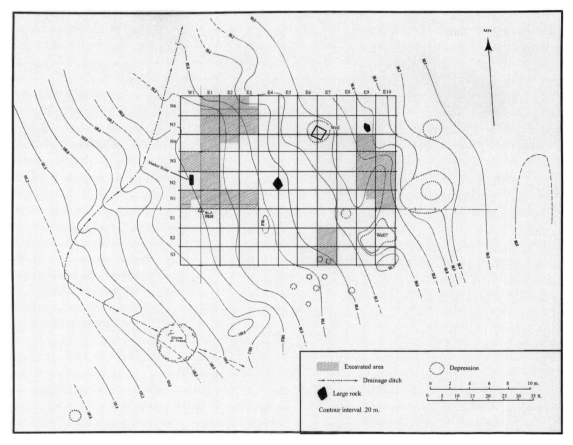

FIG. 4-5. Map of Fort Shirley, showing the archaeological grid and the excavated areas. The shallow ditch surrounding the site probably marks a palisade. The "marker stone" was placed at the site by the Heath Historical Society about 1901.

the area at a depth that almost never exceeds 50 cm. Thus, the soil is continually waterlogged, and the path from Hosmer Road to the site quickly turns with use into mud. It is a wonder that the fort *as* a fort lasted as long as ten years (figs. 4-4 to 4-8).

There are no visible architectural remains or artifacts on the surface, other than the large marker stone (in our square N2W1) and Anna Norton's small, schist headstone 50 meters to the northwest of this. The ground is hummocky, with several noticeable depressions, including the water-filled excavation left by previous investigations of the well found by Arthur Perry. After we had cleared the area reputed to be the site of the fort from its cover of ferns and small trees, two very shallow ditches became apparent. One is to the west of the marker stone and heads downhill in a NNE direction; the other lies at right angles to this, and connects with it. A third such ditch was found 35 m east of the marker stone, parallel with the first ditch. These three features are possibly the remains of a palisade ditch, but there is no documentary evidence that this blockhouse-type fort was ever picketed; their purpose may perhaps have been to divert water draining down from above

FIG. 4-6. Plans of the excavated areas of Fort Shirley: (*a*) northwest cut, with large chimney foundation; (*b*) south-center cut; (*c*) east cut. The presence of bricks along with scattered schist indicates that chimney bases were present in all three cuts.

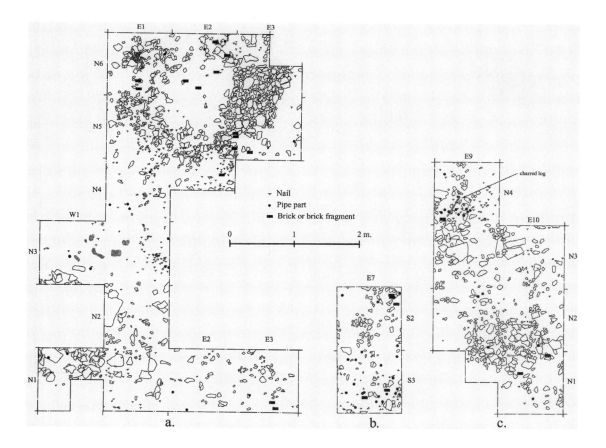

FIG. 4-7. View of the Yale excavations in Fort Shirley. Because the fort was occupied for only ten years, the deposits are very shallow.

away from the fort. Nonetheless, the possibility of a palisade should not be rejected out of hand.

A much larger manmade ditch was discovered in the woods west of the child's grave. This ditch is at least 70 meters long and is slightly curved toward the northwest. Even today it carries water during spring and early summer, and must have been a measure taken by Fort Shirley's soldiers to make their damp residence a little more habitable.

Excavations and Stratigraphy

Archaeological work began on Fort Shirley on 1 June 1974, and continued until 1 August of that year, with numerous interruptions caused by rain, which filled the excavations and often made digging impossible. We sometimes felt that we were engaging in underwater archaeology. A grid of two-meter squares was established for the site, oriented to 6° East of Magnetic

North, and centered on a survey station placed 2.7 m SSE of the marker stone. In conformity with the system previously used by the University of Massachusetts team at Fort Pelham, these squares were designated by directions and by consecutive numbers from the survey station, and were divided into quadrants for excavation and recording. The northwest quadrant was designated A, the northeast one as B, the southwest as C, and the southeast as D. Every artifact was individually plotted according to this system, and all digging was by "natural" layers rather than by "metrical" ones.

Only 24 squares were actually excavated, some of these only partially, so that less than a third of the area probably covered by the blockhouse has been investigated. This should be kept in mind when the architecture and activity areas at the site are discussed below.

The stratigraphy of Fort Shirley is very straightforward, as its ten-year period of occupation has produced only a very thin cultural layer, with some variability resulting from forest action and the activities (including construction) of the fort's occupants. The entire site is overgrown with ferns, bushes, and small trees, the fern roots in particular causing a rather uneven ground surface. Some erosion has also taken place, apparently during the nineteenth century when it was open pastureland. Beneath the surface vegetation is a very thin layer of black topsoil, often indistinguishable from the

FIG. 4-8. The best-preserved chimney base is in the northwest corner, but even it is in very poor condition.

underlying brown or black subsoil; these two strata exist almost everywhere in the site, and occur at widely varying depths. Most of the artifacts were recovered within them, and together they are considered to be Layer I.

About 80 percent of the artifacts came from within 15 to 20 cm of the surface; they are rarely to be found on the surface or below 30 cm. It is worth noting that the brief testing for phosphates carried out during the excavation season by Janice Weeks and Joyce McKay showed that most of this chemical activity was confined to Layer I. A few cultural items were recovered from greater depths, but disturbance from root and animal action in such a site is to be expected. Where our digging probed deep into rock concentrations (that is, in the remains of chimney bases), artifacts were almost nonexistent.

At depths from 6 to 25 cm, Layer I is replaced by Layer II. This stratum shows a wide variety of color changes, and is the layer in which we would expect to see evidence of different structural and activity zones. The first of these color variations consists of a dark, brown-black soil; is fairly rare; and occurs on the peripheries of structures (in Quadrants N3E10-B and N3W1-A). The second is deep yellow and is found only in the interior of the rock concentration centering on Square N5E2. At first we thought that this was a kind of fill, and the structure was further excavated in hopes of finding a floor beneath it; this operation was futile, for the underlying feature proved to be nothing more than hardpan, and no artifacts were found. The deep yellow soil thus constitutes the floor.

The final soil category in Layer II, burned earth, is readily recognized for its bright red and yellow hues. It is always accompanied by charcoal, often in considerable quantity. Greenish soil, probably ash, is frequently in association, while a few concentrations of very red earth might be decayed brick. Burned earth is commonly found in two areas. The first is associated with the rock concentration surrounding the marker stone; it is found through all of N2E1 and most of N3W1 and N3E1. If the excavations had gone deeper, virtually all of Squares N3E9, N3E10, NN2E10, and N1E10 would show the same intensity of burned earth as N2E9, which went to a considerable depth.

The probable meaning of the features uncovered will be discussed below.

Excavation of the Well

The surface depression visible in the eastern half of N5E6 and in most of N5E7 suggested to us the presence of a well, and it was decided to excavate it (figs. 4–9 to 4–13). We had before us the somewhat long-winded yet vivid account left by Perry of the well that he had uncovered at Fort Shirley in 1886:

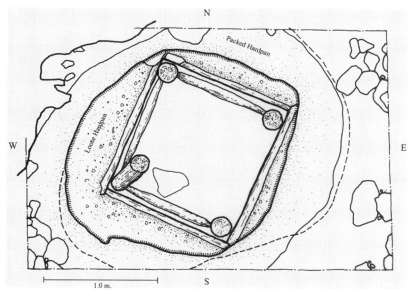

FIG. 4-9. Looking down to the top of the square wooden well just after excavations had revealed its presence.

FIG. 4-10. Vertical plan of the well.

Almost three half-centuries have already passed since the well was dug and the water first drunk by the thirsty workmen around it, and yet the risk is very slight in predicating for substance, that four forest staddles about six inches in diameter, one for each corner of the well, were set upright on the ground, and then ash planks, rived from a log about five feet long, were pinned or spiked on the outside of these staddles, beginning at the bottom; and this frame being placed on the ground where the well was to be, the earth was

FIG. 4-II. View into the well after excavation. The sides were of ash planks. Even before we reached bottom, water began gushing in. George Frideric Handel was still alive when this well was filled in and sealed.

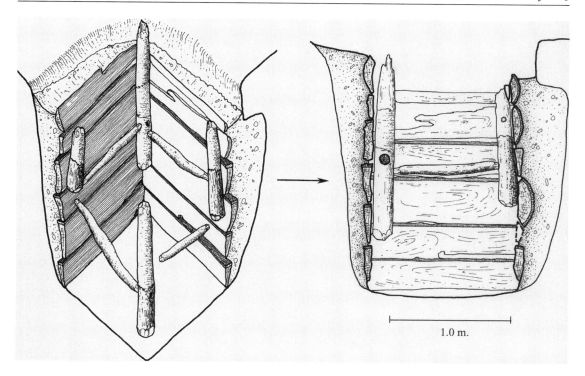

FIG. 4-12. Isometric and side views of the square well in Fort Shirley.

thown out over the sides, and so the well was gradually sunk to the required depth, the plank siding being gradually added upward as the shaft was lowered. These rived planks and the tops of the four corner-poles, that can now be seen and fingered less than two feet below the surface of the ground, were not very uniform in thickness, and of course have rotted off at the top by time and exposure; but enough of both has been preserved till this time by constant submergence in the water and in the unusually moist soil above it to reveal the nature of the materials used and in the mode of their employment. One of the corner-posts was a black birch, and the bark on it was in a good state of preservation at and below the surface of the water in 1886.[8]

Judging by our own findings in the second well, Perry's account would seem to be both accurate and perceptive.

The depression that we observed in N5E6 and N5E7 was almost perfectly circular, and measured two meters in diameter and 20 centimeters in depth. An indication that this might be a well, perhaps brick-lined, came from a brick fragment found lying on the surface of the depression. Tests were made with a probe, and showed that there was stone and possibly wood underlying it.

On 4 July Kloppenburg began actual excavation on the site of the supposed well. He began digging N5E7-D with a trowel, in anticipation of

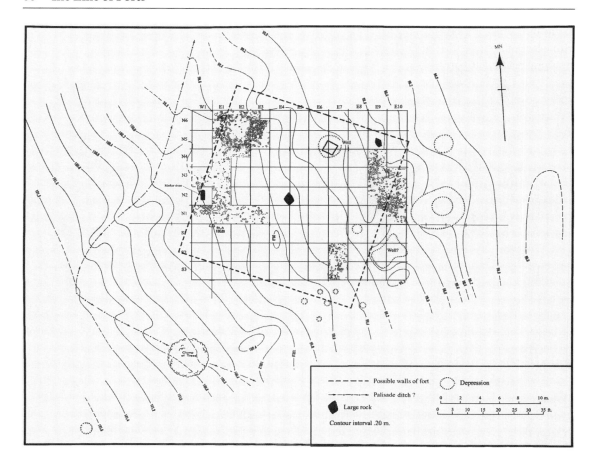

FIG. 4-13. Most likely placement of the Fort Shirley
"blockhouse," on the basis
of excavated chimney foundations and the 1744 order.
The square well would have
been located inside the
parade.

heavy artifact concentration; but other than a pipe stem just below the surface, this and other quadrants in the square proved almost completely sterile. However, a distinct color change was reached at 6 to 10 cm. The soil of
Layer I was the dark brown humus typical of this stratum throughout the
site. Layer II proved to be of a greenish color, and had a claylike consistency.
Digging was stopped at this depth, and all of Quadrant D was cleared to
the beginning of Layer II.

By beginning with N5E7-D, Kloppenburg had hoped to approach the
wall of the depression horizontally, so as to preserve its stratigraphy. Having
found the greenish layer, he moved to Quadrant C and began digging there.
On the level ground surface, the green soil of Layer II again appeared, but
within the depression itself this soil was somewhat deeper. Near the surface,
a bone fragment was recovered.

Deciding that the work was going too slowly, Kloppenburg began digging both Quadrants A and C with a shovel, but it was necessary to remove
a tree stump and a large number of roots with an axe. Down to a depth of

80 cm below datum, he encountered nothing but the greenish soil, along with occasional small stones. At about 90 cm, the tip of the shovel hit stone in several places, and brought up a mixed yellow and blue–stained soil. From this depth on down, the well would always have water in it; as a consequence, from then on, the digging would be in mud.

The next day (5 July), Kloppenburg brought the water down to a workable depth by draining it with a bucket. Continuing digging, he came across what will be called Plank 1 of the well's north wall. Cleaning around it with trowel and brush, he discovered the north corner post: clearly this was going to be a square wooden well of the kind described by Perry. However, the easterly end of the board was still covered by a large overburden of dirt because it extended into N5E7-B, not yet excavated.

As the well had now been located, the manner in which it was to be uncovered had now to be considered. It was decided that all the quadrants (N5E6-B, N5E6-D, N5E7-A, N5E7-C, N5E7-D) should be taken to the level of the hardpan found in N6E6, so as to give a solid base on which to work, and to show the well in clear outline.

Clay hardpan was found at a depth of about 45 cm in the western halves of Quadrants B and D in N5E7, but the greenish soil in the eastern halves disappeared, and the soil returned once again to the brown soil of Layer I. Furthermore, this loose soil continued down alongside the packed hardpan, so that a sharp contrast was visible at their juncture. It appeared that this line was no natural phenomenon, as it generally followed the contours of the well. It thus seemed that the hardpan indicated the limits of the excavation that the soldiers had made in order to build the well shaft, which was presumably square or rectangular. Accordingly, Kloppenburg dug B and D down until a level of about 45 cm was reached throughout the squares, and the contrast between the soils showed clearly. Cleaning the edges of the well with a trowel, he found that the hardpan constituted a virtual "rim" around the well, sloping down to well sides. In order to reveal the entirety of the well and this hardpan enclosure, N5E6-B and D were excavated, demonstrating that a ring of hardpan totally surrounded the well in a rough oval. The well itself was not placed in the center of the oval, but rather pushed to its northern and eastern edges, while the northwest, northeast, and southeast corners of the well were partly obscured by the hardpan rim.

Excavation in the body of the well proceeded. Soon, all four corner posts and the four boards of the first (topmost) course of planking had been uncovered. Plank 1 on the south side had partly fallen in on its western end, apparently because the western corner post had also fallen somewhat toward the center of the well. The wood was well preserved thanks to waterlogged conditions. Now that all four sides of the well had been found, it was possible to see that it was about 120 cm (slightly under 4 ft.) square.

From this point on, excavations were carried out solely within the confines of the actual structure. The greenish soil of Layer II disappeared at an average depth of 95 cm, being replaced by what seemed to be loose hard-pan (Layer III); this was characteristically yellow, and liberally stained with spots of brown and blue. The Layer III stratum contained many large stones of schist, as well as a great deal of wood debris, most of it uncut and some it apparently charred. Two clay pipe fragments, a handwrought nail, and two bones were found in Layer III. By this time, the well was being dug in arbitrary 30 cm levels, as it was too muddy to see stratigraphic changes exactly as they occurred. Layer II, however, was very consistent throughout.

While removing Layer III, several facts were learned about the well. The west corner post turned out to be only 62 cm long, and was supported by braces from the north and east corner posts; braces were also found on the north and east walls, although the one on the east was only fragmentary and not in situ. The braces on the south, west, and north walls were all in place, with tapering ends that fit into holes carved into the posts to which they were attached. As the excavation went deeper, preservation became remarkable: bark could be seen on all the posts and on the braces. The north post was in such perfect condition that it could be identified as yellow birch (*Betula lutea*).

At a depth of 1.72 cm, a definite and abrupt stratigraphic change occurred. The yellow hardpan ceased, and was replaced by a gray-green clay the color of wet concrete; this was thick and viscous, and very fine-grained. This stratum, Layer IV, contained mainly small stones and bits of charcoal. But the most striking feature of Layer IV was that in its final 20 cm were found a number of wooden artifacts and cut pieces of wood in a perfect state of preservation (see fig. 6-20); these were washed, and then conserved by soaking them for two weeks in a solution of Carbowax 4000.

The well bottomed out with Level V, reaching a depth of 2.80 m below datum. This was a very hard, gravelly layer of gray clay and many small stones. The wooden lining stopped just above this layer, indicating (along with the stratum's very hard consistency and cultural sterility) that this was indeed the bottom. A soil sample for pollen analysis was taken from Level V and analyzed at Yale University for an indication of the floral composition of the Fort Shirley site at the time when the well was constructed (appendix 2).

Interpretation of the Excavated Well and Its Construction

As in the well dug by Professor Perry so many years ago, the horizontal planks of this well were made of white ash (*Fraxinus americanus*), all surely split from a single log that still retained its bark.[9] The southernmost corner post was red maple (*Acer rubrum*), as was a brace on the north wall. In a particular course, the planks were all about the same size, with minor variation. Because they were split, they were wedge-shaped in profile; most of them were so well preserved that they would be usable today.

The purpose of the corner posts is a continuing mystery: not one reaches the real bottom of the well. They are staggered in length; the one on the north measures 1.61 m, that on the east 1.64 m, and the west one .62 m. It seems that well's builders relied not so much on these posts, but more upon the degree to which the boards themselves bound each other. The posts, with their bases never touching the bottom of the well, were held in place by the braces that pressed them away from each other and against the walls. But for such a structural system to work, the gap behind the boards must have been filled with earth. It thus seems that the soldiers built their wells from the bottom up, not from the top down as Perry would have had it.

Such an interpretation is supported by the shape of the original excavation. This appeared as the earth behind the walls began to dry out: as it dried, it sheared off from the earth behind it, revealing the contours of a large pit that Kloppenburg believes was dug by the colonials. One this pit had reached an adequate depth, they began construction of the actual wooden shaft, filling in the walls of the well as they built up. This interpretation would explain the loose hardpan soil between the boards and the pit walls; they certainly would have utilized their own backdirt. When the walls had reached a height where they could no longer support themselves unaided, the corner posts were placed in and braced. This procedure might not have been part of their original plan, but might have been improvised as groundwater pressure exceeded the strength of the sides alone (such pressure was sufficiently great to force us to dismantle the well shortly after it had been dug). We believe that this would explain why the posts do not reach all the way to the bottom.

I still do not understand why the hardpan "rim" in N5E7-B and D contrasts so sharply with the brown soil (see fig. 4-9). If it had been the limit of the original excavation, one would have expected it to have caved in. A possible explanation is that in making a well head of stone, the builders needed a firm foundation, and so took extra pains to fix a solid, hardpan rim to that side. In fact, it is highly probable that there actually was a stone well head, as a number of fairly large stones were recovered from around the well's mouth. The rest of them were undoubtedly removed by Samuel Higgins when he converted the "fort site" into a farmstead.

Stratigraphic interpretations of the well fill are open to debate. The wooden artifacts (including roof shingles) were probably dropped in while the well was in use. When it was abandoned, for whatever reason, it was filled with ash and dirt from hearths and firepits. The decomposing ash became the sticky, green-gray clay of Layer IV, which would explain the charcoal fragments in this stratum. Layer III presents more of a problem.

The artifacts suggest that this stratum was accumulated while Fort Shirley was still inhabited, perhaps by Archibald Pannell and family. By this time, the well seems to have been used as a refuse dump for stone and trees. There is, of course, the possibility that the filling was carried out in the early nineteenth century by Higgins to keep his sheep from tumbling into the well. Layer II cannot now be explained: its greenish earth is unique within the stratigraphy of Fort Shirley, and may be a form of ash mixed with other soil.

Architecture and Activity Areas

The documentation for the construction of Fort Shirley in 1744 is extraordinarily detailed, even though no plans of the fort have ever surfaced. The orders of 20 July 1744, given to William Williams, specifically state that the fort was to be 60 feet square, the "houses" (barracks) 11 feet wide, the mounts 12 feet square and seven feet high, and the barracks roofs to be shingled. Williams's accounting following the completion of Fort Shirley is equally specific; in it, the fort is called a "Block House"; that is, its sides consisted of planking with the mounts raised on opposite corners. Of the more than 54 laborers involved in raising the fort, several had special jobs. Five of them were busy making the four chimneys; Alexander Herren and Joseph Brooks laid the stones for the chimney bases, while "Chamberlain & others" were paid for "Diging the Clay Carrying the Morter & Stone Making the Catts etc." Nine horseloads of straw were purchased for use in chimney construction. Thus, we know with some certainty that there were two barracks, each 11 feet wide, and each with two chimneys raised on the old English pattern with double (back-to-back) stone fireplaces, the chimneys themselves formed of a mixture of clay, stones, and straw contained in a pole structure.

As per the specifications given to Williams, 12,000 shingles were employed to roof the barracks; these were laid over lath, and held with 16,000 nails. Doors for the barracks and perhaps for the walls of the fort are implied in the accounting for five pairs of hooks and hinges, five hasps and staples, three padlocks, and two pairs of small door hinges.

Between the barracks was a parade, which was floored over with hewn or sawn timbers, so that much or perhaps all of the space within the walls not occupied by houses was covered over. Such may account for the relatively small number of artifacts recovered by our excavations at Fort Shirley, in contrast to the abundant finds at Fort Pelham, which had no parade.

Of the six hewn timbers or planks that were saved by Colonel Asaph White from the blockhouse walls of Fort Shirley, only portions of three have survived. The rest have suffered the vicissitudes of time, as well as the actions of well-meaning persons following their dispersal from Colonel White's old barn during the 1930s. For instance, at that time two were cut up and fitted into fireplaces by an "artistic" lady of Heath, and are lost beyond retrieval. The survivors are all very similar, although all three have been cut down and lapped (probably when they were incorporated into the White barn). They were scored and hewn with broad axes from white pine (*Pinus strobus*), and are extraordinarily regular in workmanship and in their dimensions, measuring 5–6 inches (12.7–15.2 cm) in thickness, and 13–14 inches (33.0–35.6 cm) in width. The longest specimen is 11 feet 8 inches (4.09 m), but this had been cut down at some time in the past, so that the full length of the original timbers is unknown. Large oak dowels, originally square in crossection but now 1½ to 1¾ inches (3.8–4.5 cm) in diameter fastened the edge of each plank to the one above or below to make the walls. One small end timber piece in the collection of the Heath Historical Society has been notched and slightly chamfered, and this is undoubtedly the way the corners of the blockhouse wall were fashioned. An unexplained feature of these timbers is that all three have irregular rows of holes filled with square oak dowels; I hazard the guess that these formed part of the outer walls of lean-to barracks, and that the dowels served as pegs on which to hang clothing and gear.

There is ample evidence that the large concentrations of stone found in our excavations represent the remains of the four chimneys and their fireplaces, at least what have been left by depredations committed since 1754. One of these centered on Squares N5E2 and N6E2, and another centered on N2W1 (which could not be excavated because of the marker stone sitting on it); both of these must have been chimneys for a single barracks placed in a northeast to southwest direction. The other two concentrations centered on N4E9–N3E9 and S2E7–S3E7 respectively, and would have been chimneys for a matching barracks on the other side of the parade. We found these concentrations by regular probing with a steel rod; the area between the hypothetical barracks had no such features.

As can be seen from the detailed plan (see fig. 4-6), a considerable amount of charcoal was recovered from the vicinity of these ruined structures; samples of it proved to be ash (*Fraxinus* sp.; see appendix 2). A charred ash log lay in the southwest quadrant of N4E9. Further evidence that wood fires had occurred in and near these features is the presence of burned earth in Layer II, almost always associated with the rock concentrations. Unfortunately, not enough was left to delineate the boundaries and appearance of the chimneys accurately, but small, very decayed fragments of bricks suggest that the hearth floors were of brick, all of which must have been removed when the fort was decommissioned (or by Samuel Higgins in the next century).

Both board and shingle nails—all handwrought—were found on the peripheries of the rock concentrations, and between them, although their frequency is far lower than at Fort Pelham. There is no sure explanation for this, as the putative dismantlers of Fort Shirley did not resort to the (perhaps legendary) New England practice of burning old buildings down to get the nails. The more likely way of salvaging nails comes from information on Fort Massachusetts, which Seth Pomroy found in ruins by November 1759; in his report to Governor Pownall, Pomroy said that he had ordered the roof to be taken off one of the abandoned fort's mounts, "ye Shingles & nails to be carefully sav'd & Carryed to west Hoosuck, & put on yt which I think will do well for it; that Sav'd ye time of making Shingles and fetching nails at a Distance."[10] If this had been the practice at Fort Shirley, its shingles and nails probably ended up in one of Colrain's forts, as that was the native place of its last soldier, Archibald Pannell.

Certainly one item that would have been taken away from the decaying fort is window glass, as it was so costly in colonial Massachusetts. There must have been at least four two-sash windows in each of the two barracks, giving a total of 16 sashes; a sash of the period might have contained 12 lights, thus amounting to 192 panes of glass. While more window glass was excavated at Shirley than at Pelham, its general paucity means that a 1754 rescue effort must have taken place. Probably only those sashes with broken panes would have been left behind. The high incidence of window glass fragments in N4E9-C (24 in total) makes it virtually certain that a window sash was left in situ in this square, to fall to pieces—along with its remaining broken lights—with the rest of the fort. The same might be said of N2E9-A (10 fragments), although it is unfortunate that most of these glass shards were recovered on the screen, and so do not appear on the plan.

There were doubtless four rooms in each of the Shirley barracks. In a letter to Ephraim Williams, Sr., written on 2 June 1747, on the eve of his departure from the command of Fort Massachusetts, William Williams instructed the incoming Ephraim Sr. on how to build a barracks there: the building was to be "divided in the middle with a Teer of Timber, place a Chimney in the Center of the East part with two fire places to accommodate those Rooms. In the West part place the Chimney So as best to accommodate the two Rooms on that part."[11] One of the barracks rooms was supposed to be partitioned off to make a storeroom, and in all likelihood this is how stores were kept at Fort Shirley.

Given that the second well at Fort Shirley was oriented not to True North, but to 24° East of Magnetic North, the two barracks could have had a like orientation, as roughly indicated by the chimney remains. Thus, the entire fort seems to have been oriented to this direction. In figure 4-13, I have attempted such a reconstruction based on this and upon the specifications of July 1744. My own guess is that the blockhouse was somewhat larger than 60 feet on a side, as the spread of rocks fallen from the decayed chimneys goes well beyond its borders. The second well, which was probably the original one, would have been near the north side of the fort and within it, while Perry's well would have lain outside the walls—perhaps it might have been dug at a later date when the second well went sour or bad. There may be other wells yet to be discovered; in particular, the surface depression in N1E12 and N1E13, and in the squares to the north, should be investigated.

I have no idea of where the gate would have been, but suggest a location on the east side, as the road from Colrain would have led in from that direction. There is also no evidence for the placement of the mounts that are specified in the 1744 orders.

Bearing in mind that much of the interior of the fort was covered by planking (that is, by the wooden parade and the barracks floors), it is little wonder that so few artifacts other than nails were found in our admittedly limited excavations. The distribution of those that were recovered show little patterning. There is a moderate concentration of glass, pottery, and pipe fragments in the southwest quadrant of N4E9, where we suspect the presence of a fireplace. Cooking activities are suggested by the high frequency of small pieces of charred and calcined bone in S2E7-A and S3E7-C, and it is reasonable to suppose that one or both fireplaces on the southern end of this barracks were used as kitchens. Particularly fine examples of apothecary vials came from N2E10-B and N1E10-B, so that a dispensary for ailing soldiers might have been located there.

Returning to the problem posed by the faintly visible ditches that surround Fort Shirley on three sides, and that conform to its general orientation: had they been found only on the west and the north, one might reasonably infer them to be drainage ditches. But the presence of the third ditch on the east raises doubts about this interpretation, and suggests that the fort was in fact picketed. According to a plan conserved in the Yale University Library, the approximately contemporary Fort No. 4, in Charlestown, New Hampshire, was a blockhouse surrounded by a palisade, although the ground plan of the stockade was apparently more complex than that of Shirley. At No. 4, two of the wells, shown with sweeps, were inside the stockade walls, while the third lay between these and the palisade.

According to Dr. Stanley South, such arrangements were not unknown in the southern colonies during the French and Indian Wars, or slightly later.[12] Fort Ninety Six in Charleston, South Carolina, was a palisaded fort with a barn inside that served as a blockhouse. Fort Dobbs, in North Carolina, occupied from 1755 to 1764, was a large blockhouse (53 ft. by 40 ft.) on the order of Fort Shirley, and was surrounded by a diamond-shaped picketed ditch; and the blockhouse-like Fort Prince George in South Carolina was also enclosed by a palisade. In fact, in a letter of 23 February 1973, Dr. South had predicted to me that we should find such ditches. I suspect that the Fort Shirley ditches, dry or not, are the result of picketing, not drainage; in fact, all other documented forts in the Line of Forts were so picketed. Excavations in the ditches might well disclose the stumps of the pickets themselves.

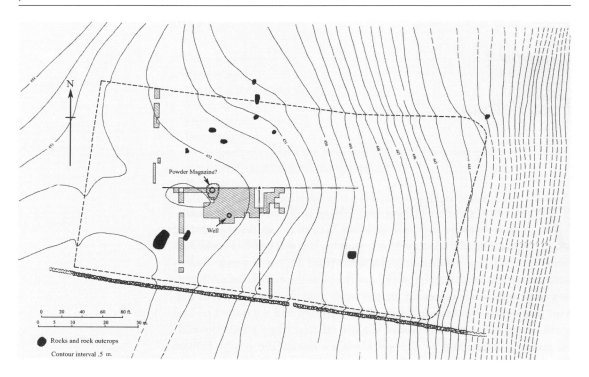

FIG. 5-1. Map of Fort Pelham, Rowe, Massachusetts.
The dashed line indicates
the palisade ditch described
by Arthur L. Perry. On
its south side is the post-
occupation wall that incor-
porates most of the fort's
stone architecture. The
hatching indicates areas
excavated by the Univer-
sity of Massachusetts field
school. Elevations are in
feet. Courtesy Daniel Ingersoll.

In February 1762, the General Court put up for sale nine townships plus
10,000 acres. The Reverend Cornelius Jones, a graduate of Harvard in the
Class of 1752, made the winning bid for the last parcel, and became the
owner of what was then called Myrifield Plantation, comprising what was
to become the town of Rowe after its incorporation in 1785. Jones moved
to the area, becoming Rowe's earliest settler and its first Congregationalist
minister. According to local tradition, he camped out in the ruins of Fort
Pelham while surveying his new lands. Jones must have been incompetent
as a real estate operator, however; in 1779 he sold most of his land, including the site of the fort, to William Parkhurst & Co., removing to New York
State where he died a poor man.

The land transactions recorded in the Franklin County Registry of Deeds
show that the next owner of the Fort Pelham site was Dr. Pardon Haynes
of Rowe, the town physician from 1788 until his death in 1834.[2] His estate
inventory indicates that he was not only a "gentleman," but a wealthy one,
and by the time of his death he had acquired a great deal of land over many
years. There is no way of knowing exactly when the Fort Pelham tract was
cleared, or when the stone walls that run across it were erected; perhaps this
was done around the turn of the nineteenth century. At that time, the schist
stones remaining from the chimney and fireplaces of the barracks would
have been incorporated in the field walls, accounting for the fact that there

is even less architecture to be discerned in Fort Pelham than in Fort Shirley. The heirs of Dr. Haynes sold the property during the 1840s and 1850s to the Gould family. By the first two decades of the twentieth century, it had passed into the hands of Edward Wright, when it was known as the Fort Pelham Farm.

In fact, local oral tradition had never allowed the location of the long-disappeared fort to be forgotten. "Fort Pelham" appeared on maps published as late as the Beers Atlas of Franklin County in 1871. It is said in Rowe that during World War I, two German spies turned up in the town, looking for the fort.

The most distinguished visitor to the fort was Professor Arthur L. Perry of Williams College, who first "critically examined" the site in 1878, perhaps even before he became interested in Fort Shirley. His companion on that trip was John H. Haynes, a Rowe resident and presumably a descendant of Dr. Pardon Haynes. Perry made a second inspection in 1885 with his son Carroll Perry, then a freshman at Williams.[3] His observations are especially important for several reasons. First, the site was then open pasture; by 1956, when it was given to the Rowe Historical Society, it was difficult to find because of the undergrowth. Second, Perry was a remarkably astute scholar with a knowledge of old forts and with a firsthand familiarity with the relevant documents. And last, while more than 220 years had passed between Pelham's abandonment and modern archaeological work, there was a lapse of only 122 years since the act of demission and Perry's visit; he is thus likely to have seen surface features that would be less visible today.

Perry's most important contribution was that he saw the clear outline of the palisade ditch, now not entirely visible, and was able to measure it. It formed a parallelogram 12 rods by 24 rods in extent (198 by 396 ft., or 60.3 by 120.7 m). According to Perry, "a trench, perhaps a foot deep, had been dug around the four sides, and posts of a pretty uniform size (perhaps hewed) were set upright into the trench, unless natural trees of the right dimensions were already growing in line, and then the earth was thrown back into the trench and upon both sides of the staddles, which now forms the pillow of turf that can be traced almost unbroken, particularly on the south and east sides."

Perry also noted the well, suggesting that "the removal of four or five large stones that now choke the opening would practically restore the digging of 1745, and discover with certainty whether it were originally walled up within or constructed with corner-posts like the corresponding well at Shirley." He identified the large, somewhat circular depression to the northwest of the well as either the powder magazine or the beginning of an unfinished well thwarted by underlying ledge, and suggested excavation to determine this. Finally, Perry felt that the main opening into the fort was on the north side, as to avoid the swampy ground that was subsequently to become Pelham

FIG. 5-2. View of the stone field wall at Fort Pelham, probably built at the beginning of the nineteenth century. Most of the fort's masonry ended up here.

Lake, the otherwise straight military road from Shirley would have had to bypass this by curving to the north.

The Fort Pelham Farm was sold in 1942 to Florence E. Neal, who presented it to the Rowe Historical Society in 1956. The site (which had been open pasture until about 1930) had returned to second-growth bush and trees, and was not easy for the casual visitor to find. Today, much of the brush has been removed, and the site is marked by a large boulder with an inscribed stone plaque.

Surface Features of the Site

Perry's palisade line can still be traced in part, and is especially visible when the ferns have died down in mid-autumn. It forms a parallelogram with its long axis oriented east and west; actually, the whole figure is tilted slightly more than 8° East of Magnetic North. The more recent stone wall to the south also conforms to this orientation (fig. 5-2). The entire area enclosed by the palisade line is about 7,278 m^2 or slightly more than an acre and a half. Excavations disclosed that archaeological remains were confined to the western half of the enclosure, where the ground is fairly flat. In all likelihood, the precipitous eastern half was reserved for the grazing of horses, cattle, and other animals. Some large boulders and schist outcrops are found on the surface, but away from the site of the barracks; their presence precluded the construction of a planked-over parade like that at Shirley.

What the palisade or "picket line" would have been like is suggested by a document detailing the construction of the one at Fort Massachusetts in 1751.[4] There they dug a trench 1½ feet deep, and set in it 3,000 pickets (stakes) 6 inches in diameter and 9½ feet long, that had all been burnt 2 feet up from the bottom to preserve the wood. Finally, they were bound together by ribs that had been attached to the stakes by pins.

On the eve of excavation, the two most visible features of Fort Pelham were the well described by Perry, and the large depression just northwest of it that he had suggested might be the location of the powder magazine. As at Shirley, there were no surface artifacts to be seen anywhere, and there were no indications of chimney foundations or other architectural features. Whoever had built the stone wall (probably in the late eighteenth or early nineteenth century), had taken advantage of the schist incorporated in the chimney or chimneys, and moved it into the wall.

Excavations and Stratigraphy

The first season of archaeological research conducted by the University of Massachusetts (designated UMASS in this report) field school at Fort Pelham began on 28 June 1971, and was concluded by 10 August of that year. The second season began on 1 July 1972, and was completed by the end of that August. Both seasons were directed by Dr. Daniel Ingersoll, then on the UMASS faculty.

The site was laid out for excavation in five-foot squares, on a grid oriented to Magnetic North. Each square was divided into 2.5 ft. quadrants. The designation of squares and quadrants was in the same system that was later used by the Yale group at Fort Shirley, and began from the intersection of the east-west and north-south datum lines (figs. 5-1 and 5-3). Altogether, 97 squares were excavated during the two seasons, covering an area of 2,425 square feet or 225.5 m². From our computer analysis of the artifacts (see below), this excavation took in most of the area of occupation, but not all of the major area of trash disposal. In addition, the UMASS team ran a narrow, interrupted trench north along the W21 line that opened up another 225 square feet within the palisade line, but the team encountered no artifacts in it.

The stratigraphy was somewhat similar to that of Fort Shirley, but the clay hardpan of Shirley was missing, the cultural layers resting directly on the underlying glacial till; this reflects Pelham's far better drainage. On the

FIG. 5-3. View of the University of Massachusetts excavations at the close of the 1971 field season. The site was excavated in five-foot squares. Courtesy Daniel Ingersoll.

surface was a zone of leaf litter, containing only a few recent artifacts discarded by modern visitors. Beneath this was Layer I, a dark, yellowish-brown (10 YR 4/4 in the Munsell system) loam approximately four inches thick. Layer II was a yellowish-brown (10 YR 5/8) sandy silt about six inches in thickness. The final artifact-bearing stratum was Layer III, similar to Layer II but 10 YR 5/4 on the Munsell scale. The UMASS excavators identified what they termed "Displaced Layer III" in areas surrounding the well and the "powder magazine"; this was a C-zone–like soil or till that they thought to have resulted from the eighteenth-century excavations for these structures. It was also found in and over hearths in S6W5 and S3W8.

Rocks were found scattered throughout the excavated areas; except for the "powder magazine," these never formed anything definitely suggesting a structure, and no chimney bases could be plotted. However, there did seem to be a significant increase in rock density in the squares S1W8 through S1W5, and S1W7 through S2W4, suggesting that a building with a single chimney once existed in this area. We shall examine this proposition later.

Other stratigraphic features noted were "hearths" and stained areas.

Because of the nature of the UMASS excavation records, however, it is difficult to trace these features from one square into the adjacent square. We have the feeling that none of these are surely hearths or fireplaces, but may just represent fires casually set out-of-doors for burning trash, singeing pigs, or the like.

The "Powder Magazine"

It is a tragedy that most of the notes and plans of the alleged powder magazine, the most interesting feature of Fort Pelham, were carried off by the student excavator and never returned, in spite of determined efforts to get them back on the part of the UMASS and Yale archaeologists. Consequently, what is reported here is based upon the observations of Daniel Ingersoll, and upon the catalogue of artifacts found in this feature. Plans exist for the east profile of S2W10, Quadrant B, and for N1W11, Quadrant A. As can be seen from figures 5-4 to 5-7, the depression believed by most (but not all) observers to be the site of the powder magazine was centered on S1W10, but extended into neighboring squares. Apparently, the original sides of

FIG. 5-4. Plan of the central excavated area at Fort Pelham, showing the distribution of nails and pipe parts. There are notable concentrations of both in the northwestern part and in squares S1W6 and S2W6. Both may indicate two-story structures.

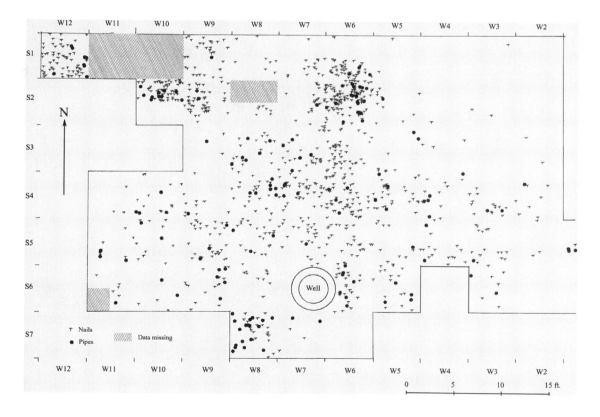

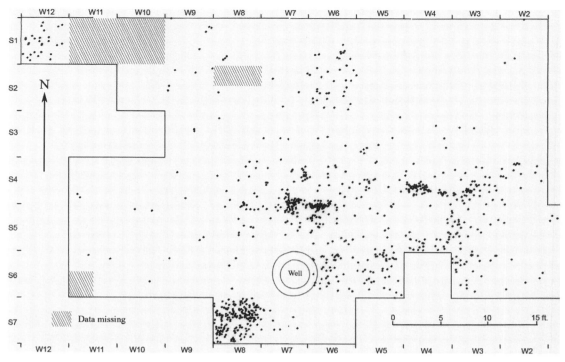

FIG. 5-5. Distribution of animal bones, central part of Fort Pelham excavations. The drainage from the concentration in S7W8 must have contaminated the well.

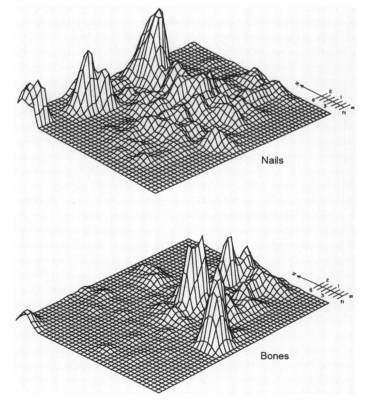

FIG. 5-6. Computer-produced maps of nail and bone distributions, Fort Pelham.

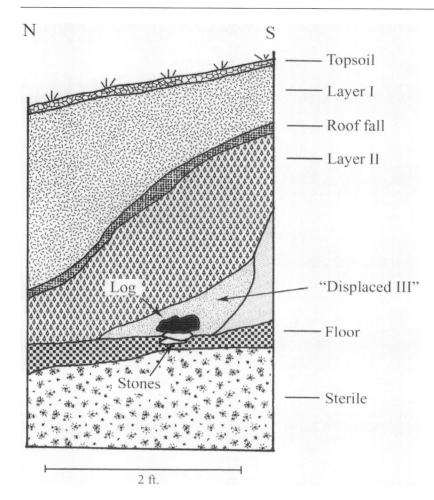

N S

— Topsoil

— Layer I

— Roof fall

— Layer II

Log

"Displaced III"

— Floor

Stones

— Sterile

2 ft.

FIG. 5-7. Stratigraphy of the east wall of S2W10, quadrant B (northeast). This is the only available record for what was probably a cellar rather than a powder magazine. There is no information on the named layers. The vertical scale is the same as the horizontal.
Courtesy Daniel Ingersoll.

the ancient excavation were vertical, and were lined with roughly placed stones and perhaps logs. Layer I extended below the leaf litter and was more than two feet thick as it dipped down toward the center of the depression. Between Layer I and Layer II was what the excavator labeled "roof fall," about two inches or less thick; he presumably identified this feature from wood fragments and stain. Layer II, rich in nails and other artifacts, was about the same thickness as Layer I, and was occasionally underlain by "Displaced Layer III," at least on the outskirts of the excavation; both of these strata rested upon the original dirt floor of the magazine. This floor was flat, two to three inches thick, and was stained dark black in places; it contained significant numbers of bullets and gunflints.

I interpret this as a cellar, not a "powder magazine." This would have been a subterranean, dirt-floored storeroom, about 15 feet square and oriented to 45° east of north. The large number of nails recovered implies a two-storied

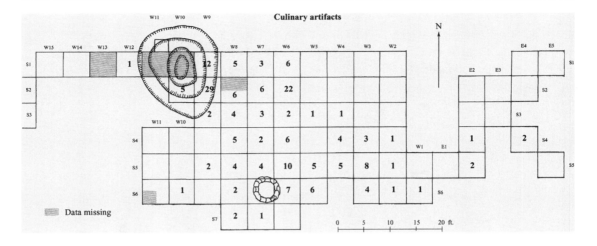

FIG. 5-8. Frequency of culinary artifacts, Fort Pelham. These include knives, forks, spoons, and pottery. The incidence of table implements was particularly high in S2W6.

superstructure that must have had a residential function: there was a significant concentration of domestic items such as buttons, knives, forks, spoons, coins, white salt-glazed stoneware, bottles, and pipe fragments (fig. 5-8). Surely no one in his right mind would have lived over a powder magazine. When the historian Francis Parkman visited the site of Fort Massachusetts in the early 1840s, he found a similar depression that he also interpreted as a cellar hole.[5]

The Well

The Yale group began excavations within the well on 31 August 1976. The Pelham well proved to be strikingly different from the two at Fort Shirley. Instead of a square well with wooden sides, we found here one constructed of coarse field stones; the builders had obviously intended it to be approximately circular. The opening itself varied from 2 to 2½ feet in diameter. By the fall of that year, we had reached a depth of five feet, but digging proved to be very difficult and dangerous as large stones clogged the well down to this level. Accordingly, work was stopped at this point; it might be possible to proceed further with a block-and-tackle rig, but in view of the constricted diameter of the well, future work will be hazardous.

The "Garden" Area

As previously mentioned, a sporadic trench was run by the UMASS team along the W21 line from Squares N15W21 to N19W21, to sample an area that Dr. Ingersoll felt might have been used as a garden by the fort's inhabitants.

In favor of this interpretation are the following: (1) the soil is deep, dark, and loose, and contains very few rocks; (2) few if any artifacts were discovered; and (3) the area supports a vegetation different from that of the rest of the fort site, the association including crabapples, hawthorn, and many ferns. These facts suggested to Ingersoll a landfill project for agricultural purposes. However, another possibility would have been a leveling operation to dry out an area of low and wet soil within the palisade walls.

Artifact Density and Distribution

The excavation of Fort Pelham produced large quantities of mid–eighteenth-century artifacts, especially nails, but little or nothing in the way of architecture. In 1977, Reid Kaplan of the Yale Computer Center (YCC) suggested to me that information about the life and activities within the fort, and possibly the plan of the barracks itself, could be extracted from the distribution of these remains by appropriate use of image processing.[6] Plan view maps were created using the Calcomp 826 Plotter attached to YCC's IBM System 370/158. Maps were made of all the data, individual subsets of the data by artifact type, and certain groups of artifact types that were thought to have a functional relationship. An example of the latter would be gunflints and bullets, both military in character (fig. 5-9).

Although artifact types such as gunflints and pipe parts were found helpful in suggesting the uses to which an area of habitation was put, displays of nail and bone density were the main diagnostic tools used to delineate those areas (fig. 5-10). Nails were the only reliable indicator of structures, as stones and window glass had been scavenged for reuse, and the UMASS excavators did not distinguish between window-glass and bottle-glass fragments in their plans.

FIG. 5-9. Incidence of military artifacts, Fort Pelham. Included are gunflints, bullets, lead wire, and lead spree (from casting bullets). There was a high incidence in and near the large depression (a probable cellar) in the northwest of the main excavations.

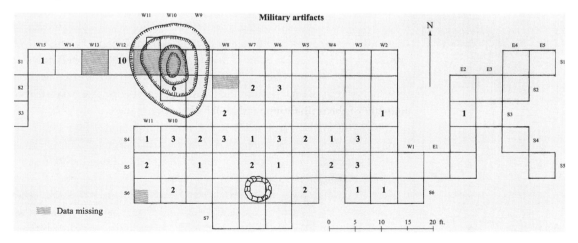

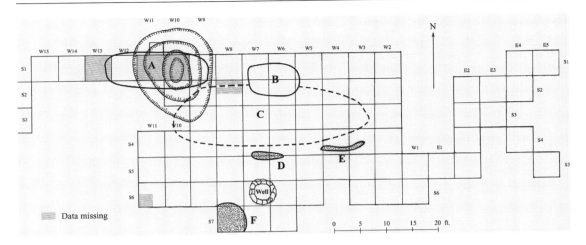

FIG. 5-10. Interpretation of the artifact and bone distribution at Fort Shirley: A, probable two-story structure with a cellar hole at eastern end; B, two-story structure, possibly officers' quarters and dining area; C, possible location of the men's barracks, c. 40 feet long; D, E, and F, dumps for animal bones.

As can be seen from figure 5-6, the faunal remains cluster very tightly. There is a low peak in the area of the "powder magazine"; a very high one to the southwest of the well (in Square S7W8); and two high peaks in the center-west of the site that are roughly on an east-west line. In addition, there is an area of animal bone fragments to the north of the central peaks (in S1W6 and S2W6) that, although low in density, is very clearly outlined. To the east of the well is a separate area of medium density. The maximum density of bone was along the W16 line, in S12W16 and S13W16; this is plainly part of a large midden area of food remains connecting with the bone concentration to the southwest of the well (in S7W8).

The most striking effect of the displays based on nail density consists of the peaks that range along the northern edge of the main excavated area. In front of the eastern peak (which centers upon S1W6 and S2W6) is a north-south ridge that diminishes in height toward the southwest, extending over the edge of the well. The "mound" on the southwest side of the well is obviously part of the midden. To the east and south of the ridge lies an area of low density. These features are most easily seen in heavily filtered displays. Because excavation data are lacking for Squares S1W10 and S1W11 (the area of the powder magazine), the two nail-density peaks in the northwest corner are in reality only one; we believe that they represent the southeast corner of a building that probably had a complex inner structure with many nailed joints.

The central nail pattern surely represents the remains of the collapsed barracks structure. Daniel Ingersoll, the excavator, interpreted the two bone peaks, aligned east-west, as part of the drip line of a building before its collapse; his reasoning is supported by the clustering along the line of other artifacts (excluding nails, which would necessarily have been deposited *after* the collapse). Their extreme concentration and their shape, however, offer additional possibilities for interpretation. It seems more likely that these bone concentrations mark the positions of two doors that would have been situated at either end of the southern side of the barracks. The faunal debris would thus be the result both of sweeping out the living quarters, and of the common Anglo-American practice of "air-mailing" uneaten portions of food out the nearest door.

It will be noted that the area to the north of the eastern bone peak is almost devoid of nails. If this marks one door, where is the building to which it gave access? The answer to that requires formation of a model for the collapse of wooden buildings. Observations of derelict houses and barns throughout the New England countryside show features of collapse common to abandoned, old-frame or log cabin–type structures. Almost invariably the downfall is initiated at one corner. In framed buildings, this results in considerable rotation around the diagonally opposite corner post, and in shear along common wall planes. The roof is carried in toward the originally defective corner. The end result is a parallelogram or perhaps trapezoidal figure both rotated and displaced from the original position.

If one were to shift the central nail area to the east by eight feet, a reasonable estimate of wall height, and then slightly rotate its southwest-northeast axis to coincide with the supposed "drip line," one would find that the "doors" suggested by the bone peaks are aligned precisely at the ends of a rectangle approximately 20 feet long and 10 feet wide, situated about 6 feet north of the well. While admittedly small, these dimensions are consistent with the documented width of the Fort Shirley barracks, 11 feet. This shifted area has a median nail density of about one nail per square foot, which is an acceptable value for a roof.

That the barracks would have fallen generally southward is ensured by the presence of the structure represented by the highest nail peak, as this would have acted as a buttress on the north. Such a structure could not have been larger than eight feet on a side, as is indicated by the extreme localization of all the artifacts found in Squares S_1W_7–S_1W_5 and S_2W_7–S_2W_5. From this, and considering the very high peak density of 13–14 nails per square foot, I believe that we can infer a multistoried structure. The north-south nail ridge almost certainly represents its collapsed form superimposed on the barracks debris; the notch between peak and ridge (see fig. 5-6) confirms this superimposition. As the attached barracks gradually collapsed and shifted, the "tower" would have been drawn southward. It should be noted that the only significant concentration of rocks in the site was in just this area.

Architecture and Activity Areas

The density displays have suggested something of the long-lost architecture of Fort Pelham. The barracks consisted of a single building to the north of the well, measuring not much more than 10 by 20 feet, and oriented approximately east-west. No trace of a chimney base was found, but it could have been placed in the middle of a north-south partition that would have divided the barracks into two equal spaces, each room warmed by a single fireplace. Alternatively, it could have been situated at one end, leaving a single, large, but not efficiently heated room. Whatever the floor plan, there would have been room for four bunks, perhaps triple-decker. In garrisons along the Pennsylvania frontier, according to Bouquet's 1758 orders, for every two men there were to be one bedstead, one bed (mattress), one bolster, and three blankets.[7] Thus, the Pelham barracks could have slept up to 24 soldiers, although at times the atmosphere must have been a little close.

The muster rolls for Fort Pelham confirm this interpretation for the barracks. In the spring of 1746, there were 21 men posted to Pelham.[8] By November 1748, the roster had increased to a total of 30, and comprised one lieutenant (Samuel Childs), a clerk, a sergeant, and 27 enlisted men.[9] Following the signing of the Treaty of Aix-la-Chapelle in that year, the military population of Pelham dropped precipitously, so that there were only five persons (one sergeant and 4 men) in the muster roll of December 1749 to June 1750.[10] Finally, from June 1751 until the decommissioning of the fort in 1754, only George Hall, and perhaps his wife and children, inhabited what was left of the barracks.

As for the structure to the north of the barracks, measuring eight feet square, it was doubtless two-story, possibly surmounted with a watchtower; as the barracks occupied high land in the approximate center of the palisaded area, this would have given a good view over the palisade walls. While the ground floor of the structure may have been stone-lined, the rock concentration could be the remains of a chimney with fireplace on one side. This seems to me to be the most likely explanation, as it is almost certain that meals were taken in this building. The artifact distribution maps (see figs. 5-8 and 5-9) show significant concentrations of pottery, knives, forks, spoons, buttons, and glass within its bounds. The room or rooms must also have been a place of relaxation and enjoyment; there is also a high density of pipe fragments.

The cellar ("powder magazine"), if that is what it really was, lay northwest of the barracks, and was separate from it. This again seems to have been a two-story structure, with a dirt floor. Either the ground floor or the upper story—or both—was used as a residence, most likely by the commanding officer and his family. The same concentration of culinary items (knives, forks, and spoons) that was seen in the "tower" area is to be seen here, along with numerous buttons, glass fragments, and pipe parts. But military matters were also important here: there is a far higher density here than in the "tower" of bullets, gunflints, and lead sprue. The exact size of the structure is impossible to determine due to the absence of crucial excavation data.

Within the palisade walls, the only other structure for which there is the slightest evidence would have been a small outbuilding or shed just southeast of the barracks; but this evidence is extremely tenuous. If it did exist, it might have provided shelter for some of the fort's livestock during the severe winters of the northern Berkshires.

Household refuse was swept or thrown out of the barracks doors. There was, nonetheless, a definite area for dumping food remains, beginning just southwest of the well and extending in that same direction for more than 60 feet. Effluent from this garbage and trash would have drained into the well, so that the fort's drinking water, like that at Shirley, must have been badly contaminated.

NOTES

1. Brown 1960:20.
2. Brown 1960:93.
3. Perry 1904:97–99.
4. Perry 1904:245.
5. Parkman 1892, 2:258 n. 1.
6. A detailed account of this project along with the computer-generated plans can be found in Kaplan and Coe 1976.
7. James and Stotz 1958:106.
8. Williams Papers, Massachusetts Historical Society.
9. Brown 1960:226.
10. Williams Papers, Massachusetts Historical Society.

Chapter 6

The Artifacts of Shirley and Pelham

Prefatory Remarks

*I*N THIS SECTION, I have grouped the artifacts of Fort Shirley with those of Fort Pelham, with both components treated as though they were a single component. This arrangement can be justified on these grounds:

- The two sites, as the crow flies, are only 4.7 miles (7.5 km) apart.

- They were not only occupied by people of the same cultural and sociopolitical world, but to some extent the occupants of the two forts were interchangeable.

- Their material culture came from the same source, namely, the retailing and commissary system of the Williams family, based in Deerfield.

- The forts were occupied for exactly the same time span, from 1744 to 1754, only a brief moment given the immensely long time scales of prehistoric and historic archaeologists.

Ceramics

Pelham had large quantities of fragments from simple brown-or-green-glazed earthenware (fig. 6-1*f–r*); Shirley had only a few such shards. The shapes include open bowls with plain or thickened rims, cream or milk pitchers, and handled mugs. This rough-and-ready ware was probably made in eastern Massachusetts for local consumption. According to Watkins, Charlestown was the most important producer of red earthenwares in the eighteenth century, until its destruction by the British in 1775, but similar pottery was turned out in the area from Boston to Cape Cod, as well as in Essex County.[1]

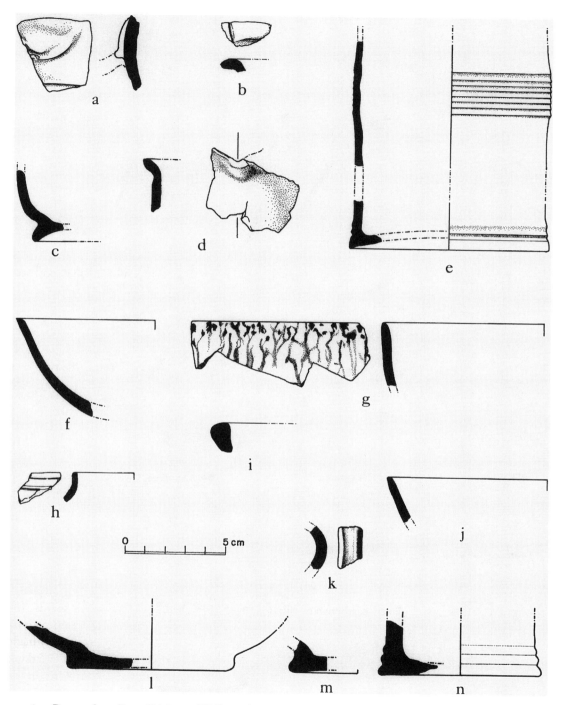

FIG. 6-1. Pottery from Forts Shirley and Pelham: (*a*, *b*, *d*, and *e*) Jackfield ware; (*c*) Delft ware. (*f–n*) brown or green-glazed earthenware.

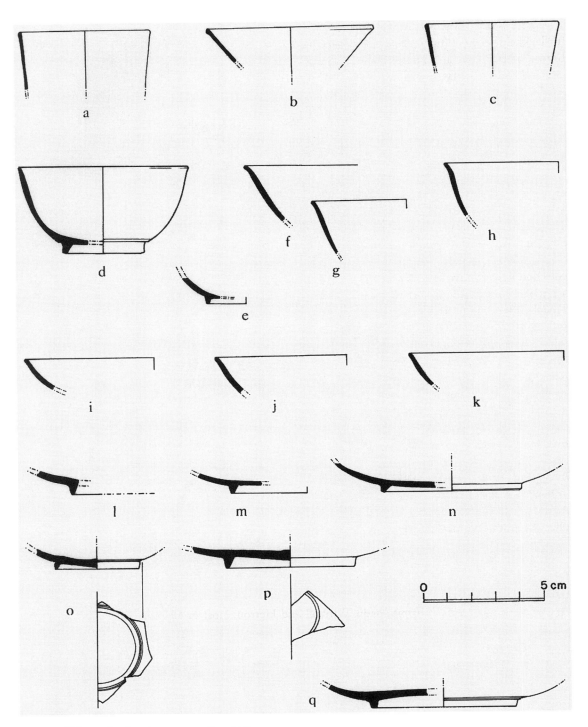

FIG. 6-2. White salt-glazed stoneware, Fort Pelham.

Where Shirley was low in this relatively coarse ceramic, it was high in "Jackfield" pottery (fig. 6-1*a, b, d, e*), a very hard, thin, ware with a dark brown to black glaze and a purplish-brown paste. Most of the shards recovered belong to one large tankard or mug, but there is also a bowl with a rounded lip and a modeled vessel of unknown shape. "Jackfield" ware was produced in some quantity throughout Staffordshire in the mid–eighteenth century.[2]

The finest ceramic in the forts—confined to Pelham—was white, salt-glazed stoneware, a hard, almost eggshell-thin ware of great refinement, with a glossy, pitted glaze resembling the surface of an orange peel. There are only two shapes in our collection: handleless teacups and their saucers (fig. 6-2). I estimate that the entire group of shards represents four teasets. The chief centers of manufacture in England were Fulham and Lambeth, Norringham, and Staffordshire; by 1762, hundreds of different potteries were turning this ware out, in an attempt to simulate porcelain.[3] Identical teacups and saucers have been found at Fort Ligonier,[4] Brunswick Town (in a 1730–60 context),[5] and Fort Michilimackinac,[6] where it was used by the French as well as the British, testifying that its popularity was not confined to Englishmen in America. One problem: why is there a total lack of white, salt-glazed plates in our forts? The answer probably is that the militia and officers were eating from pewter plates, which must have been removed when the forts were decommissioned.

The few fragments of brown-on-yellow pottery from Shirley seem to have come from posset cups or mugs. Known both as "English slip-decorated earthenware"[7] and as "combed-and-dotted-yellow slipware,"[8] this was made in the west of England as well as in the Staffordshire area, and was widely distributed in British America; it remained in use well into the period of the Revolution, as it was found in quantity in 1776–77 context in Fort Montgomery, New York.[9] A handful of Delftware shards from Pelham appear to be mainly from bowls, but one may have been a small pot for pharmaceutical ointment (fig. 6-1*c*).

Glass

By comparison with the illustrations in Turnbull and Herron, most or all of our clear glass fragments appear to be from baluster or balustroid wineglasses with knops (fig. 6-3*a–e*), but a few might be from tumblers.[10] They would be post-1720 and pre-1750 in date. Identical glasses are held by the tipsy participants in Hogarth's famous 1735 painting of the indecent revels in the Rose Tavern.[11]

There is a high frequency, especially at Pelham, of pieces from olive-green beverage bottles (fig. 6-3*g–l*). All would appear to be from round-

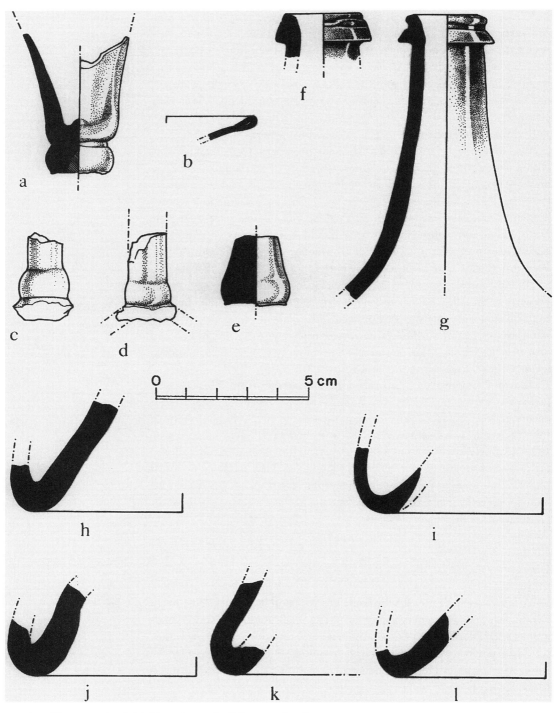

FIG. 6-3. Glassware: (*a–e*) drinking glasses. (*g–l*) beverage bottles.

sectioned wine or rum bottles, somewhat squat with large pushups or basal kicks; the string rim of the neck is sometimes tooled down. They measured about 18 cm (20½ in.) in height, and held a fifth (of a gallon). Such bottles are certainly English, and are virtually identical to examples dating from 1736 to 1740.[12] Most likely they held rum rather than wine, but in their country of origin they may have been intended for a sparkling or fast wine, as the function of the string was to tie down the cork when the bottle was filled with effervescent liquor.[13]

Other common artifacts at Pelham and Shirley are fragments of small, thin-walled flasks of a light blue-green color, with pushups and either straight or everted rims (fig. 6-4). The only decoration consists of vertical ribbing, gadrooning, or tear-drop-shaped protuberances. All this pharmaceutical glassware is most likely of English make, and was probably taken to the forts by Dr. Thomas Williams, the surgeon to the Line of Forts. A ribbed flask identical to fig. 6-4*a* and *b* was found in the excavations of an eighteenth-century trash deposit outside his Deerfield house.[14]

There seem to have been more windows in the barracks of Shirley than of Pelham, as window glass was more than three times as common in Shirley, even though the area excavated was far smaller. All of the panes or lights are of crown glass. Such windows were probably twelve-over-twelve, a tradition that carries well into the nineteenth century in New England.

At Pelham there were pieces of small mirrors, identified as such because they were silvered on one side. The 216 mirror fragments at Michilimackinac came from oval, round, square or rectangular, and even octagonal originals that were beveled on one or both sides, and never more than 7 to 8 cm (about 2¾ to 3¼ in.).[15] The Pelham mirrors were probably similar to these—not even large enough to shave by.

Table Implements

There was remarkably good preservation of knives and forks at Pelham, other than the usual iron rust. Iron or steel table knives (fig. 6-5*e–g*; 6-14*k–m*) have bone plates on the handle, attached to the flat tang by rivets. The butt end of the handle is either cut on a bias or ends in a "pistol grip"; at the heft is an iron cap, while the end of the blade has the usual "scimitar" shape of the period. Such cutlery is characteristic of mid–eighteenth-century England and British America

Table forks (fig. 6-15*a–e*) are steel and two-tined, and were probably set into bone "pistol-grip" handles (now missing). Comparable forks have been found at many British American sites, including Rosewell,[16] Fort Ligonier,[17] and Fort Michilimackinac.[18] Three-tined forks do not appear until later in the century.

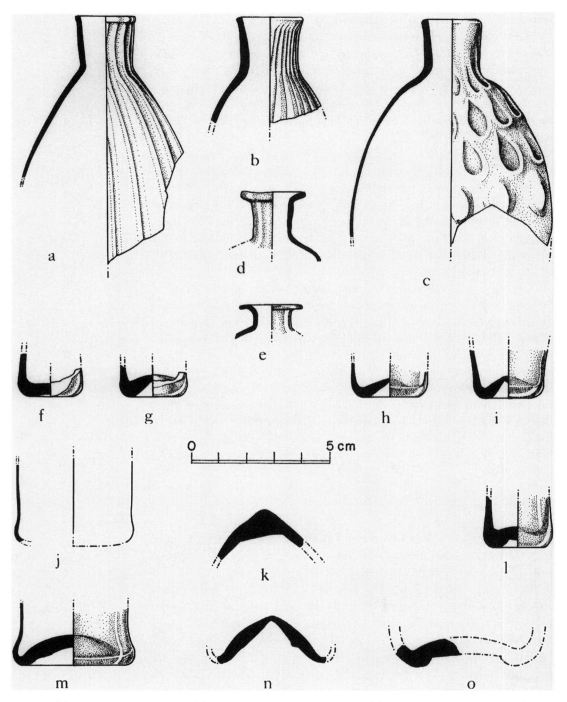

FIG. 6-4. Blue-green apothecary vials. These probably once belonged to Dr. Thomas Williams, surgeon to the Line of Forts.

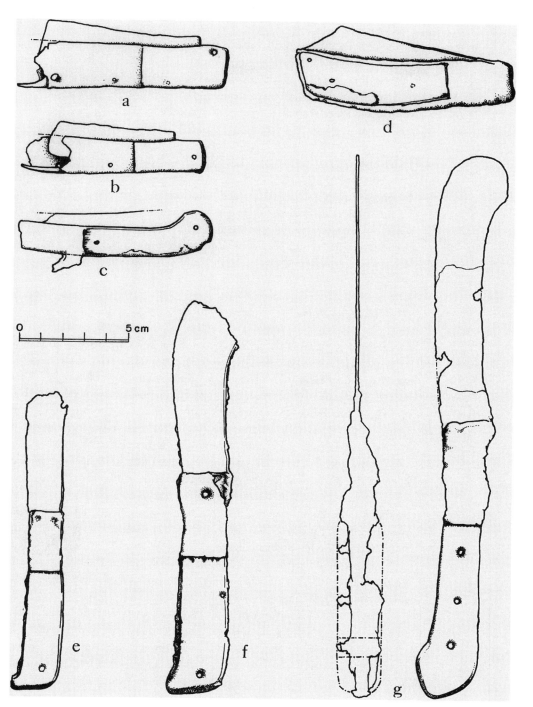

FIG. 6-5. Bone-handled knives from Fort Pelham: (*a–d*) jackknives; (*e–g*) table knives. These are also depicted in fig. 6-14.

The majority of Fort Pelham's pewter spoons (fig. 6-6) have egg-shaped bowls and rattail junctions on the underside; their handles have flaring, rounded ends and a decorative spine running down the middle of the upper surface; this spoon type was introduced into British America around 1710 and maintained its popularity throughout the century. One specimen, however, is the size of a small teaspoon, with no decoration.

Jackknives

Seven jackknives (sometimes called "clasp knives") were lost or discarded by the soldiers in Pelham. These are bone-handled, hinged pocket knives, with iron parts now highly corroded. The inlaid bone has been attached to the iron by small rivets. Very similar ones have been found at other military sites in British America.

Clay Smoking Pipes

Other than handwrought nails, clay smoking pipes were the most common artifacts in our two forts (fig. 6-7). The vast majority of the fragments were from heelless, kaolin pipes—the familiar "churchwarden pipes"—all surely of Bristol manufacture. Six bowl fragments are stamped with RT and eight with R TIP PET, and are clearly products of the Robert Tippett family of pipe makers in Bristol, England. One bowl fragment is stamped with an asterisk and a W, almost certainly the first letter of WILSON; this was John Wilson, also an important pipe maker in Bristol. The Tippetts had been in the business since the end of the seventeenth century[19] and were enormously successful in getting their pipes marketed over much of British America and even in French Canada; in fact, a whole cargo of Tippett pipes was aboard the French frigate *Machault* when it was sunk by the British at the mouth of the Restigouche in 1760.[20]

One fragment has the remains of tobacco cake inside the bowl, and still gives off a strong odor of tobacco—a small souvenir of what the barrack interiors and the soldiers probably smelled like!

It has long been known by historical archaeologists that the bores of clay pipe stems progressively diminish in diameter from the mid–seventeenth century to the end of the eighteenth, and this has been used by several researchers to assign absolute dates. A formula proposed by Lee Hanson is $Y = 1894.88 - 32.98X$, where X is the mean diameter of the bore in sixty-fourths of an inch, and Y is the desired date.[21] I applied this to 87 pipe stems from Fort Shirley and came up with a mean date of 1746.80; and to 250 examples from Fort Pelham, producing a mean date of 1752.08. Both of

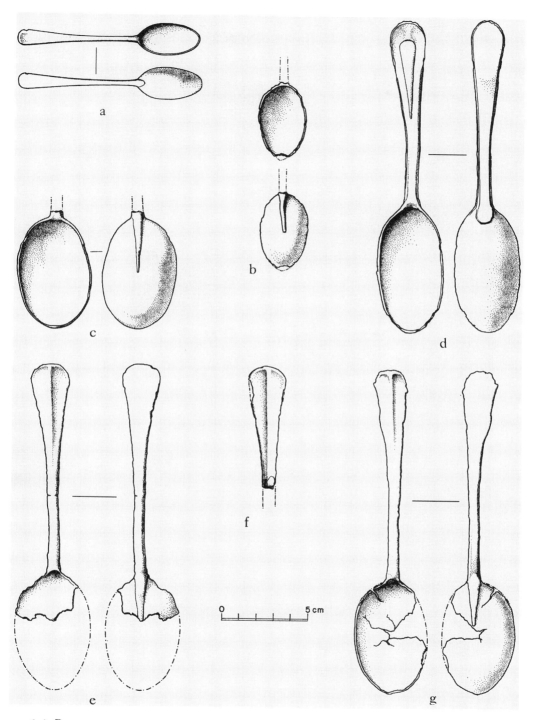

FIG. 6-6. Pewter spoons.

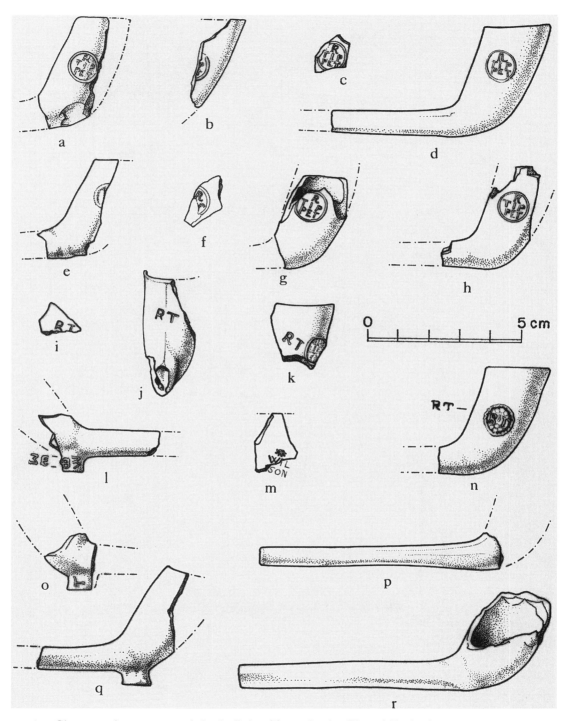

FIG. 6-7. Clay pipes, the majority made by the Robert Tippet family of Bristol, England.

these are within the known time span of these sites. They suggest to me that the human population of Shirley dwindled somewhat earlier than that of Fort Pelham.

Coins

A relatively large amount of coinage managed to get itself lost in such small and short-lived sites as Shirley and Pelham; possibly the nature of the barracks floors contributed to the monetary leakage. The most interesting specimen is a much-worn silver coin from Pelham (fig. 6-8*b*) with a bust of Louis XIV of France on the obverse, looking right, and the inscription LUDOVICUS XIIII.D.GRA; on the reverse is a crown above four fleurs-de-lis, and the inscription 16 (crown) 75 FRAN. ET NAVARRE. REX. Richard L. Dotty, curator of modern coins at the American Numismatic Society, identified this for me as a four *sols* piece. According to him, the American colonists were so short of specie that they would readily accept anything, as long as it was a coin. The Fortress of Louisbourg has French coins that date back to

FIG. 6-8. Coins from Forts Shirley and Pelham: (*a*) English copper farthings; (*b*) Louis XIV silver four *sols* piece; (*c–l*) English and Irish copper halfpennies.

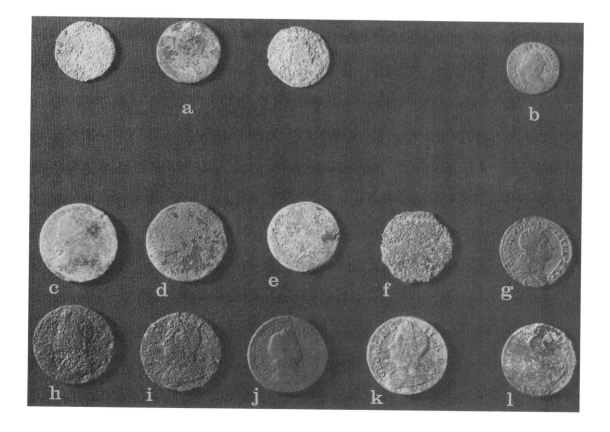

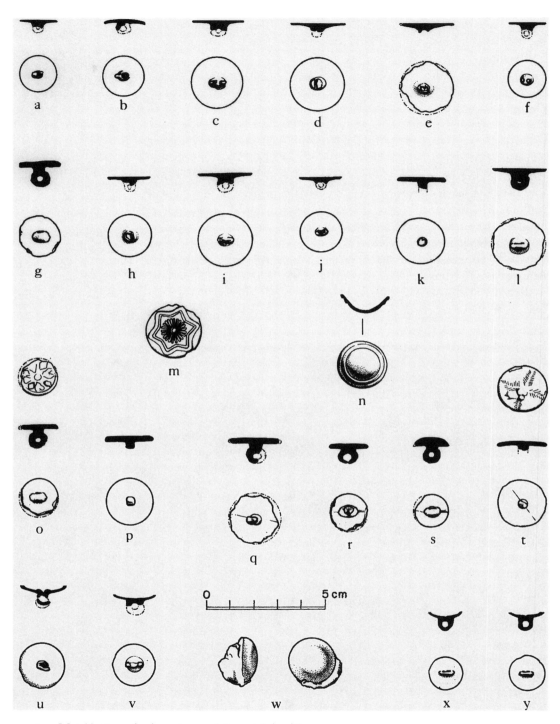

FIG. 6-9. Metal buttons: (*a–t*) pewter or white metal; (*u–y*) brass.

the 1650s, often completely worn; our piece might have been obtained during the New England capture of that stronghold in 1745.

The other coins are British copper farthings and halfpennies (fig. 6–8*a*, *c*–*l*). While the farthings are totally worn on both sides, the halfpennies can be identified as having been struck during the reigns of George I and George II, and also bore the signs of long use.

Clothing Hardware

Like their European and colonial contemporaries, the men in the forts wore clothing rich in buttons that could be lost or discarded. Some are of pewter or white metal (fig. 6-9*a–t*), and the rest of brass (fig. 6-9*u–y*). All were of typical mid–eighteenth-century English type. There are no regimental buttons, as numbered buttons do not make their appearance in the British Army or provincial militia until 1768.

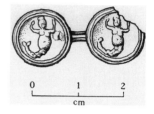

FIG. 6-10. Brass cufflink, Fort Pelham.

Two sleeve links or cufflinks (fig. 6-10; fig. 6-12*d*) came from Pelham. One is of brass, and has a chubby mermaid on each button; the other is octagonal, and very fragmentary. Unconnected sleeve buttons are very easy to confuse with other buttons, but sleeve links are probably common in British American military sites.

Almost as ubiquitous in eighteenth-century sites are shoe and clothing buckles (fig. 6-11). One (fig. 6-11*a*) is probably the frame of a shoe buckle of pewter or white metal. All others are brass clothing buckles; the best preserved is a knee buckle with intact, hook, tongue, and hinge bar (fig. 6-11*b*).

Miscellaneous Brass Artifacts

Two brass artifacts from Pelham are probably military. One is a finial (fig. 6-12*a*); I had originally thought that this might have graced the end of a small flagpole, but I now think it is most likely the cap for a powder horn. The other (fig. 6-12*b*) can be identified as a ramrod guide, for an American-made rifle rod.

But the prize artifact in either of the excavated forts is a snuffbox lid from Pelham (fig. 6-12*g*). This is complete with hinge; the three-dimensional, rococo ornamentation on the upper surface is based on floral designs. The form exactly matches a number of examples from the early and mid–eighteenth century given by Snowman,[22] but all of his illustrations are of enameled and/or jeweled works of art, rather than the plainer but still elegant type represented by the Pelham specimen. The box may once have been gilt, and probably belonged to an officer rather than to a "centinel."

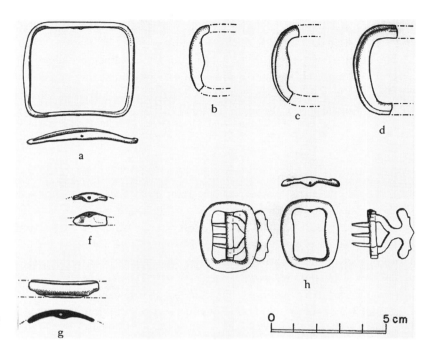

FIG. 6-11. Shoe and clothing brass buckles.

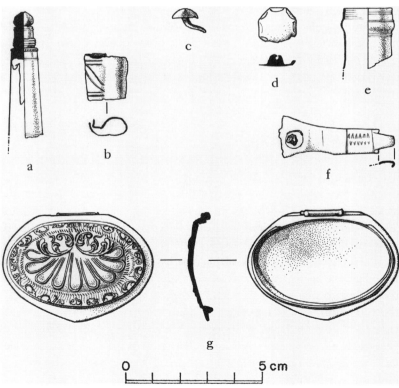

FIG. 6-12. Miscellaneous brass artifacts: (*a*) finial; (*b*) ramrod pipe; (*c*) uphol-stery tack; (*d*) octagonal button; (*e*) tube; (*f*) gun finial? (*g*) snuffbox lid.

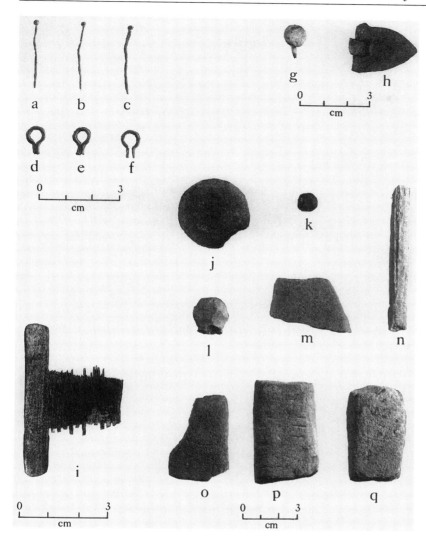

FIG. 6-13. Miscellaneous objects, Fort Pelham: (*a–c*) iron or steel pins; (*d–f*) cotter pins? (*g*) brass upholstery tack; (*h*) brass hinge; (*i*) bone or ivory comb; (*j*) mud concretion; (*k*) garnet? (*l*) shaped fragment of schist; (*n*) ground and incised serpentine or green schist; (*m* and *o–q*) whetstones.

Bone or Ivory Comb

Also from Pelham is a double-edge comb with a different size of teeth on each edge (fig. 6-13*i*). Combs of this type have a long history: they became popular in England in the twelfth century, although they first appear in Roman times. In fact, I have seen identical examples in late Etruscan grave lots in the Villa Giulia, Rome. In the eighteenth century they were used for combing one's own hair; wig combs were far coarser. No fewer than 46 of these were found at Fort Michilimackinac, from both British and French and British occupations.[23] I suggest in chapter 7 that they may have had a secondary function: to comb lice and other vermin from the hair.

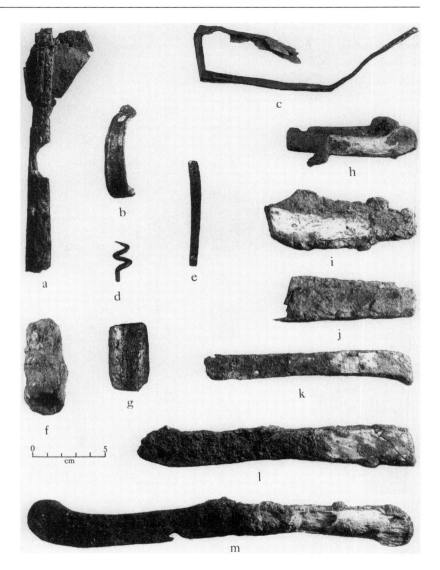

FIG. 6-14. Iron artifacts, Fort Pelham: (*a*) tin-plated spatula; (*b*) tin-plated cup handle; (*c*) tin-plated strap; (*d*) gun worm; (*e*) curved strip; (*f–g*) iron tubes; (*h–j*) jackknives; (*k–m*) table knives.

Tin-plated Iron Artifacts

British American military sites usually produce objects of tin-plated iron, and Pelham is no exception. We have no canteens, but one artifact is a handle from a tin cup, and there may be a section of a cooking spatula. The rest are bits and scraps, and impossible to identify (fig. 6-14*a–c*).

Miscellaneous Iron Artifacts

In addition to the table implements and jackknives, an amazing variety of iron artifacts came from Pelham. The only one of direct military significance is a gun worm (fig. 6-14*d*), a corkscrew-like tool that was once fitted on to a ramrod. The function of worms or scourers was to extract damp and unfireable charges from muzzle-loading guns, and to engage a bit of rag for cleaning purposes.[24] Other identifiable tools include an awl, a router blade, a piece of a hoe or adze, and a small wedge, as well as a currier's slicker. Even though there were no fish bones at Pelham, the relatively large size of the single iron fishhook (fig. 6–15*g*) suggests to me that the soldiers took advantage of the great salmon run that existed 250 years ago in the nearby Deerfield River.

Shirley and Pelham produced fragments of cast-iron cooking pots (fig. 6-17*t–u*). Of a type in use throughout the eighteenth and nineteenth centu-

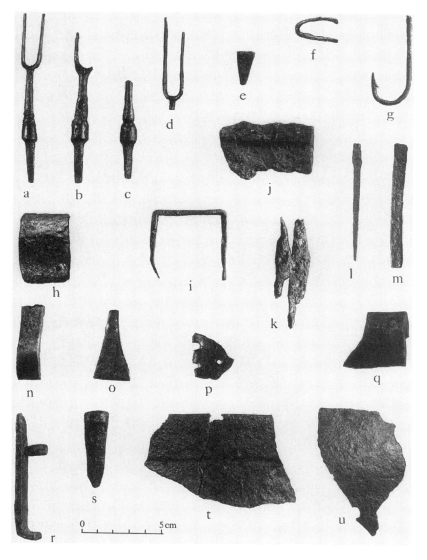

FIG. 6-15. Iron and steel artifacts, Fort Pelham: (*a–d*) forks; (*e*) pyramidal object; (*f*) spring? (*g*) fish hook; (*h*) cylindrical object; (*i*) latch keeper; (*j*) currier's slicker; (*k*) unidentified; (*l*) awl; (*m*) flat bar or strip; (*n*) unidentified; (*o*) router; (*p*) plate or hinge; (*q*) hoe or adze? (*r*) bent bar with rivet; (*s*) small wedge; (*t–u*) cooking pot fragments.

ries, these would have had tripod feet and been suspended over the fire by S-shaped pot hooks attached to the handle. Another domestic artifact from Pelham is a solid, heavy object superficially resembling the modern flat iron (fig. 6-16*f*). But flat irons are a relatively recent invention, the older form having been the box iron; this contained a crude iron element (like our specimen) which was made red-hot, then inserted into the "box."

Not surprisingly, the collection from Pelham includes iron harness buckles (fig. 6-16*c–e*), horseshoes (fig. 6-16*j, k, m*), and even an ox shoe (fig. 6-16*l*—keep in mind that oxen have cloven hoofs!). One of the horseshoes has neither heel nor nail holes, evidence that this was hand-turned by the

FIG. 6-16. Iron artifacts, Fort Pelham: (*a–b*) mushroom-headed spikes (door studs?); (*c–e*) harness buckles; (*f*) heating element for box iron; (*g*) L-headed nails; (*h*) washer; (*i*) cylindrical bar; (*j, k,* and *m*) horseshoes; (*l*) ox shoe.

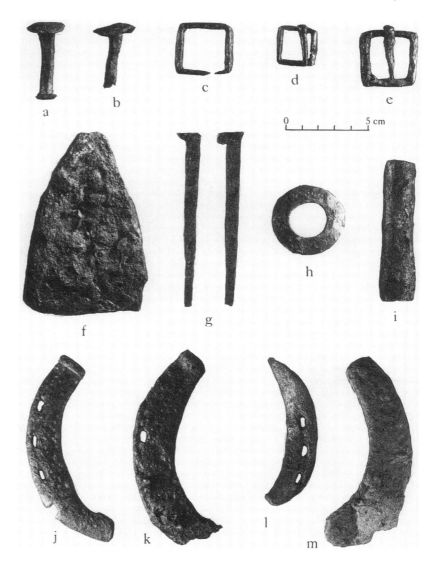

fort's farrier, who would have made the fullering and punched out the holes at his own forge fire.

By far and away the largest category of artifacts in both forts consists of several thousand shingle and board nails, thoroughly rusted. All of them are handwrought, with rose heads and drawn, pointed ends. An analysis of a "grab-bag" sample of 180 intact nails from randomly selected pages of the Fort Pelham field catalogue produced the following result: 70.5 percent measure between 1 inch (2d) and 1¼ inches (3d), and thus were shingle nails; 19.2 percent range from 1½ inches (4d) to 3 inches (10d) and so were board nails for various purposes. The rest are smaller than these, and are of unknown use.

More interesting are two L-headed nails (fig. 6-16g) from Pelham. Their length—4.4 inches and 6.6 inches—makes it certain that they were 20d nails used for nailing down floor boards. In the 1744 account of William Williams for the construction of Fort Shirley, there is an item for "5 at of 20d Do [nails]." In northwestern Massachusetts, until recently, 20d nails were sold in hundredweight (properly abbreviated "cwt") kegs, each containing about 3,000 nails. Thus, there were once some 15,000 of these at Shirley alone. What happened to them? We can only assume that almost all were rescued from the floors of both forts, as well as from the parade at Shirley, when the forts were decommissioned. Apparently the shingle and board nails were of little interest.

Lead

Lead, gunflints, and gunpowder were what these forts were all about. With so much lead about in the form of bullets and shot, and with the constant need to cast bullets, and with certain drainage into the drinking wells, it is difficult to believe that some individuals, particularly any children in the forts (such as little Anna Norton in Fort Shirley), would not have suffered some form of lead poisoning, however mild.

All the bullets were made for use in muzzle-loading weapons, and were apparently cast in gang molds, probably of soapstone; a number of examples still show the casting nubbin. Several are impact-flattened, and eleven specimens of bullets and shot were miscast. I have graded these into four categories, depending upon size:

1. Small shot (fig. 6-17a), 3.3 to 5.0 mm, 8 percent.

2. Large shot (fig. 6-17b), 6.0 to 7.1 mm, 12 percent.

3. Small bullets (fig. 6-17c), 7.8 to 10.0 mm (.31–.39 caliber), 49 percent.

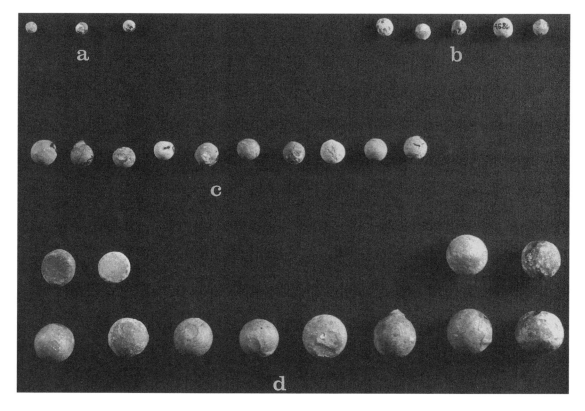

FIG. 6-17. Bullets and shot, Forts Shirley and Pelham: (*a*) small shot; (*b*) large shot; (*c*) small bullets; (*d*) large bullets.

4. Large bullets (fig. 6-17*d*), 13.2 to 17.0 mm (.52–.67 caliber), 31 percent.

Exactly what kind of weapons were these projectiles made for? With the shot, there is little problem as this was often poured on top of a bullet charge to give added effect, whether animals or humans were the target. It was very effective against the enemy during night attacks on the forts.

In the time of William III, the average caliber of a military flintlock was about .75 caliber. The famous "Brown Bess" musket of the same caliber was adopted after 1702, in the days of Queen Anne, and remained in use by the British Army for much of the century; they fired bullets of about .70 caliber.[25] On the other hand, early American rifles had bores that were considerably smaller. The calibers of 32 Pennsylvania rifles described by Lindsay, dating from 1761 to the first half of the nineteenth century, range from .34 to .67.[26] Incidentally, 13 of Lindsay's "rifles" are actually smoothbore. This suggests to me that there were few if any muskets in the Line of Forts, but a variety of arms of lesser caliber including smoothbore fowling pieces and rifles.

As one would expect, there is fairly abundant lead sprue—waste scrap from the casting of bullets—in both Shirley and Pelham. Sows are described by Grimm as "lead that solidified in the channels carrying the molten lead to the bullet mold."[27] We have two of these (fig. 6-18*l*, example on the far right); the spacing of the nipples from which the bullets were cut after cooling suggests that the molds were for casting small bullets. There also two lead gunflint patches (fig. 6-18*f–g*), pieces of flattened lead that have been folded over to hold gunflints. There is a small hole piercing each along the folded edge.

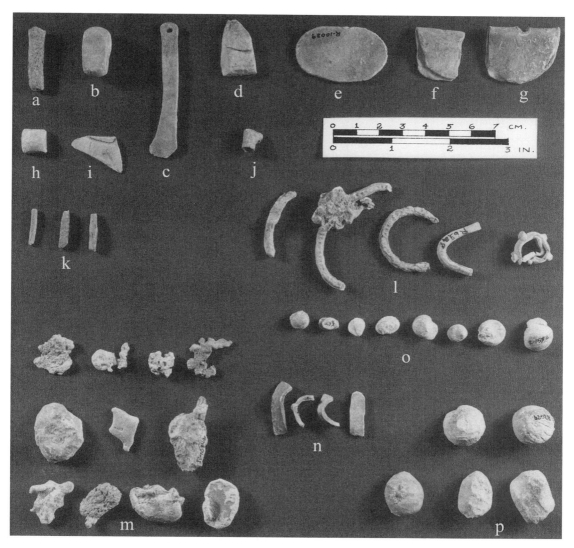

FIG. 6-18. Lead artifacts: (*a*) cylindrical bar; (*b*) oblong bar; (*c*) pierced lead bar; (*d*) wedge-shaped piece; (*e*) flattened oval; (*f–g*) gunflint patches; (*h*) square; (*i*) piece of lead; (*j*) small cylinder; (*k*) lead pencils; (*l*) wire (4 specimens on left); sow (on right); (*m*) spree; (*n*) lead strips; (*o*) miscast bullets, (*p*) lead ingots?

I surmise from specimens of lead wire in our forts that lead for melting down and casting into bullets and shot was in the form of wire coils, and not lead ingots. It would have greatly speeded up the melting process; for just this reason today's lead solder comes in this form.

Gunflints

In their exhaustive and definitive study of eighteenth-century gunflints in North America, Hamilton and Emery[28] have proved that all those in British American military sites fall into three categories:

1. French gunflints made on blades, honey-colored and generally translucent.

2. French spall gunflints, made of the same raw material, but with a prominent bulb of percussion.

3. English spall gunflints, of the same workmanship as the above, but ranging in color from a fine gray to a coarse, grayish tan. In his pioneering study of colonial gunflints, John Witthoft suggested that such flints were Dutch-made, but this is now known not to be so.[29]

All of these were imported across the Atlantic from France and Great Britain.

In the combined sample from Shirley and Pelham, 64 percent of the gunflints were French, and made on blades, and the remaining 36 percent were English-made spall flints. The question might be raised, How did these French products, found in quantity throughout British North American military sites right through the American Revolution, manage to find their way there, given the international situation? Elijah Williams was probably selling these in his Deerfield store along with British spall flints (fig. 6-19). In provincial Massachusetts forts, the answer probably lies in the extensive smuggling from French Canada that was carried out by Boston merchants during all these hostilities.

The Wood in Fort Shirley's Well

Every historical archaeologist hopes to find a treasure trove of otherwise perishable materials preserved at the bottom of wells and privies. This is often the case, but it must be admitted that at the bottom of Shirley's square wooden well we found only a motley collection of artifacts, mostly

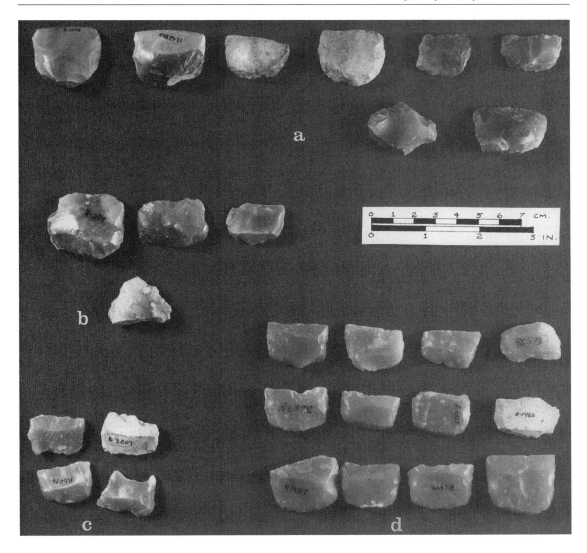

of unknown use (fig. 6-20). The wooden stick incised with Xs is probably a gaming piece, to be used with other sticks as a primitive form of dice. There are two fragments of shingles from a barracks roof; these had been split with a froe.

FIG. 6-19. Gunflints: (*a–b*) English spall gunflints; (*c–d*) French blade gunflints.

Overview

When I began this project, I was under the impression that the militiamen manning these forts would have been Natty "Hawkeye" Bumppo types, clad in a mixture of Yankee homespun and fringed buckskins. From the artifacts

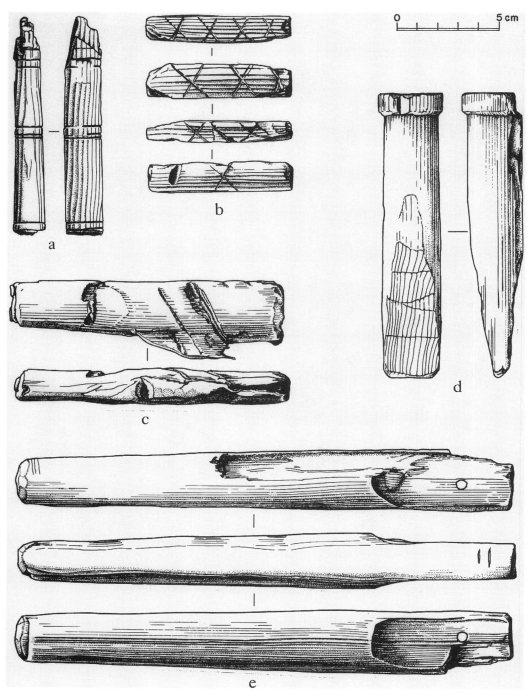

FIG. 6-20. Wooden artifacts from bottom of square well, Fort Shirley: (*a*) decorated rod; (*b*) gaming piece? (*c*) whittled piece; (*d*) wedge? (*e*) handle?

of these two forts, nothing could have been further from the truth. This was not an "Age of Homespun" but an "Age of Consumerism." There is hardly an item in the collection that could not have been unloaded from British ships on the docks of Boston. Writing about the many forts of the period along the waterway that runs from the Richelieu River in Canada to Albany, New York, David Starbuck has rhetorically asked whether all the material culture in military sites on the frontier was already "outdated."[30] On the evidence from the Line of Forts, the answer must be a resounding no.

I had also anticipated evidence for contact with the Native Americans who constituted an ever-present threat to the forts and to the settlements that they protected. I would have expected at least some trade beads. There are none whatsoever. Unlike the French in Canada and the Great Lakes region, the English-speaking people of northwestern Massachusetts were not inclined to adapt to American Indian culture, or to listen to what the other side might have to say. There was just too much bad blood—literally—between the two groups. These frontiersmen might wear Indian moccasins and travel on Indian snowshoes during their "scouts," but that was as far as it went. They were first and last Englishmen, living on the outer fringes of the empire.

NOTES

1. Watkins 1950:24–33.
2. Mankowits and Haggar 1957:117 and Noël Hume 1969:123.
3. Mountford 1973:197–215.
4. Grimm 1970:pl. 66.
5. South 1969: pl. 3*d*).
6. Stone 1974:169, fig. 91.
7. Miller and Stone 1970: fig. 33*a, c*.
8. Stone, Little, and Krael 1973: figs. 1–2.
9. Fisher 2004:136 and fig. 12.13.
10. Turnbull and Herron 1970.
11. Phillips 1964: pl. 10.
12. Noël Hume 1970: figs. 10–11.
13. Brown 1971:106.
14. Blades n.d.: pl. XII.
15. Brown 1971:179 and table 7.
16. Noël Hume 1963, fig. 21(*9* and *10*).
17. Grimm 1970, pl. 61(*16*).
18. Maxwell and Binford 1961:pl. 10*b*.
19. See Walker 1974 for a complete description of the Bristol pipe-making industry; clay pipes were still being manufactured in Bristol as late as 1921.

20. Sullivan 1986:90.
21. Hanson 1969 (this is his Formula 6).
22. Snowman 1990.
23. Stone 1974:fig. 72.
24. Peterson 1968:73.
25. Peterson 1956:165–96.
26. Lindsay 1972.
27. Grimm 1970:109.
28. Hamilton and Emery 1988.
29. Witthoft 1966.
30. Starbuck 1999.

Chapter 7

Daily Life in the Line of Forts

The People in the Forts

*V*IRTUALLY ALL of the men in the forts were citizen soldiers: colonial militia from Hampshire County, or else recruits and impressed men usually on their way to a military expedition; during the term of the conflict (1744–63), probably not one red-coated, regular British army officer or enlisted man ever saw the inside of any of these forts. The militia was a very old institution in Massachusetts, known since the earliest days of the colony.[1] In 1693 the General Court in Boston enacted the General Militia Act, which laid down the rules for the colonial army; this act was in effect through the peace of 1763. All males between the ages of sixteen and sixty were required to bear arms and attend military exercises, with the exception of certain categories of persons such as physicians and surgeons, ministers, sea captains — and Harvard College students! Each militiaman was required to provide his own firearm, 12 gunflints, 20 bullets, and one pound of gunpowder. Some of those in the Line of Forts would have been militiamen of this sort.

But in times of crisis, the militia officers were required by law to impress (that is, draft) soldiers for service, especially on the frontier. As with the draft during the American Civil War, one could buy one's way out of this, and again there were many exemptions. In addition, there were many volunteers for specific campaigns, such as the siege of the Fortress of Louisbourg, the Crown Point campaign, or the final conquest of Canada.

The muster rolls for the Line of Forts are fairly complete.[2] Each covers 26 weeks, that is, a half-year. In the muster roll of June 1746, there are listed by name one captain (Ephraim Williams, Jr.), three lieutenants, eight sergeants, six corporals, one clerk, and 214 "centinels," that is, privates. The pay scale was set by the General Court, in the revenue act of 1742. In the March–September 1748 muster roll of Captain Ephraim Williams, Jr., and his company, annual wages were as follows:

Capt. ------- £62/6, then increased to 80/

Lieut. ------- 60/9

Sergt - - - - - - -	52/9
Corpl - - - - - - -	52/3
Gunner- - - - - -	53/3
Clerk - - - - - - -	52/9
Centinel - - - - -	40/0

The 6 April 1749 muster roll specifies that the chaplain and the surgeon (Dr. Thomas Williams) were each to receive £44/7/6 per annum.

However, as Wyllis Wright has pointed out, there is a problem in using these records, as "men moved between the militia and the regimental ranks and rose and fell in rank at the hazard of patronage as much as of experience."[3] Scouting and garrison duty might be carried on by a combination of militia and men recruited for but not used in a larger military operation, such as the Louisbourg expedition, and men were often transferred from one fort to another.

With a few notable exceptions, the surnames of the officers and soldiers were either English or Scots in origin (or Welsh, in the case of the Williamses), as they were throughout New England prior to 1830. Surprisingly, two of these exceptions were Algonkian Indians: Connewoonhoondelo Sedaudy, listed as a resident of Deerfield, and George Quaquaquid, a native of New London, Connecticut—perhaps a Pequot. Both served throughout the period, and probably would have been expert scouts and trackers. Their pay was the same as for any other "centinel," as was that of one Moses Peter Attucks, who might have been Native American, African American, or, like the famous Crispus Attucks of the 1770 Boston Massacre, of mixed heritage. Two of the soldiers were definitely not free, as they were listed as "servants." These were Cesar Negro and John Crooks, again with standard "centinel" pay, but whether this went to them personally or to their masters cannot be determined. Crooks may have been an indentured white servant, but Cesar Negro was one of Deerfield's many slaves.

But the muster rolls do not tell the whole story. We have documentary evidence that women and children—the families of some of the officers and soldiers—were also in the forts. When Fort Massachusetts fell to the French and Indians in August 1746, among the captives were the wives and children of three of the defenders; another captive, the Reverend John Norton, had left his family, which included four children, back in Fort Shirley. And as Shirley and Pelham gradually lost their importance within the Line and the complement of soldiers began shrinking, these garrisons became more and more a family affair. On the eve of their decommissioning, there were only Archibald Pannell at Shirley, and George Hall at Pelham, each with his family.

Factionalism occasionally reared its ugly head in the Line of Forts, most especially in Forts Massachusetts and West Hoosuck during the decade of the 1750s, as rancor grew between Williams loyalists like Captain Isaac Wyman and an anti-Williams group led by Seth Hudson. This sometimes involved whole families, as this probably prejudiced report from Hudson (dated 25 April 1757) illustrates:

> Samuel Taylor at this time was Soldier at fort Massachusetts & had his family there & tho he had manner or right in this fort yet he came by Captn Wymans order & pulled out Jabez Warren & family out of a Room of Mr Chidester's House that Warren had agreed with Chidester for in order to go in himself & his family & order his Soldiers to assist him & Halled out man, woman, & Children Store [stole?] their Cloaths & broke to bitts & Destroyed some of Mr Chidesters goods & because some refused to assist in that affair, Captn Wyman Came over & with him Leiuy Barnerd, & threatened to Punish us if we Did not obey Taylor & Captn Wyman owned at the head of the Company that Taylor Had done according to his Orders, justified him therefore.[4]

Material Culture

Almost all artifacts in the archaeological record for our two excavated forts—Shirley and Pelham—could have been obtained in one of Deerfield's three retail stores, and that is obviously where these items were purchased. The leading storekeeper of the village was Elijah Williams. As Elijah was a cousin of William Williams and Ephraim Williams (the senior officers of the Line of Forts), as well as the commissary for the forts, Elijah's store was simultaneously a depot for military supplies and *the* place where soldiers and townsmen alike bought the things they needed.

Elijah's detailed "day books" (account books) for the period of King George's War, the peace, and the French and Indian War have survived, and they are a treasure trove for finding out what all these people bought and owned. Here are the day-to-day transactions—many thousands of them over the entire period—in which all the major players in the drama appear, including the officers and men in the muster rolls, as well as Deerfield's leading lights, such as the Reverend Jonathan Ashley. In modern terms, Elijah's store combined features of today's Wal-Mart with those of Home Depot: in it one could buy just about everything from fine silks to chamber pots to ginger to building nails, to musket balls and gunflints. As with the Sears Roebuck and Montgomery Ward catalogues of the first half of the twentieth century, Elijah's account books afford a fairly complete picture of mid–eighteenth-century material culture on the Massachusetts frontier. Here we will confine ourselves to that part of Elijah's accounts that run from early 1744 until the beginning of 1746.[5]

The origin point of this cornucopia of consumer goods pouring into western Massachusetts was, of course, the mother country. The overwhelming majority of Elijah's sales consisted of English-made textiles and other yard goods, at reasonable prices; this was definitely *not* the "age of homespun." The store's sales of ribbon, needles, pins, thread, knitting needles and the like showed that these stuffs and yarns were worked up into dresses and other articles of clothing by the wives of the soldiers and officers in their Deerfield homes. Nonetheless, a great deal of indigo was sold (by the pound and half-pound), so that there must have been a fair amount of home dyeing and weaving, perhaps for bed coverlets. Shoes and heavy boots also were local products, as there were sales of leather, hobnails, and shoe nails, but no shoes.

British-made hardware of all sorts—nails, axes, sheep shears, buckets, and so forth—could all be bought in the store. Jackknives, certainly of the same kind that was found at Fort Pelham (fig. 6-5*a–d*), were a frequent purchase, with prices ranging between three shillings and four shillings sixpence.

The culinary artifacts excavated at Fort Pelham had surely been obtained from Williams and the other Deerfield storekeepers. Elijah sold knives and forks in combination: for instance, 3 knives and 3 forks for 15 shillings, or one dozen knives and forks for 31 shillings sixpence ("cheaper by the dozen"!). Creamware plates are absent from his accounts, as they were from the two forts; in fact, Josiah Wedgewood only perfected his creamware in the 1760s, and it was not to become common in Anglo-America until later in the century. What one ordinarily ate and drank from prior to the creamware revolution was pewter, and this would have held true in the forts—but except for spoons, there was no pewter in the excavations. Why was this so? After all, vast quantities of pewter manufactured items were imported into America from England; in 1760 alone, about 300 tons were brought into the colonies, the weight equivalent of one million eight-inch plates or 300,000 quart mugs.[6] Both Elijah Williams's account books and the inventories of people who served in the forts show that pewter was a common possession in every class on the frontier. Elijah sold them plates, serving dishes, basins ("basons") of various capacities, porringers, mugs and tankards, but relatively few spoons.

Most people on the frontier including the denizens of the forts, seem to have had their own pewter spoon molds. Thus, although these were the most easily breakable category of pewter, there were easily replaceable, using old pewter scraps for raw material. All other pewter, no matter how damaged, would have been salvaged as the fortunes of Forts Shirley and Pelham declined, either for repair of existing pewter objects or for recycling into spoons.

The large number of metal buttons recovered at both Shirley and Pelham simply reflects the fact that a man's clothing in those days was button-rich. In 1753 William Williams had a coat and breeches made by the establishment of John and Richard Billings in Boston; the detailed bill includes 18 coat buttons and 12 "small buttons."[7] We can be sure that everyone in the forts wore their everyday, homemade clothing (this was long before militia uniforms appeared in America), tempered to the realities of the season. For men, this would have consisted of pants or breeches of leather or worsted, buckled just below the knee, a shirt, stockings, a wool vest, and a wool coat. It is doubtful if any but the officers wore three-cornered hats, as none were sold in the Deerfield stores; in contrast, wool caps often appear in Elijah's account books, especially in the colder months of the year. And last, locally made shoes and heavy boots, buckled but not laced.

Military Artifacts

Because these soldiers were militia, they would have been expected to provide their own smoothbore guns, bullets, powder, and gunflints. At the outset of King George's War in 1744, there was almost a run on these supplies in Elijah's store, as militiamen and civilian residents of Deerfield, Colrain, and other frontier settlements prepared for hostilities. Flints were usually sold by the dozen, as one would expect from the General Militia Act. They were cheap enough, at twopence each. Powder was sold at 16 shillings a pound. Also available in the store were bullets, bullet molds, shot, and lead (perhaps in wire form, see fig. 6-18*l*), but the soldiers seem to have made and provided their own powder horns.

Documents do not tell us what military stores were sent to the forts by the province, but we do know that the colonial government provided artillery, particularly breech-loaded swivel guns. These were relatively small (half-pounder) naval weapons mounted on swivels and placed in the fort's mount or mounts, and were highly effective in protecting a fort against Indian attacks. In 1747, the General Court provided two swivel guns for each "blockhouse," except for the two west of Fort Pelham, which were to have one swivel gun and one four-pounder each.[8]

Moccasins and snowshoes, used by all those men engaged in "scouting" (patrolling between the forts) have left no archaeological trace.

Food and Drink

During King George's War, the rations allowed the troops in the Line of Forts were:

> *In garrison:* one pound of bread, one-half pint of peas or beans per day, two pounds of pork for three days, one gallon of molasses for forty-two days.
> *On the march*, one pound bread, one pound pork, one gill of rum per day.[9]

We do not know whether scouting counted as being "in garrison" or "on the march." We also are ignorant of whether there was allowance for the wives and children who sometimes accompanied the men in the Line of Forts.

Elijah Williams at one time supplied military loaves of bread made from his own mill to the soldiers in the Colrain forts; but in the more distant ones, bread was presumably baked in brick fireplace ovens within the barracks. Dried peas provided by the Deerfield commissary (again Elijah Williams!) would have been eaten as a thick porridge or gruel with pewter spoons. In appendix 1, Joanne Bowen presents the data on meat consumption at Fort Pelham, based on faunal remains. As in the rest of British America, there was heavy reliance on domestic animals, especially pork, followed by beef, with mutton a poor third—in almost exactly the same proportions as at Fort Michilimackinac. At least some of the pork came from military rations, but the forts' denizens may have kept pigs, which do well in the forest, and certainly had milk cows and perhaps even steers in the clearings.

Except for the flour, the military rations had to be shipped to the frontier from Boston, a difficult and expensive proceeding. Here is an account of a shipment brought to Fort Massachusetts in 1748 by William Williams in his capacity as commissary:[10]

103 Bushells Flower at 42/	£216- 16-
Transport from Sheffield to S^d Fort	
£14-10 for every 10 Bushell	149- 16-8
2324 lb Pork at 2/	232- 8-
5 Bushells Salt at 112/.	28- -
To Scalding & Packing 10. Bbls of Pork at 11/.	5- 10-
To Driving the above pork to the Fort	23- 10-
To 72 Gall^n Rum at 60/	216- -
To 13 Bushells of Peas at 40/	26- -
To Transporting ye Same	13- 10-
	911-0-8
To my Trouble & Expences in procuring & hiring ye Transport of the above articles, with the risque &c	89
	£1000- -8

Delay or parsimony in the provision of military rations could lead to complaints and unrest, as witnessed by a petition made in 1757 to the General Court by the residents of West Hoosuck (modern Williamstown), complaining about the supplies sent to that fort from Fort Massachusetts by Captain Wyman:

> . . . a Number of us Have not Had any bread for three weeks past, only what we are forced to Provide for our Selves. . . . furthermore our allowance is but Small and not Sufficient to live on, for we receive but 5 lbs and a half of flour for Seven Days allowance of Bread and six pounds and 2 ounces of pork per week and six gills of rum for Seven days and a half a pint of pease pr Day wine measure, which is the Whole that we get for allowance.[11]

As Bowen shows, food resources included game animals like ruffed grouse, passenger pigeon, woodchuck, and deer, easily available to skilled hunters like Aaron Denio, John Hawks, and Gershom Hawks. These could have, temporarily at least, relieved some of the food shortages.

However, a diet consisting only of pork, dried beans, and dried peas would have led to scurvy. Military rations tell only a fraction of the story, for there is ample evidence that some, perhaps most, of the forts operated as small farms (see chapter 8), and certainly had gardens inside or outside the stockade line. In 1757 Colonel William Williams, who had not only overseen the building of Forts Shirley, Pelham, and Massachusetts, but commanded them at the beginning of King George's War, ordered these garden seeds from a Boston merchant: four different kinds of cabbages; two of lettuce; two varieties of turnips; onions; Dedham squash; cucumber; "squash pepper" (perhaps a variety of bell pepper); four kinds of peas; radish; parsley; parsnips; beans; asparagus; and an assortment of herbs.[12] Potatoes, often bought in the Deerfield stores, would certainly have been propagated around the forts. The diet available to the soldiers and their wives may have been far more varied than one would think, especially if many of these items were preserved for the winter. Turnips and potatoes would surely have been stored in cellars like that at Fort Pelham, along with apples and cider.

Details of the cuisine of the Massachusetts frontier are missing, as we have no surviving recipe book, but some of the large variety and amount of spices sold in Deerfield, such as black pepper, cinnamon, nutmeg, cloves, ginger, and allspice, would have found its way to the forts. The same is true with sugar. Other sweeteners available to them were maple syrup and maple sugar; in March, Sergeant John Hawks took time off from his duties in the Colrain forts to go "a-shugerin" (appendix 5), a laborious task now but even more so in those days long before the invention of metal spiles, plastic tubing, and galvanized evaporator pans.

In fact, the soldiers in the forts may actually have had much better fare than that indicated by the stark record of military rations. For example, in a letter of 3 August 1748 written from Fort Massachusetts to his wife, Seth Pomroy tells her:

> I Shant want any Thing Sent to me: we live at This Fort well; my Diner yesterday was a Biscake Suitt whertlebury Pudden & a good Peace of Corned Beef with Squashes & Turnip; no Syder, But a good appitite.[13]

The province was lavish in allocation of rum to the forts. In the winter of 1755, among other supplies given out by Elijah Williams in his role as commissary were nine gallons of rum to Lieutenant Hawks for Morrison's Fort in Colrain; 19 gallons to Lieutenant Burk for Sheldon's Fort; and 20 gallons to Ensign May for Rice's Fort in Charlemont.

Apart from the military ration of liquor, rum must have flowed freely from private stocks. On the testimony of the account books, this was indeed a bibulous frontier, in spite of its sternly puritanical ideology.[14] Rum sales on every scale, even to the Reverend Ashley, were an important part of Elijah's income. This was largely Massachusetts-made, as part of the infamous three-way trade among Africa, the West Indies, and New England. The "wine bottle" fragments excavated in the forts (fig. 6-3*g–l*) would most surely have contained rum, as wine was prohibitively expensive to all but the River Gods and their close relatives.

Although we cannot prove they used it, another and quite cheap source of alcohol easily available to the soldiers in the Line of Forts was spruce beer. This was made by boiling spruce chunks until the bark peeled off; removing them; adding molasses and boiling it again; adding yeast while it was lukewarm; and finally pouring the liquid into a barrel that was bunged up and left to ferment for anywhere from two days to two weeks.[15] Widely used during the French and Indian War by British troops and American militia, it might have accounted for the unusually large quantities of molasses in military rations to the forts and in Elijah's over-the-counter sales in Deerfield.

Chocolate, tea, and coffee were non-alcoholic drinks, but quite dear and thus probably not used much by the yeomen soldiers. The commissioned officers were another matter. It is impossible to say which of these hot drinks were contained by the very thin-walled, delicate, salt-glazed cups and saucers from Fort Pelham (fig. 6-2), but it could have been any one of these (chocolate appears in the accounts with more frequency than the other two). The owner might well have been Lieutenant Samuel Childs, in charge of Pelham and its complement of 29 men in 1748. I like to think that he (and his family?) occupied the two-story structure we have inferred from artifact concentrations.

Health and Sanitation

From a modern perspective, conditions in the forts must have been remarkably unhealthy for their occupants. Packed in as they were into small barracks, with most or all officers and men furiously smoking their clay Robert Tippett pipes when in garrison, the atmosphere must have been rank indeed, especially in winter months. Although there are no records, the incidence of lung disease, particularly emphysema and cancer, must have been high for these men, at least in later life. The sheer amount of rum imbibed must also have taken its toll.

Perhaps the worst health hazard here and elsewhere in the military barracks and camps of British America was bad sanitation. There was obviously little or no concern with the drainage into wells from privies and garbage disposal areas. Although we do not know where the Fort Shirley and Fort Pelham privies were located, a glance at figure 5-5 will reveal that culinary trash must have contaminated the Fort Pelham well. The Reverend John Norton's account of the August 1746 capture of Fort Massachusetts tells us that half of the 20 defenders under Sergeant John Hawks were ill with the "bloody flux," that is, dysentery.[16] In a letter written to his wife from Fort Massachusetts on 3 August 1744, Seth Pomroy (armorer to the Line of Forts) has this to say:

> I enjoy my heth well Tho many of ye Soldiers have Ben (& now are) trobled with ye Bloody Flux: But none Daingerous.[17]

The situation was probably not very different in any of the other forts. The disease may well have spread into settled communities like Deerfield. Historian James Henretta notes: "There were severe outbreaks of infectious dysentery in New England in 1745, 1756, and 1775, as soldiers and militiamen carried the contagion out from their crowded barracks and camps. Many towns had one-half of their inhabitants stricken in these epidemics. The infection was so debilitating (especially to the very old and the very young) that epidemics normally took the lives of 5 to 10% of the population."[18]

Personal hygiene was probably rudimentary. Cakes of soap were expensive in Elijah Williams's store (four shillings apiece). Probably few soldiers washed very much at any time, either themselves or their clothes, adding body odor to the prevailing fug of tobacco and fireplace smoke. Bathtubs were nonexistent here, and rare everywhere in America until the close of the century. When they did wash, it may have been an occasional rubdown using a washcloth and basin. But clothes *were* washed from time to time, as testified by the heating element for a box iron from Fort Pelham (fig. 6-16*f*).[19] They probably never made much effort to clean their teeth, and dental caries and its attendant pain and tooth loss were probably rife in the forts.

It would be surprising if lice infestation were not a problem in the forts. Examples identical to the fine-toothed ivory comb seen in fig. 6-13*i* have been identified as "lice combs" by some historical archaeologists. Elijah Williams sold many such combs in his store, priced from six shillings sixpence to seven shillings sixpence. Probably everyone in the forts possessed one of these combs, either to remove head lice or simply to comb one's own hair, or both. Coarser, single-edged combs were used to comb wigs, but wigs were unlikely to have been worn in the forts, even by gentry like Ephraim Williams.

Deerfield historian George Sheldon affirmed that he had never met with any reference to a military hospital in the Connecticut Valley, and suggested that the sick and wounded were cared for by private families; for example, Ezekiel Wells, wounded at the siege of Fort Massachusetts in 1748, spent 10 weeks and two days in Deerfield boarding in the house of one William Arms.[20] Archaeologist David Starbuck tells us that while eighteenth-century military hospitals "performed an essential function in treating soldiers and officers in the field, the mortality rate was so high that soldiers may have had a better chance of recovering by remaining in their huts and barracks."[21] By modern standards, wound care was rudimentary and brutal. Ezekiel states the following, in a petition to Governor Shirley and the General Court:

> ... on the 2nd Day of August in the same year [1748] being calld to engage the Enemy near said Fort he received a Shott in one of his Thighs near to his Body, which fractured the Bone in such a Manner as that Chyrurgeon [Surgeon] has been obligd to cutt off at Sundry Operations a considerable Piece from the same ... that tho' having labourd when much Pain & Weakness by the Blessing of God & the Help of the Chirurgeon his Life is spard, & his Wound healed. Yet he is thereby become a Criple, & renderd unable to Earn his daily Bread.[22]

Supplies intended for the sick in the Line of Forts are quite surprising to modern eyes. Here is a memorandum from Colonel William Williams covering the period from 10 December 1745 to 10 December 1746[23] (costs have been omitted here):

> At each of the Forts for the use of the Sick
>> 12 gallns Rum
>> 14 lbs Rice
>> 1 Bushel Oatmeal
>> 20 lbs candles
>> 2 lbs Pepper
>> 14 lbs Sugar
>> 4 Buckets
>> 2 Axes

In 1749, Ephraim Williams sent in a bill for "sundries for the sick" that included one firkin (a small cask) of butter, a half-barrel of New England rum, one peck of oatmeal, a half-pound of rice, and a half-pound of sugar.[24] Rum was obviously thought therapeutic: on 5 March 1755 Elijah Williams charges Lieutenant John Hawks "five quarts of rum for Daniel Ward, a Sick Soldier, and one quart for his Lame Leg."[25]

Dr. Thomas Williams, Ephraim's brother, was surgeon for the Line of Forts, and his account books have been preserved; these list every single prescription and medical treatment that he administered to the people of the Massachusetts frontier over many decades.[26] Williams had little formal medical training, as medical schools did not exist in the Colonies, but in general he followed a general tradition stemming with little change from classical authorities such as Hippocrates and Galen. These founding fathers of Western medicine looked on health as arising from a proper balance of the four corporeal "humors": blood, phlegm, black bile, and yellow bile. Sickness was an imbalance of these in one form or another. Common Galenic treatments included purgatives, "phlebotomies" (bleeding), and diet. Williams is known to have been an admirer of the Dutch physician Hermann Boerhaave (1668–1738), renowned not only for his diagnoses at his patients' bedside, but also for his extensive knowledge of supposedly therapeutic chemicals. It thus comes as no surprise that Williams's medical kit included a large chemical pharmacopeia, contained in the same kind of thin-walled glass bottles and flasks that ended up in the forts.

His phlebotomies and those of his successors as surgeon probably did little harm to the soldiers, unless the incisions became infected, but some of the medicines prescribed by Williams contained highly deleterious substances like mercury and lead compounds. In all, the soldiers and the residents of Deerfield would have been far better off confining themselves to the herbal medicines and treatments of the Indians they so much feared and despised.

Recreation and Self-improvement

As anyone who has been on or near a battle zone knows, war consists of very long stretches of boredom punctuated by short intervals of sheer terror. The same must have been true of the Line of Forts. In a year laid out in an unending weekly cycle of Sabbaths, with no holidays like Christmas[27] or Thanksgiving or July 4, probably no newspapers, and certainly no USO troupes or radio or television, the monotony must have been considerable, above all in those forts (Shirley and Pelham) that were never attacked.

Abundant clay pipe fragments bear witness to the amount of smoking that went on. Huge quantities of pipes were sold to all classes of Deerfield society and to the soldiers of the forts. These were often bought by the half-dozen, but they were cheaper by the dozen, selling for between two shillings sixpence to three shillings. The cheapest of all were "short" pipes (one dozen cost only one shilling). All, of course, had originated in Bristol, England. Curiously, very few sales of tobacco are recorded in Elijah's "day books," suggesting that it must have been grown locally at little expense; in fact, the Connecticut Valley was and still is ideal for tobacco cultivation. Some took snuff, which was sold either as loose powdered tobacco, or in its own snuff-box; these latter selling for the surprisingly small price of two shillings (see fig. 6-12*g*).

Drinking of alcoholic beverages, whether rum, cider, or home-brewed beer, was probably a fairly constant daily activity. We know from the account books that the surgeon to the Line of Forts, Dr. Thomas Williams, was a particularly heavy imbiber of rum, as was William Williams. Wineglasses were present at both Shirley and Pelham, but it is likely that this very expensive drink was available only to the officers.

Music must have played a role in the soldier's lives, but we have no archaeological data to prove it. Hymns, psalms, and anthems would have been sung on Sabbath days, and it would be surprising if none of the men had a fiddle to while away the time, or play at weddings. What is almost certain is the playing of Jew's harps; Elijah Williams bought these by the dozen from his Boston wholesalers, and often sold them from his Deerfield store.

Reading material was sparse everywhere in frontier New England during the seventeenth and eighteenth centuries. Nonetheless, as measured by "signature literacy" (the ability to sign one's name), the evidence is that three-fourths of the male rural population of New England in the mid–eighteenth century had reading fluency—a figure much higher than that for contemporary rural England or continental Europe.[28] This ratio of reading literates to illiterates must have held true for the soldiers in the forts. Of course, this measure does not mean that they necessarily had *writing* fluency; a perusal of John Hawks's journal will show deficiency in this regard. But what could they have read in the forts? During his disputation with Ashley (see below), the French Jesuit Saint-Pé states, "You felicitate that there is no one under your ministry who does not have a Holy Bible at home," and then goes on to ask skeptically, "But of what use is reading without understanding?"[29] Surely those who had their families in the forts would have had their Bible. But Bibles were expensive: in the Williams store in 1745, while a New Testament could be purchased for 10 shillings, a Bible cost as much as 37 shillings sixpence. My guess is that most of them would have read their Testaments, at least on the Sabbath.

The only other books sold by Elijah were almanacs (one would like to think Benjamin Franklin's "Poor Richard's Almanac" among them) and primers, the latter perhaps used by parents in the forts to teach their children how to read.

What I have said applies only to the yeomen. As for the officers and River Gods themselves, that is another story. The Williamses and their relatives had the benefit of higher education, either at Harvard or at Yale, and Ephraim Jr. is said to have traveled in his youth to England and the Continent, where he would have enlarged his knowledge of the world. He was a very well read man in many subjects, as testified by the inventories of his estate and his military chest made following his death at Crown Point in 1755.[30] Among the books in his chest were four volumes of *Cato's Letters*; this is a collection of political and philosophical essays by John Trenchard and Thomas Gordon, and a major work of Whig liberalism that advocated freedom of conscience and freedom of speech. Ephraim's Whiggish outlook—surprising for a member of a family that generally leaned toward downright Toryism—is confirmed by his ownership of two volumes of the *Independent Whig*. Ephraim was definitely a man of the Enlightenment; in his estate were the works of Addison and Steele. Yet he was also a man of Protestant New England; he had with him on the march a psalmbook and a New Testament. But there is no doubt that he was a cultured and liberal gentleman, which accounts not only for his popularity among the soldiers in his command, but also for the bequeathing of his estate to found the school that was to eventually become Williams College.

Religion on the Massachusetts Frontier

There can be no question that the officers and men of the Line of Forts took their religion very seriously. In John Hawks's journal of 1756–57 (appendix 5), every single Sabbath day is carefully marked. Because his fort in Colrain was located among the Scots-Irish settlers with their local Presbyterian meetinghouse, he usually went there for the "meeting" and Sunday sermon. When in his native Deerfield, he attended Sunday services there, where he could listen to the Reverend Jonathan Ashley thundering from the Congregational pulpit with his Calvinist message.

All of the 250 men in the Line of Forts were Calvinist Protestants. During the recruitment of soldiers for the Crown Point expedition in 1755, Shirley himself had specified to Ephraim Williams, Jr., that there be no Roman Catholics among them.[31] The struggle with the French and Indians was a sectarian as well as a territorial war. Having arrived in New England from religiously torn Ulster, the Scots-Irish Presbyterians of Colrain were perhaps even more fervently antipapist than were the Congregationalist Puritans of Deerfield and the more western forts. Assigned to the Line was a Congregationalist chaplain, the best known being the Reverend John Norton, taken prisoner at the 1746 capture of Fort Massachusetts, and author of a book about his captivity.[32] Such chaplains must have traveled among the forts, preaching at a different one each Sabbath day.

The Reverend Jonathan Ashley played a key role as the leading ideologue of the Massachusetts frontier. His sermons have been preserved, but so has the record of a fascinating exchange of letters with Father Jean Baptiste Saint-Pé, one of the Jesuit leaders of French Canada.[33] Saint-Pé had shown kindness to John Norton during his Canadian captivity, and Ashley wrote to thank him for what he had done for a fellow minister. This developed into a polite and broad-ranging argument, neither side conceding anything to the other. The main point of contention, other than the authority and role of the Pope, was whether their respective flocks should be allowed to read the Bible (Ashley's point of view), or whether it should be interpreted for them by their priests (Saint-Pé). Ashley stressed that every family in *his* church owned the Holy Book.

There was, however, a schism within the Calvinist camp, pitting the more traditional Congregationalists like Ashley against the evangelical fundamentalists led by Jonathan Edwards, who had been expelled from his Northampton pulpit by John Stoddard, a mighty River God and ally of the Williamses. The Great Awakening did not get very far in Deerfield or with the Williams clan, as this comment on Edwards by Ephraim Williams, Jr. (writing to Ashley from Fort Massachusetts) shows:

> He [Edwards] was a very great Bigot, for he would not admit any person into heaven, but those that agreed fully to his sentiments, a Doctrine deeply ting^d with that of the Romish church.[34]

In a way, Ashley saw the situation on the frontier as a holy war, with the barbarian Indians and the French "papists" on one side, and his people on the other. Here is part of his famous 1744 sermon on the matter, telling his Deerfield flock that their calamities at the hands of the enemy were a consequence of sin and that they could only be saved through repentance:

> Your enemies shall come upon you from the north with bow & spear; they shall be cruel and merciless; your hands shall wax feeble & anguish shall take hold of you. You shall not be able to go forth into the fields, for the sword & fear shall be on every side, & the spoiler shall come suddenly upon us, — when men shall be pursued out of their houses, their fields taken out of their hands, & their wives ravished and they themselves shall fall in Battle.[35]

Even Ashley's great enemy Jonathan Edwards—"apostle" to the Stockbridge Indians—agreed with him in believing that the Indians were in the grips of a satanic religion, that "the devil sucks their blood."[36]

Chaplain John Norton was Ashley's protégé (he had been ordained by Ashley), and must have brought that pastor's message to all the soldiers and officers in the Line of Forts. Later chaplains were the Reverend Joseph Strong, a native of Granby, Connecticut, and the Reverend Stephen West, both headquartered in Fort Massachusetts. These made sure that Sunday for the soldiers was truly the Lord's Day: the journal of Captain Isaac Wyman for 17 May to 10 July 1756, records that Mr. Strong conducted two "Exercises" each and every Sunday.[37] And in May of the following year, Captain Seth Hudson, commander of the fort in West Hoosuck, part-time surgeon, and thorn in the side of the Williamses, petitioned the General Court to send a chaplain as they had none at that time; the nearest service available to them was at Fort Massachusetts, four miles distant.

On 8 August 1755, Lieutenant Matthew Clesson sent for Mr. McDowell (Presbyterian minister in Colrain) to come to Fort Morrison and pray with his scout of fifteen men before they went out on their patrol.[38]

These men of God in the Line of Forts were conscientious about their duties, even in captivity, as a petition of 25 January 1748 to Governor Shirley and the General Court shows:[39]

> The Memorial of John Norton of Springfield in the County of Hampshire, Clerk, humbly showeth That in the month of February, 1746, he entered into the Service of the Province as a Chaplain for the Line of Forts on the Western Frontier and continued in that service until the Twentieth day of August following, when he was captivated at Fort Massachusetts and carried to Canada by the enemy, where he was detained a prisoner for the space of twelve months, during which time he constantly officiated as a chaplain among his fellow-prisoners in the best manner he was able under the great difficulties and suffering of his imprisonment, and your Humble Petit'r begs leave to further to inform your Excell'c. & Honors that besides the great difficulties and Hardships that your Petit'r induced during his captivity abroad, he and his family by means thereof are reduced to Straight and Difficulties at home. He therefore prays your Excell'c. and Honors would take his distressed Circumstances into your wiser Consideration and grant him such Help and Relief as your Excell'c, and Honors in your Wisdom and Goodness shall deem meet, and your memorialist as in duty bound shall ever pray.

His petition was granted to the sum of £37 10s., not for his and his family's sufferings, but "in consideration of his officiating as Chaplain to the Prisoners whilst in captivity in Canada."

There can be little doubt that these men on the northern frontier of British America felt themselves to be in a kind of crusade against the forces of evil. In a letter written to Israel Williams from Albany on 15 June 1755, Seth Pomroy (by now a lieutenant colonel) asks the following:

Sir, as you have at heart the Prodistant interest so I ask an interest in your prayers that the Lord of Hosts, the God of Armys would go forth with us, and give us victory over our unreasonable incroching barberous mordering enemies & return us in due time to safety.[40]

NOTES

1. See Millar 1967 and Whisker 1997 for historical surveys of the institution.
2. Most are in the Israel Williams Papers collection of the Massachusetts Historical Society (Boston) and in the William Williams Papers in the Berkshire Athenaeum (Pittsfield). Additional muster rolls from the Line of Forts also appear in Perry 1904 and Brown 1921.
3. Wright 1970:18.
4. Israel Williams Papers, Massachusetts Historical Society.
5. PVMA 5380: Elijah Williams Account Book of April 26, 1742, to January 16, 1746. Collection Pocumtuck Valley Memorial Association.
6. Cooke n.d.:3–4.
7. William Williams Papers, Pittsfield Athenaeum.
8. Patrie 1974:27.
9. Perry 1904:92.
10. Israel Williams Papers, Massachusetts Historical Society.
11. Perry 1904:414.
12. Coe and Coe 1984:42.
13. De Forest 1926:94. "Whortleberry" is an English name for the European blueberry or bilberry (*Vaccinium Myrtillus* L.), but here obviously applies to our native wild blueberry (*V. nitidum*), still a major crop in the northern Berkshires. Pomroy was enjoying what would today be called "deep-dish blueberry pie," or perhaps "blueberry cobbler."
14. Ibid:45–46.
15. See http://canadahistory.com/sections/documents.
16. Perry 1904:125.
17. De Forest 1926:93.
18. Henretta 1973:14.
19. According to Whisker (1997:78), in the opinion of Jeffrey Amherst's seasoned, professional officers, the American provincials not only were "utterly ill-mannered and ungentlemanly," but "men and officers alike stank for they failed to bathe and wash their clothing."
20. Sheldon 1972, 1:568.
21. Starbuck 1997:33.
22. Copy of original manuscript in Williams College Library. At that time, the surgeon for the Line of Forts was Phinehas Nevers of Stafford, Connecticut, and Deerfield.

23. Perry 1904:106.
24. Perry 1904:235.
25. Sheldon 1972, 1:633.
26. They are now in the Pocumtuck Valley Memorial Association.
27. "By the eighteenth century, New England seems to have been the only place in the Christian world where Christmas (December 25) was no longer observed either publicly or privately" (Purvis 1999:284).
28. Grubb 1990:453, 456; Purvis 1999:248.
29. McClellan 1954:470.
30. Wright 1970:167–73 gives these inventories in toto.
31. Perry 1904:295.
32. Norton 1870.
33. McClellan 1954.
34. Perry 1904:630.
35. Sheldon 1972, 1:536.
36. McDermott 1999.
37. Perry 1904:277.
38. Sheldon 1972, 1:640.
39. Perry 1885:104.
40. Wright 1970:106–7.

Chapter 8

Summary and Conclusions

*T*HE CONFLICT that raged on the northern frontier of New England during the mid–eighteenth century, and that resulted in the Line of Forts, can be put into not just one, but a multitude of perspectives. At one and the same time, it was a religious war between Protestantism and Catholicism; a clash of two or perhaps three cultural systems (taking into consideration the Native American point of view); a competition between the British Parliament and the provincial interests of New England in the future of British America, and in how war should be waged; a method of enriching the River Gods and further consolidating their control over western Massachusetts; and a successful real estate operation on the part of the ubiquitous Williams family, and their adherents.

To fully understand what archaeological excavations have uncovered in two of the forts in the Line of Forts, we must consider the large questions of (1) political and military patronage, (2) rampant consumerism and the colonial economy, and (3) social differentiation in Hampshire County. I shall finally turn to the as yet unanswered question of why the American Revolution followed so swiftly on the heels of Great Britain's greatest victory ever, over her greatest enemy.

The Patronage Pyramid

During the conflict, the ultimate source of political power in the American colonies was not the king but Parliament in London's Westminster, and its then leaders, the two Pelham brothers. Thomas Pelham-Holles, First Duke of Newcastle, was secretary of state, a post that he held for three decades. An enormously rich, landholding aristocrat, according to historian J. H. Plumb he was "the century's greatest exponent of the art of patronage."[1] His younger brother Henry Pelham (for whom Fort Pelham was named) was prime minister from 1743 to 1754; on his death in 1754, he was succeeded in office by the duke.

In Massachusetts, Governor William Shirley was Newcastle's man. By far the most able and most popular of all the royal governors in the colonies, and known for his personal honesty, Shirley was nevertheless a master of the same game that the Pelham brothers played in the mother country. A historian of Shirley says of him in this role:

> As a career administrator, Shirley conceived of the problems of government primarily in terms of the manipulation of patronage; indeed his success as a colonial executive was grounded in his astute distribution of political awards and favors. ... Shirley used the French war, land and timber speculation, expanding trade, and the advantages of office to keep his friends together. ... [The coalition] was fed a rich diet of profits and was challenged at the same time to noble purpose.[2]

Although by training a lawyer, Shirley showed remarkable ability in military matters (the mighty victory at Louisbourg was largely his doing). The "French war," from which so many New England merchants, real estate operators, military suppliers, and ordinary citizens profited, was indeed popular, in both senses of the word. Even the common people benefited by Shirley's policies, not least the debtors whose burdens were eased by his inflationary measures (in particular, printing paper money to pay for the war).

On the next lowest level in this patronage pyramid were the River Gods, in particular Colonel Israel Williams of Hatfield, the de facto head of the mighty Williams network of relatives and adherents. They were the creators of the Line of Forts, under orders from Governor Shirley. Robert Zemsky has said of the River Gods: "Only two things seriously concerned them: military affairs, for which they had a genuine aptitude; and the politics and distribution of power within the valley. Among themselves they could fight over political spoils with a gusto befitting feudal barons. Hampshire County was their preserve, and they remained the final arbiters of what the provincial governor and General Court could or could not do within the valley."[3] This was a dangerous frontier at a dangerous time, and the commissioned and noncommissioned officers of its provincial militia were looked up at and respected—and, perhaps more important, voted into office by the freemen of the county.

The Williamses and their circle were important dispensers of military patronage, as well as receivers of it. The economic advantages accruing to them are summarized by Kevin Sweeney:

> Commissions in expeditionary regiments and in garrison companies stationed in forts along the Hampshire frontier gave officers a steady income and a financial incentive to raise troops. Merchants who secured appointments as sub-commissaries received ready access to government bills of credit

and the use of much-needed operating capital. During the 1740s and 1750s, four Williamses and two of their in-laws served as sub-commissaries. Military commissions and commissary contracts offered holders the opportunity to reap financial awards beyond those allowed by the government. In addition to such mundane practices as inflating accounts submitted to the government, members of the Williams family concocted some rather imaginative schemes to use underemployed soldiers and unspent government funds for personal gain.[4]

In a footnote, Sweeney indicates that Colonel William ("Billy") Williams, the builder of Forts Shirley and Massachusetts, and later of Fort Anson in Pittsfield, was an adept in the latter practice, but the principal beneficiary of the system must have been Elijah Williams of Deerfield: as the military sub-commissary for the Line of Forts and the principal storeowner in this frontier town, he surely found this war or series of wars tailor-made for profiteering.

The Consumer Revolution on the Massachusetts Frontier

When I began my excavations in Fort Shirley, I had naively thought that I would have been dealing with the material culture of a self-sufficient frontier society. In a study of the material culture of Plymouth, Massacusetts, the late James Deetz maintained that in the American colonies between 1660 and 1760, there was a distinctive "Anglo-American" system, less English than what had preceded it, and that it was a "typical folk culture," marked by strong conservatism, resistance to change, and considerable regional variation. Deetz further maintained that this system had continued relatively unchanged "in more isolated rural areas of New England until well past the middle of the eighteenth century."[5] In a 1927 study of clothing in American provincial society during the period 1690 to 1763, the respected historian James Truslow Adams made the following claim: "Farther out on the frontier of all the colonies, conditions of every sort were, of course, much more primitive, even the costume changed and the use of the Indian hunting shirt was general. Indeed, in the later years of the Indian wars many of the young pioneers adopted more of the native dress."[6]

But when I examined what we had actually dug up and compared it with the more abundant artifacts from Fort Pelham, I was nonplussed. Hardly one item, with the probable exception of the brown- or green-glazed earthenware, and perhaps a few iron artifacts, could be proved to have been made on this side of the Atlantic. We found nothing at all that would suggest Indian costume, but rather a plethora of brass buttons and buckles and a sleeve link obviously "made in Britain." And then I came across the account books of Elijah Williams. This was hardly Deetz's "folk culture" or the "Age of Homespun" that I had been reading about.

We now realize that between 1690 and 1750, "something had happened ... to change the course of social and economic history throughout the English-speaking world and beyond. . . . It changed people's standards and style of living from Wellington to Surinam."[7] This change was the Consumer Revolution, a democratization of material culture resulting from the Industrial Revolution: during these decades the British Empire became an "empire of goods."[8] The Acts of Trade and Navigation in passed by Parliament in the second half of the seventeenth century ensured that the American colonies would supply nothing but raw materials to Britain and the rest of the world, while their need for manufactured goods produced in the home country would continue unabated.

For New England, which produced nothing that was not also available in Britain (except for ship masts), this commerce thus remained one-way, with the distribution of goods handled by Boston merchants.[9] Fabrics were one of the region's volume imports (as can be seen in Elijah's account books), and a major item in the chronic trade deficit between the region and Great Britain. By the early 1740s, Boston had more than 166 warehouses, and the port was already a huge entrepôt for a vast territory from Nova Scotia and Newfoundland to North Carolina. In 1743 alone, on the eve of King George's War, some £600,000 worth of British goods came to Boston.[10]

This flood of "popular" (as opposed to "folk") consumer items poured through Deerfield and in rapid fashion into the forts (see chapters 6 and 7). Ivor Noël Hume has suggested that once this merchandise reached the colonies, there was no appreciable time lag between its acceptance on the coast and its availability in the frontier settlements, even going so far as to speculate that contemporary English taste may have manifested itself at Fort Michilimackinac before it became the vogue in Williamsburg.[11] This surmising may be an exaggeration, but at least for the larger forts staffed by regular officers and soldiers, the British military supply system was amazingly efficient.

Over the years of the conflict, Elijah Williams had several wholesaler suppliers in Boston, but the principal one was the firm of Joseph Green and Isaac Walker. It must have been no easy task to transport these goods from Boston to Deerfield and then get them into the Line of Forts: in Massachusetts and beyond the frontier both the mountain and river systems generally run from north to south, so river transportation is out of the question. The distance from Boston to Deerfield is about 98 miles over today's roads; 250 years ago, it would have been considerably longer given the terrain that would have had to be crossed by ox-teams hauling wagons. Even more formidable would have been the difficulty of getting supplies and rations to the forts by horse and oxen. But so they did: the presence of delicate pharmaceutical bottles and eggshell-thin, white salt-glazed ware at these remote outposts speaks to the high degree of professionalism in this transport system.

Social Differentiation

While Hampshire County and the frontier were far more democratic than Great Britain, they formed no populist democracy. There were considerable economic gaps between the college-educated, elite, River God families and the lesser commissioned officers in the forts; between the commissioned and noncommissioned officers; and between the noncommissioned officers and the men. Consider these figures, taken from the probate records of Hampshire County:

- John Stoddard of Northampton, the original organizer of the Line of Forts, died in 1748, leaving an estate valued at £35,433.8.10, one half of which was in real estate. £428.16.0 of this was in silverware alone. He owned a vast amount of clothing, including three suits of clothes and no less than 35 shirts.

- Lieutenant Matthew Clesson of Deerfield died in 1756, leaving an estate of £569.13.5, of which £409.1.8 was in real estate. His clothing ("wearing apparel") was worth only £16.5.0, but he did own some books and writing materials, so he was literate.

- Joshua Hawks of Charlemont, a soldier ("centinel") in Fort Pelham from 1747 to 1748, and a farmer in civilian life, died in 1762. The estate inventory totaled £244.15.1, of which £147.4.0 was in real property (250 acres of land). Only £45.12.1 was in personal belongings. He had no complete suit of clothes, and only one shirt and one pair of breeches to his name. Hawks had no books or writing materials, and his wife was completely illiterate, having signed the inventory with an X as administrator.[12]

Yet in spite of this economic division, all modern scholars seem agreed that relations between every rank of society, in or out of the military, were far easier than they were within the British regular army (that pretty much took over the conduct of the war in 1755). The gap between the regular commissioned officers and the men in their charge was not only large, it was insurmountable: they were more than two separate classes, but almost like almost two different species. The enlisted soldiers were only too often treated by their aristocratic officers with a harshness and brutality that few would inflict upon animals. Many of the Redcoats (or "Lobsters" as the provincials derisively called them) had been impressed or shanghaied in the old country, and were in for life. The penalty for desertion was death by hanging.

By contrast, the provincial militia was what social historian Fred Anderson has called "a people's army."[13] He has found that during the 1755–63 phase of the conflict, more than one-third of all Massachusetts men of military age served in the provincial army, and that of these, 90 percent were volunteers (see the Hawks journal, appendix 5). They were mostly young men of middling social and economic status. On the positive side, they were well recompensed financially. Officers and men were bound up into an amicable, informal fellowship by kinship, friendship, and contractual relationships, very different from what prevailed in the regular armies of Europe and Britain. Egalitarian, yes, but there was a downside, too, as the British generals recognized. The provincials were poorly trained, lacked the iron discipline of the regulars, and unlike British regulars, had no idea of proper hygiene and sanitation (this latter was also true of the Line of Forts: see chapter 7).[14]

Nonetheless, in comparison with British army forts such as Fort Edward and Fort William Henry, the little wooden blockhouses in the Line of Forts would have seemed like miniature paradises to the provincials who manned them.

The Line of Forts as a Real Estate Venture

In spite of many years of searching, I have never been able to locate a plan of any of the structures in the Line of Forts. However, I did find in the Massachusetts State Archives a surveyor's map from the mid–eighteenth century that had on it both Fort Shirley and Fort Pelham (fig. 8-1), albeit indicated in the most sketchy fashion. The tract in which a tiny Pelham is situated is labeled as "Land Petition'd for by J Green, I Walker, T. Bulfinch"; just below (east of) the fort is the annotation "W. Williams Farm." The tract in which an equally imprecise Fort Shirley appears reads: "These lines include G & Walkers Lands."

I have already commented in chapters 4 and 5 about the role of Elijah Williams's Boston wholesalers, Messrs. Green and Walker, in the post-occupation history of these two forts. Apart from their role in the defense of the Massachusetts frontier, the Williamses were up to their ears in the rampant speculation in frontier lands that was in force even before the Treaty of Paris in 1763.

The transition from the settlement policy for "wild lands" that had prevailed in seventeenth-century Massachusetts to one of speculation had taken place in the early years of the eighteenth: group migration began to be replaced by the migration of individual families.[15] By the middle part of the century, land grants were made largely to speculators—individuals or

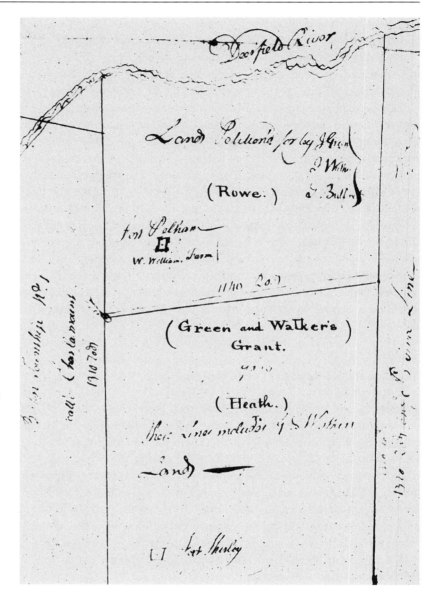

FIG. 8-1. Map of real estate tracts, mid–eighteenth century. The forts of Shirley and Pelham are sketchily indicated, along with the names of the land speculators. "Plan of a tract on Deerfield River adjoining Charlemont, petitioned as a new township, showing locations of Fort Shirley and Fort Pelham, dated November 1749," Series SC1/50, Maps and Plans 1638–1986, Third Series, v. 32, p. 12, no. 638. Massachusetts Archives.

groups to whom the province was indebted. This policy produced a division of huge tracts of land into townships of uniform size and geometric shape. In this system, land acquisition depended on an individual's or a group's ability to pay up, not on a social right as before. The grantee usually had no intention to settle, but to resell at a profit. Although in the end such speculation often proved disastrous to those who had bought large tracts, it nevertheless did stimulate pioneering.[16]

Except for Fort Shirley, where the waterlogged soil conditions were completely unsuitable, the forts in the line were surely surrounded by their own farms, to the profit of William and Elijah Williams, along with the commissioned and noncommissioned officers under their command. It was definitely in the Williamses' interest to attract soldiers and their families to settle in these places permanently, and so they did. On 11 July 1756, Israel Williams reported that "Sergt. Chidester, his son James Chidester, and Capt. Elisha Chapin went from ye block-house at West Hoosuck to seek their cows, were soon fir'd upon and all killed or captivated."[17]

So, the Williams clan had the best of both worlds: the world of the speculators, with Elijah profiting by (and probably receiving kickbacks from) his connection with Green and Walker, and with William Williams attracting militiamen and their families to the western "wild lands" to settle and farm.

Aftermath: Twilight of the River Gods

The years between 1763 and 1776 saw the alienation of the colonies, which until then had enjoyed a period of "salutary neglect." Bent on maintaining a true empire, the obtuse British ministers insisted on enforcing old and rightly neglected colonial laws and inventing new and unpopular ones, while keeping the much-disliked regular army on American soil.

The response to this by those who had been concerned with the Line of Forts is interesting. The aristocracy of western Massachusetts, especially the Williams family and their relatives by marriage, was stoutly loyalist throughout the period of unrest. The most famous Tory in these parts was Israel Williams of Hatfield, a close friend and confidant of the unfortunate Governor Thomas Hutchinson, who had been his classmate at Harvard.[18] With his son William Williams and Colonel Oliver Partridge, Israel, the "Monarch of Hampshire County," exerted every effort to undo the work of the hotheads in Boston. After 1772, he was more than once the target of mobs stirred up by the fiery preacher Joseph Lyman, but he refused to recant, even when imprisoned. The old Tory did not succumb until 1788, when he suffered a fall down the stairs.

Deerfield was another center of Williams family loyalism, with Major Elijah Williams as a leading proponent. The Reverend Jonathan Ashley inveighed against the revolutionaries throughout the struggle, and had the temerity to suggest in a sermon that the patriots who had recently fallen at Lexington were damned to perdition. The Williamses in Stockbridge and Colonel William Williams of Pittsfield (the old Pontoosuck) also remained true to the Crown.

Yet, unlike many loyalists in eastern Massachusetts, New York, and other parts of the new nation, the Williamses were not forced to emigrate to

England or Canada by American independence: although they lost their political role, they retained at least some of their economic and social importance. Perhaps their services in King George's War and in the French and Indian War had saved them from a more profound local enmity. And certainly the benevolence of Ephraim Williams, Jr., who in his will left a legacy to the people of West Hoosuck for a school, was long remembered; this school was to become Williams College, and West Hoosuck would be renamed as Williamstown in his honor.

On the other hand, the enlisted men in the Line of Forts were usually Whigs or revolutionaries, as were many of the junior officers. Most of the latter were not of the aristocracy and had come up from the ranks. Their letters and other writings prove them to have been poorly educated, barely semiliterate in some cases. Seth Pomroy of Northampton, raised in a family of blacksmiths, is a case in point. He became a delegate to the Massachusetts Provincial Congress in 1774 and 1775, and in 1775 he was made a major general in the Massachusetts forces. Until his death in combat in 1777, he was active in raising and training militia in behalf of the Continental Congress. Men like Seth Hudson of West Hoosuck and Samuel Connable of Bernardston (formerly Fall Town) played lesser parts on the American side. The only prominent aristocrat to side with the Revolution was Joseph Hawley, who may have been motivated more by his dislike of the Williams family than by his zeal for independence.

The most lasting legacy of the great struggle between France and England that ended in 1763 was thus not the yawning social cleavages in New England or even independence. Rather, it was this opening up of new lands for permanent settlement. The population of Deerfield shot up after 1763, and town after town was founded in western and northern New England. The older settlements had been pretty much confined to the river valleys where the inhabitants came under the domination of River Gods like Israel Williams and John Stoddard. The newer and more democratic towns gradually spread through the hill country of western Massachusetts in a regularly spaced pattern closely conforming to the predictions of locational analysis.[19] Perhaps the best testimony to the importance of King George's War and the French and Indian War in the founding of New England as we know it was provided by General Epaphras Hoyt, a native of Deerfield and a knowledgeable student of the subject:

> More than fifty towns border the Connecticut above the northern boundary of Massachusetts; and the whole upon the river are not less than eighty; in most of which are compact villages, many exhibiting taste, elegance, and wealth. And if those on the highlands and smaller streams, are less compactly situated, they are not inferior in point of wealth and respectability. While we in tranquility enjoy the boon acquired by our fathers, let us remember their

toils, their dangers and their sufferings; and that this has been obtained, at the price of their blood.[20]

I shall end my account of this remote place and time on a personal note. Dealing with the history and material culture of men and women who lived and died more than two centuries ago has been a revelation. Even though (with the exception of Governor Shirley) no portraits of any of them have been preserved, I feel that I have come to know and understand these people better than I do many of my contemporaries. From that stubborn old Tory Israel Williams, to the genial and brave Ephraim Williams, Jr., down the social ladder to that great frontiersman John Hawks and to ordinary militiamen like the hunter Aaron Denio, I can picture them all in my mind's eye in a way that would be absolutely impossible in the study of prehistory (by its nature bereft of documents and of the individual humans who make history). These insights are why so many of us find historical archaeology such a worthy and satisfying pursuit.

NOTES

1. Plumb 1950:36.
2. Schutz 1961:268.
3. Zemsky 1971:32–33.
4. Sweeney 1982:113.
5. Deetz 1973:15–19.
6. Adams 1970:37.
7. Carson 1978:62–63.
8. See Breen 2004 for a detailed accounting and analysis of the Consumer Revolution of the eighteenth century.
9. McManis 1975:110.
10. Gipson 1967:7–10.
11. Noël Hume 1970:25.
12. Probate records in Northampton, the county seat.
13. Anderson 1984.
14. Whisker 1997:72.
15. McManis 1975:52, 65–66.
16. Bidwell and Falconer 1925:72.
17. Perry 1904:257.
18. Bailyn 1974:252–53.
19. Swedlund 1975:31.
20. Hoyt 1824:312.

Appendixes

Appendix 1

Military Foodways at Fort Pelham, a Faunal Analysis

JOANNE BOWEN

*L*OCATED ALONG the Massachusetts northern border, Fort Pelham and a number of forts were constructed to protect the colony from attack. Abandoned after only nine years, when the area was no longer directly in the line of attack, Fort Pelham was left undisturbed until archaeologists began work in the 1970s. Given the short occupation and lack of subsequent disturbance, this site produced a large and tightly dated faunal assemblage. While this site might be thought of as an isolated outpost that remained separate from the local farming communities, documentary evidence, backed up by analysis of bones recovered from Fort Pelham, demonstrate that it maintained integral ties to the local community.[1]

Following Charles Cleland's lead in his comparative study of dietary differences among the French and British occupations of Fort Michilimackinac, this study attempts to reconstruct the provisioning system as the basis for interpreting the meat diet of Fort Pelham's inhabitants.[2] By showing that the French inhabitants maintained strong relationships with local Native populations, and the British, who remained distant from the Native populations, developed stronger supply networks, Cleland was able to demonstrate the French reliance on fish and other wildlife and the British reliance on large domesticates were determined by the strength of local relationships and the military supply system.

Analysis of the faunal remains from Fort Pelham and related documentations reveals a complex picture of provisioning at Fort Pelham, one that shows the fort's soldiers and their families maintained strong ties to the local community. Drawing on the three levels identified by Chang, Trigger, Tringham, and others, as important components of settlement systems, this study focuses on Fort Pelham as a unit of the British military system, but also how the inhabitant's meat diet mirrored their relationships with the colony and the local community.[3]

A fundamental policy of England's colonial military system was one of self-defense, where the American colonies were expected to protect themselves with their own army. Thus, when the colonies were engulfed in a war against the French and Indians in the 1740s, Massachusetts, with almost no aid from the mother country, launched a successful attack on Louisbourg. France retaliated with attacks on the New England frontier, and Massachusetts responded by increasing garrisons and building new fortifications in the west and along the northern border, where they could buffer any attack from the north. Fort Pelham was one of these forts. As long as a threat remained the colony kept garrisons at full strength, but with the signing of a treaty in 1748 threats diminished, and the number of men garrisoned at Fort Pelham was reduced from 30 to 5, and later was reduced even further to only one soldier and his family. With the onset of yet another war in 1754, Fort Pelham and its neighbor Fort Shirley were abandoned in favor of forts more in the line of attack. In this continual state of hostility, civilian and military life became intricately intertwined. From the mid–seventeenth century, when settlements were established along the Connecticut River Valley, and during the early eighteenth century, when the western part of the colony was settled, the threat of Indian attacks persisted and towns were at least partially responsible for their own defense.[4] In areas open to attack, towns built fortifications.[5] The colonial government's role was to choose the sites for forts, pay for them, and retain ultimate authority. Once built, however, these forts became the responsibility of the town, including staffing them with local militia. With the renewed conflicts in the eighteenth century, the colonial government interceded in this locally run militia by establishing regular garrisons, impressing local militia members, and making them subject to military law. Despite this, the local military forces and forts remained local in character. Frequently the soldiers and officers came from the same region, or nearby towns, and officers were given a great deal of autonomy in making decisions.

There was ongoing, continual interaction between the military and civilian populations. When threatened with attack, families living near forts could stay at the fort at night and work in their fields during the day; if attacked, families could move to the fort. It is unclear from the records under what conditions families could enter the fort, which families could come, and how long they could stay. It is clear, however, that this was not an open policy; records left by the frontier commander contain petitions by settlers to live in a particular fort. From reading these requests, it seems that families of officers and enlisted men received many benefits and had priority over civilians.

Provisioning mirrored this military system.[6] Except for specific campaigns England was reluctant to fund provisions, and thus the Massachusetts government was left with the task of funding supplies, but there was neither a permanent supply system, nor a clear chain of responsibility. Ultimately provisioning fell to the local commander, who obtained supplies wherever he could. Some provisions were obtained from Albany and Boston, but shipments were costly and dangerous to transport, and it appears they obtained most food supplies locally.

Zooarchaeologists writing about provisioning in the 1960s and 1970s have focused on rations provided during expeditions, a task requiring elaborate planning and meticulous care to transport large quantities through a forested wilderness.[7] The provisioning of garrisons, however, involved a very different set of problems, including obtaining food from local farmers, merchants, and through individual soldiers' daily subsistence-related activities. Much of this information was probably never recorded, but papers of the commander of the western Massachusetts army show evidence of supply shipments, local purchases, billeting, hunting, and farming, and several maps show evidence of gardening and structures that could have housed livestock.[8]

These documents record the complex nature of provisioning.[9] They show Fort Pelham was part of the larger commissary system, and that some provisions, including rations of wheat or flour, salt beef and pork, and peas, did come from Boston and Albany. These records also show the right to live on the fort brought with it the right to maintain a garden and to share in the fort's provisions. As seen in account books, the commissary system involved both civilian and military populations, who interacted with each other on a daily basis, exchanging and purchasing food and other goods and paying for them with cash, furs, farm produce, or labor.

Documents, including journals kept by soldiers when they were garrisoned in these forts indicate a substantial amount of food was produced on the fort itself. In a letter dated 10 May 1756, Daniel, John, and Thomas Sargents wrote to Colonel Israel Williams that at Fort Dummer,

> In our Fathers Day with Capt Kellogg we had benefit from Improving a part of the Intervale around the Fort but now the family of the Willards Pretend to own it from a Late Grant of New Hampshr & notwithstanding we hear there is a Reserve in their Charter of Ten acres of Land as a Proper District around the fort—our Two Families are confined to about Three Rods Square of Gound for a Garden Spot while the family of Willards have Severall Hundred of acres Contiguous to the Fort.[10]

Maps provide further evidence of soldiers engaging in provisioning activities. A 1749 map of the area shows land surrounding Fort Pelham was cleared for the first commander, William Williams, and additional land was marked off for other personnel. Several eighteenth-century maps housed at the John Carter Brown Library provide additional evidence, showing gardens surrounding forts.[11] Clearly, farming was very much a part of a soldier's daily routine.

To demonstrate that dietary patterns in British military communities mirror traditional patterns, data from faunal reports from three other eighteenth-century British forts will be compared to show that despite different locations and transportation problems, the soldiers' diets remained essentially English in character. Differences found in the relative proportions of various animals will be discussed, as they relate to logistical problems in supplying military communities, and the availability of local resources needed to sustain livestock.

To demonstrate the soldiers' diets at Fort Pelham were similar to those of local farmers, data from a contemporary New England domestic site in Rhode Island, the Mott Farm, will be compared to data from the Fort Pelham assemblage. Albeit tentative, and despite the Mott Farm's location in southern New England along the Narragansett Bay, this comparison reveals a striking overall similarity in the relative importance of domestic and wild fauna.

The following analysis of military foodways, which draws upon my work with faunal remains from the Mott Farm and Fort Pelham, and data from published faunal analyses shows that despite isolated locations and numerous transportation problems, the inhabitants of each fort depended primarily upon domesticates, and not wildlife.[12]

North American colonists were astounded by the New World's rich natural resources; surprisingly, however, even though they wrote extensive passages on the teeming wildlife, British colonists never seem to have made them a substantial part of their diet.[13] When compared to French colonials, who established long-term and enduring relationships with Native Americans, the British relative aloofness to the wilderness stands out. Reasons given have focused on differences in the French and British approach to colonization. The French missionaries and fur traders developed close contacts with the Indians and became intimately acquainted with the ways of the wood.[14] The British, on the other hand, arrived with families anticipating establishing homes, farms, and communities much like those they had left in England. They did not intermarry with Native peoples to the same extent as did the French, and British soldiers came prepared only to fight as they would do in European warfare. One observer, Thomas Pownall, after General Braddock's disastrous march on Fort Duquesne in 1755, spoke of reasons for their dismal failure and the success of the French:

> . . . The native Inhabitants, the Indians, of this Country, are all Hunters, all the Laws of Nations they know are the Laws of Sporting, & all the Idea they have of Landed Possession that of a *Hunt*, The French Settlers of Canada universally commenced Hunters, & so insituated themselves into a Connection

with these Natives. While the French kept themselves thus allied with the Indians as Hunters & communicated with them in, & strictly maintained all the Laws & Rights of Sporting, the Indians did easily & readily admit them to a local Landed Possession . . .

. . . When the French have by these Means established a Hunt, a Commerce, Alliance and Influence amongst the Indians of that Tract, & have by these Means acquired a Knowledge of all the Waters, Passess, Portages & Posts that may hold Command of that Country, in short a Military Knowledge of the ground, then and not before, they ask and obtain Leave of the Indians to strengthen their Trading House to make a Fort & to put a Garrison onto it.[15]

The reasons for the British reluctance to familiarize themselves with the wilderness and learn to use its many resources went much deeper than expressed by these passages. Reliance on domestic foodstuffs was not a new thing in British society. In seventeenth- and eighteenth-century British society, only the wealthy upper classes were accustomed to hunting, as the royal government had passed numerous restrictions on both the eligibility to hunt as well as its various methods.[16] In 1670 no one with less than an income of £100 a year could shoot game with a gun. Poaching existed, but apparently not to any great extent for laws prohibiting it were tightened up around 1650 and the practice was considered to be abhorrent to upright men.[17]

In the colonies, the British retained their reluctance to hunt. Most yeomen who came over were not from the upper classes; for those that tried, shooting remained a substantial problem. In England, military training through the seventeenth century had concentrated more on the movements required to load and handle the gun than on marksmanship. Targets in battle were not any single object or individual, but an entire company of soldiers. Though effective in European warfare, it proved dismally ineffective in hunting and in battle with Indians.[18]

Indian warfare and the devastation of King Philip's War had by 1675 taught the colonists the value of aiming, but faunal materials excavated from colonial domestic sites in New England demonstrate a continued reliance on domestic animals and retention of attitudes toward hunting (tables 1 and 2). A number of seventeenth-century house sites in Plymouth Colony and several eighteenth-century sites in southern New England have all shown hunting to have been an insignificant factor in colonial foodways. In every case, more than 95 percent of the faunal material was domestic.[19] William Wood talked of their skill in hunting in the seventeenth century:

The beaver's wisedom secures them from the *English*, who seldome, or neur kills any of them, being not patient to lay a long seige, or to be so often

Table 1.

Percentages of Species

Species, including % (cf. specimens)	No. fragments	%	No. individuals
Ruffed Grouse (13.16)	23	5.6	5
Chicken (2.6)	1	.24	1
Passenger Pigeon (10.5)	39	9.5	4
Snowy Owl (2.6)	1	.24	1
Woodchuck (5.3)	10	2.4	2
Beaver (2.6)	1	.24	1
Mouse (2.6)	2	.48	1
Red Fox (2.6)	15	3.66	1
Marten (5.3)	9	2.2	2
Mink (2.6)	1	.24	1
Horse (2.6)	1	.24	1
Deer (7.9)	48	11.7	3
Pig (23.7)	149	36.3	9
Cow (13.16)	105	25.6	5
Sheep/goats (2.6)	5	1.2	1
Totals (99.82)	410	99.84	38

Table 2.

Amount of Meat Provided by Species

Species % (Ind.)	No. individuals	Useable meat	Total meat
Bird			
Bonasa umbellus (.15)	5	1.1	5.5
Gallus gallus (.06)	1	2.24	2.24
Ectopistes migratorius (.08)	4	.8	3.2
Nyctea scandica (.05)	1	2.0	2.0
Totals (.34)			12.94
Mammal			
Marmota monax (.30)	2	5.6	11.2
Castor canadensis (1.02)	1	38.5	38.5
Vulpes fulva (.11)	1	4.0	4.0
Martes Americana (.11)	2	2.1	4.2
Mustela vison (.03)	1	1.05	1.05
Odocoileus virginianus (7.96)	3	100.0	300.0
Sus scrofa (29.12)	9	122.00	1098.0
Bos taurus (59.12)	5	450.00	2250.0
Ovis aries (1.3)	1	50.00	50.00
Totals (99.97)			3769.89

deceived by their cunning evasions, so that the Beaver which the *English* have, comes first from the *Indians*, whose time and experience fits them for that employment.[20]

One solution colonists found for their inability, or reluctance to hunt, was to trade with the Indians, who had proved to be excellent marksmen. Venison was often supplied by Indian hunters, and they also brought in beaver and otter, and wolves for bounties.[21]

On the other hand, the colonists proved far more effective at hunting wildfowl, as the fowling piece did not require skill in aiming. One simply had to point and fire at a flock of birds, preferably when they were on the shore unsuspecting of man's presence. There is a corresponding high occurrence of both fowling pieces found in probate inventories of the seventeenth century with waterfowl remains from archaeological sites in New England of that same time period.[22]

Faunal remains recovered from four eighteenth-century British forts— Fort Pelham located on the northern Massachusetts border, Fort Michilimackinac located on the Straits of Mackinac, Fort Loudoun located in eastern Tennessee, and Fort Ligonier located in central Pennsylvania— together illustrate the British reliance on domestic mammals. Based the number of identifiable fragments, the relative dominance of domesticates is evident in all four sites.[23] Excluding commensal taxa, the Fort Pelham faunal assemblage includes 373 identifiable fragments, of which 64 percent are from domesticated mammals and fowl and 36 percent are from wild taxa. On the basis of Useable Meat Estimates, the fort's inhabitants obtained 90.2 percent of their meat from domestic stock and 9.8 percent from wildlife (see table 3).[24] Excluding commensal taxa, the Fort Ligonier faunal assemblage contains 4,496 identifiable fragments of which 90 percent are from domesticated mammals and fowl, and 10 percent from wild mammals, bird, turtle, and fish. Similarly, the Fort Loudoun faunal assemblage contains 689 identifiable fragments, of which 94 percent are from domesticated mammals and fowl, and 6 percent are from wild taxa. Evidence for the dominance of

Table 3.

*Comparison of Wild vs. Domestic Taxa
in Percentages of Total Identifiable Fragments*

Site	Wild NISP	Useable meat weights	Domestic NISP	Useable meat weights	NISP identifiable
Ft. Pelham	36%	9.8%	64%	90.2%	373
Ft. Mich.	75%	78.8%	25%	21.2%	364
Ft. Ligonier	10%	xx	90%	xx	4,496
Ft. Loudoun	6%	xx	96%	xx	689

domesticates in the diet comes from Fort Michilimackinac. Excluding commensal taxa, the faunal assemblage contains 364 fragments, of which 25 percent are from domesticated mammals and fowl and 75 percent from wild taxa.[25] Using T. White's Useable Meat Estimates, the dominance of domesticates in the British diet emerges. Based on these data, the British obtained 75 percent of their meat from domestic stock and less than 10 percent from big game, while the French obtained approximately 30 percent of their meat from domestic stock and approximately 50 percent from big game.[26]

For the British soldier, wildlife was a secondary resource. As British colonists had done, they both hunted and traded with Indians, but the extent to which they hunted appears to have varied, from being permitted or even encouraged, to being prohibited. In western Pennsylvania, individual messes sent out their own men, who had permission to consume everything they shot; at other places, such as the advance post Loyal Haning, hunting was officially forbidden.[27] In August 1758: "Suffer . . . no hunters . . . to prevent their being taken. No gun to be fired."[28] From Fort Michilimackinac we learn the British traded with the Indians whenever possible, but that by 1779 the number of Indian hunters had decreased due to acculturation and the depletion of local game populations.[29] In eastern Tennessee soldiers at Fort Loudoun obtained not only fish, vegetables, and fruit, but also hogs from the Cherokees.[30]

Thus, by hunting and obtaining meat from local Native Americans, British soldiers consumed varying amounts of wildlife, which formed in every case considered here a secondary source of food, varying according to hunting skills, prohibitions, local resources, and relations with Native populations. Evidence from Fort Pelham hints that fur trading is represented in the assemblage; a number of animals, all valued for their furs are present. Among the bone fragments are metapodials and phalanges from a red fox, mink, beaver, and two woodchucks.

Among the Fort Pelham faunal remains are the remains of a snowy owl, *Nyctea scandiaca*, a bird of prey that, according to culinary historians, was not eaten. One of the largest and most powerful of the owls, it feeds on rodents, hares, rabbits, and some birds. It is most commonly found further north, but winters in southern Canada and occasionally in the United States. Most leave Massachusetts early in April.[31] In Great Britain, as a category birds of prey were used in falconry, an ancient skill in Egypt and the Middle East that was adopted by the Romans, who took this practice with them as they spread throughout Europe. When they occupied Britain, the local upper classes adopted this hunting activity. At the same time exotic birds reigned supreme on aristocratic tables, but culinary historians are clear that birds of prey were not among them.[32]

Other birds identified in the assemblage, as indicated by documentary sources, were no doubt food. Among them are the passenger pigeon (*Ecto-*

nistes migratorius) and the ruffed grouse (*Bonasa umbellus*), both of which were common in this area at that time. Bent says of the ruffed grouse:

> Formerly in New England and E. Canada the ruffed grouse well deserved the name of "fool hen" and was one of the easiest of birds to shoot. It would either walk quietly away or fly up into the branches of a tree and stare stupidly at the intruder. It was an easy matter for a good shot to pick off its head with a rifle.[33]

They nest almost always in thick woods or under dense cover and were therefore probably very common in that area.

The passenger pigeon was also very common and considered excellent fare. Numerous early accounts of this bird describe the abundance of these pigeons. Although no date was given for this quote, it describes the usefulness of these birds. Ashton Blackburne wrote:

> I think this as remarkable a bird as any in *America*. They are in vast numbers in all parts, and have been of great service at particular times to our garrisons, in supplying them with fresh meat, especially at the out-posts. . . . I have heard many say they think them as good as our common Blue Pigeon, but I cannot agree with them by any means. They taste more like our Queest, or Wild Pigeon; but are better meat. . . . I have been at *Niagara* when the centinel has given the word that the Pigeons were *flying*; and the whole garrison were ready to run over one another, so eager were they to get fresh meat.[34]

The British soldiers relied to a much greater extent on domestic livestock (see table 6).[35] Often situated in isolated areas, military communities were forced to rely on supply systems to acquire the bulk of their food supplies. These meats were often obtained preserved and barreled, and at times were even sent from Great Britain. Fresh meat was obtained by sending livestock to the fort, but the problems of transporting the animals and then supplying sufficient amounts of forage forced the communities to rely on at least two sources of preserved meats: that that was shipped through their transportation system, and livestock which was brought in and then slaughtered en masse.

In general, procuring food for troops, either at a fort, or in the field was a challenge, and depending on the location and its resources, provisioners maintained adequate food supplies using different approaches. One means of obtaining food supplies was establishing a commission system with civilians. After 1660, when the British sovereign had abolished purveyance, or the right of the British sovereign to exact provisions and transport at a fixed rate, supplies were obtained through direct contracts with private merchants, with prices adjusted according to current supply and demand.[36] In North

America during the eighteenth century, a system was developed where some of the provisions were contracted for in Britain, but most came from the colonies. One order made in 1754 called for:

> Transport vessels, "with Victualls & Bedding, for the said 1000 private Men, their Officers, & respective attendants . . ." To be provided them were, "100 Barrels of Beef, & 10 Tone of Butter be provided in Ireland, and put on board with the said Troops for their immediate use upon their arrival and in case They have no Occasion for them, That the said Provisions be turned over to the Navy . . ."[37]

One quartermaster, Sir John St. Clair, reported from Williamsburg in 1755 on his efforts to provide "horses, flour, sheep, fresh pork, Beefs, as well as rice, salt fish and calavances"—all of which were to go from Virginia to Will's Creek (near Fort Cumberland).[38] General Braddock wrote in 1755 of the military's dependence on commissions to obtain provisions and the problems of the system:

> My being oblig'd to draw my supplies from distant provinces lays me under a Necessity of employing a Number of Assistant Commissioners, none of which will serve without exorbitant pay and am forc'd to make more contracts than I otherwise should to guard against the failure of some, in which Contracts the People take what Advantage they can of our necessity.[39]

Fresh meat was provided by sending livestock. While this meat was preferred over salted, it was often difficult to provide, as Guilday describes the challenges of transporting livestock and finding sufficient amounts of forage for them on the trail. At times, this obstacle was impossible to surpass; as Guilday commented, hay was as important a commodity to them as gasoline is to a modern army.[40] Braddock, in 1755, wrote of plans for his campaign:

> I am to expect Numberless Inconveniences & obstructions from the total want of dry Forage from them being oblig'd to carry all our provisions with us which will make a vast line of Baggage and which tho' I will reduce as much as possible will nevertheless occasion great Trouble and retard me considerably.[41]

Another problem came in finding sufficient forage resources once the animals had arrived. Bouquet wrote from Carlisle in 1758: "I have spoken for all the meadows in this vicinity . . . some will be reserved for making Hay. The rest is more than enough for Light Horse, cattle, and all that may go there."[42] The cold winter months presented formidable odds, and often there was not enough. Bouquet wrote in 1755: "In six weeks a frost may destroy the grass on which our cattle feed and if we have no pork on what shall we live?"[43] One solution was to herd the livestock to the fort, or at least part way, then slaughter and preserve the carcasses to last the winter months. From Fort Loudoun came reports of driving their herd of cattle into the fort, slaughtering them, and salting down the meat.[44] Another report came from Rays Town Camp and the Forbes expedition in 1758: "I thought one of the easiest and last expensive ways of feeding the army in the fall and during the winter would be to send a thousand head of cattle to the other side of the mountains next month, besides the usual provisions and to smoke the meat in large chambers constructed for that purpose."[45] Thus, the presence of live animals in large part was dependent first on the logistics of getting them there and second on the feasibility of maintaining them once they had arrived.

One pattern predominating in the faunal data from all four sites is the dependence on domestic animals. Of these, the Fort Ligonier, Fort Loudoun and Fort Pelham data as a group show a strong dominance of beef. However, the Fort Michilimackinac data show a greater proportion of pork, and the Fort Ligonier data show a relatively small proportion of pork, and large proportion of mutton/lamb (see tables 4–6). Explanations for these variations rest not only in the supply system, but also regional resources, and the social and economic relationships existing between the military and local community. While it is beyond the scope of this appendix to explore the specifics of provisioning at Fort Michilimackinac, Fort Loudoun, Fort Ligonier, and Fort Pelham, some tentative suggestions for the relative proportions present in the assemblages are possible.

The transportation and supply lines played an important role. The transportation and supply system to Fort Michilimackinac, highly developed according to Charles Cleland, was mostly over waterways, where ships transported animals.[46] The other three forts required overland supply lines. Fort Pelham, which is located in northwestern Massachusetts and Fort Loudoun, which is located in eastern Tennessee, were relatively isolated and difficult to reach, and required wagons and packhorses being driven many miles

Table 4.

*Comparison of Domestic Mammals
in Percentages of Total Identified Fragments*

	Michilimackinac	*Pelham**	*Loudon*	*Ligonier*
Cow	4.1	24.3	54	57.6
Pig	22.2	35.6	31	4.3
Sheep/goats	0.3	1.1	0	21.9

*Includes cf. fragments

Table 5.

Comparison of Domestic Mammals
in Minimum Number of Individuals
(Total Number of Individuals)

	Michilimackinac	Pelham*	Ligonier
Cow	4.8	13.1	1.9
Pig	12.0	23.7	4.7
Sheep/goats	1.2	2.6	22.0

*Includes cf. fragments

Table 6.

Comparison of Domestic Mammals
in Minimum Number of Individuals
(Percentage of Domestic Animals Only)

	Michilimackinac	Pelham*	Ligonier
Cow	26.7	33.0	41.4
Pig	66.7	66.0	10.3
Sheep/goats	6.7	6.7	48.3

*Includes cf. fragments

overland through rough terrain and dense growth. And Fort Ligonier supply routes, which went through densely forested, roadless terrain also was
subject to all the problems that besieged the two other landlocked forts.[47]
However, the fort was also an army relay station between Carlisle and Pittsburgh and it played a prominent role in the Forbes campaign, which resulted
in the founding of Pittsburgh.[48] The area had long been in the forefront of
political and military battles and, compared to other regions, the overland
supply routes were relatively well established.

Meat preservation also played a role in determining which animals might
be sent as barreled provisions, which might transported live and slaughtered
at the fort, or which might be maintained as live herds at the fort. Pork, having a higher fat content than either beef or mutton, was the preferred meat
to preserve, as its fat spoiled faster than the fat in mutton and beef; some
thought pork's flavor even improved, once salted. Beef and mutton on the
other hand did not spoil so readily; consequently colonists tended to keep
this meat fresh if possible. Meat suppliers probably sent cattle and sheep
alive if possible.[49] Even so, beef was regularly salted, particularly in situa-
tions where it was difficult to maintain live cattle.

In the Fort Ligonier faunal assemblages, cattle remains make up 57.6
percent of the identified fragments, 19 percent of the total minimum number of individuals, and 41.4 percent of the domestic mammals (see tables
4–6). Sheep/goat remains make up 21.9 percent of the identified frag-

ments, 22 percent of the minimum number of individuals, and 48.3 percent of the domestic animals only. And pig remains make up 4.3 percent of the total identified fragments, 4.7 percent of the total minimum number of individuals, and 10.3 percent of the domestic animals only. These data, when combined with documentary evidence, indicates a combination of the supply system and local resources influenced the availability of meat at the fort.

Documents show that occasionally the express purpose of sending cattle to the fort was for their meat (see note 45). Other records tell us cattle were also sent live to the fort and kept there, at what has been referred to as "a very pretty place, well watered, and Grass in abundance."[50] This evidence, combined with the archaeological data showing the high frequencies of cattle and sheep/goats remains, demonstrates the military could easily have maintained, in addition to livestock brought in and slaughtered, herds of cattle and flocks of sheep.

The faunal remains show pork, either fresh or salted, was less important at Fort Ligonier than at any other fort. Guilday interpreted this low frequency of pig remains at Fort Ligonier as the result of the preservation process, where flesh had been removed from the bone before salting. However, since salting does not necessarily require the removal of the bone, another explanation is in order, one that takes the abundance of pasturage for cattle and sheep into consideration.[52]

In the Fort Michilimackinac faunal assemblage, cattle remains make up 4.1 percent of the identified fragments, 4.8 percent of the total minimum number of individuals, and 26.7 percent of the domestic mammals (see tables 4–6). Sheep/goat remains make up 0.3 percent of the identified fragments, 1.2 percent of the minimum number of individuals, and 6.7 percent of the domestic animals only. And pig remains make up 22.2 percent of the total identified fragments, 12 percent of the total minimum number of individuals, and 66.7 percent of the domestic animals only.

By any count, pigs at Fort Michilimackinac were extremely important. The NISP (Number of Identified Specimens) and MNI (Minimum Number of Individuals) estimates confirm the rank status of this meat, and however rough this estimate may be, Cleland's estimate of the Useable Pounds of Meat shows pork contributed 35.4 percent of all meat consumed by the British.[52] Why pork dominated the British diet at this fort remains a good question. Is it, as Fletcher claimed, that pigs were more easily maintained on vessels than cattle, and salt pork could be easily shipped?[53] Why do cattle appear in such small numbers? Answering these questions requires additional research, including an assessment of the more recent zooarchaeological work completed by Shapiro and Scott. Are the proportions Cleland identified accurate? What is the overall supply system, including not only supply shipments, but also local pasturage, the fort's soldiers' ability to raise livestock on their own, and the relationships they may have maintained with the local communities?

In the Fort Pelham faunal assemblage, cattle remains make up 24.3 percent of the identified fragments, 13.1 percent of the total minimum number of individuals, and 33 percent of the domestic mammals (see tables 4–6). Sheep/goat remains make up 1.1 percent of the identified fragments, 2.6 percent of the minimum number of individuals, and 6.7 percent of the domestic animals only. And pig remains make up 35.6 percent of the total identified fragments, 23.7 percent of the total minimum number of individuals, and 66 percent of the domestic animals only.

As stated previously, Fort Pelham's local commanders obtained both meat and livestock from multiple sources, including Boston and other New England cities, as well as local farmers. In addition to these resources, soldiers and their families grew gardens, and through strong relationships they maintained with nearby farmers, they obtained quite possibly a significant amount of meat.

The extent to which these different resources contributed to the soldiers' meat diet cannot be measured. What is clear, however, is that the fort's provisioning system was for the most part locally based, and local families moved in and out of the fort. Therefore, it is reasonable to assume the soldiers' and civilians' diet were roughly similar and that the comparison of this faunal assemblage with domestic assemblages from the same region would be productive. In an ideal world, several contemporary sites from northern Massachusetts would provide the best comparison, but as no faunal analysis of a mid–eighteenth century domestic site is available for comparative purposes, I chose to compare these data with faunal data from a contemporary farm site, the Mott Farm in Rhode Island. Even though this site was located in a different, more densely populated part of New England that had been occupied since the mid–seventeenth century, the Mott family and most farmers in western Massachusetts were average yeoman, and the agriculture in both areas was fundamentally the same. I concluded this comparison could be useful, provided the similarities were taken as only a very rough indicator of regional dietary patterns.[54]

Comparing data from Fort Pelham and the Mott Farm, one sees primarily similarities, a dominance of pig and cattle over sheep (see table 7). The similarity was only vaguely reassuring, however, as I knew the preservation of bones at the two sites differed. In the Fort Pelham faunal remains there were large numbers of loose pig teeth, fragmented in part by having been exposed on the ground; the Mott Farm bones, on the other hand, were relatively well preserved, and most teeth remained seated in the mandibles and maxillae, where they remained uncounted. Because these elements are so easily identified, I presumed the Fort Pelham data inflated the relative importance of pork and chose to delete the teeth from the NISP. More sta-

Table 7.

*Comparison of Domestic Mammals
in Percentages Identified Fragments,
Domestic Mammals Only*

	Ft. Pelham with teeth	Mott Farm with teeth	Ft. Pelham w/o teeth	Mott Farm w/o teeth
Cattle	40	32	47	38
Pig	57	42	49	38
Sheep/Goat	3	26	4	24
NISP	256	905	176	674

tistical manipulations should be pursued, but as seen in table 7, the modified data shows pig and cattle changed to quite similar proportions for both sites. In the Fort Pelham figures, the percentages shifted from 57 percent and 40 percent to 47 percent and 49 percent for the pig and cow. The Mott Farm figures shifted from 32 percent and 42 percent to 38 percent and 38 percent for pig and cattle.

The similarity is best seen in the pig and cattle data, which show both pigs and cattle thrived in both areas of New England. As omnivores, well adapted to forests, pigs did well in both these locations, including the fort where soldiers could care for them, and on the island where the Motts lived. As grazers, cattle preferred pastures; like pigs, however, they could flourish in forested areas, and they too thrived on the Mott Farm, where the Motts kept them in wooded pastures, and around Fort Pelham, where farmers were establishing their farmsteads.[55] Together, these livestock were mainstays in the New Englanders' meat diet. If one adjusts for the large number of sheep present on the Mott Farm, the proportions of the two sites seem remarkably similar, and if the amount of useable meat per carcass is taken into consideration, then it becomes clear beef was far more important than pork.

Despite the overall similarity, there were differences, which are visible in the different proportions of sheep/goat remains. Located in a densely wooded area, Fort Pelham was ill suited to sheep, which require grasses to thrive and protection from wolves. Consequently soldiers and farmers kept very few sheep.[56] But in Rhode Island, where farmers had been plowing soil for several generations, extensive pasturage did exist, and sheep farming had grown to the extent that there were extensive sheep farms producing animals to export to the West Indies.[57] Documents show the Motts owned 73 sheep, which was a large number for a yeoman farmer, but as they farmed near Newport where merchants were active, they took advantage of this opportunity and raised sheep for sale. It is not a far-fetched interpretation that the Motts' meat diet reflected this activity.

Another difference is seen in the proportion of deer, which appears in sizable quantities (7.9 percent of all identifiable fragments and 8 percent of Useable Meat) in the Fort Pelham data, but only one fragment (cf. *Odocoileus virginianus*) in the Mott Farm data. The discovery of other variables will have to wait; this level of research requires the analyses of faunal assemblages from numerous sites to uncover colonial New England foodways in its many different contexts and manifestations.

While current archaeological approaches focus more on diversity and variability as it relates to status, ethnicity, and individual agency, I wondered about the utility of this comparison. However, given the similarity existing between the Fort Pelham and Mott Farm data, and the striking differences between these data and data from Fort Michilimacknac, Fort Loudoun, and Fort Ligonier, it seemed this comparison still has some validity in that it could illuminate broad regional patterns. More research needs to be done, and more careful assessments of the strengths and weaknesses in each data base need to be conducted.

By comparing proportions of domestic animals at these different sites and integrating these data with information on the supply system and forage resources, we might be able to determine how logistics, resources, and the very important relationships soldiers and their families living in the fort maintained with their kin, neighbors, and friends living in the nearby area influenced subsistence.

The British supply system's ability to sustain its soldiers, who could be reached only through great effort, is astounding. With only relatively small variations British colonists were able to feed their military forces foods they were accustomed to. Further documentation on each of the forts and supply system could strengthen these ideas, or possibly suggest other alternatives, but the comparison of the remains from four different forts has allowed us a certain number of insights into the British effort to remain British, even when circumstances made it less than easy.

NOTES

1. I want to thank Dr. Michael Coe for giving me the opportunity to analyze these faunal remains and to make revisions on a report, which I submitted in 1976. Since this time the field of zooarchaeology has developed new analytical techniques (such as biomass) and an increased awareness of taphonomic modifications; theories have shifted away from idealized patterning. Extensive reworking of the data from multiple sites is prohibitive, so I have made only minor changes, including referencing more recent zooarchaeological work on forts and incorporating two professional papers presented on these data: Bowen 1976; 1977.

2. Cleland 1970. Even though subsequent research by scholars has largely discredited the archaeological analysis of the contexts Cleland studied, the essential distinction between the French reliance on wildlife and the British reliance on domesticates have been supported by subsequent archaeological work and zooarchaeological analyses by Scott 1985; Shapiro 1979; Martin 1991; Jelks, Ekberg, & Martin 1989.
3. Chang 1967; Trigger 1967; and Tringham 1972.
4. Garrison 1991:17–18; Innes 1983.
5. Shy 1963; Anderson 1983; Pargellis 1969.
6. Israel William Papers 1728–1785, Massachusetts Historical Society. Letters contain requests to Boston for provisions, especially for marching allowances, also several describing soldiers engaging in farming activities.
7. Guilday 1970; Parmalee 1960.
8. Israel Williams Papers, Massachusetts Historical Society.
9. Israel William Papers, Massachusetts Historical Society. Letters contain requests to Boston for provisions, especially for marching allowances, although some describe government stores kept at forts. Other letters describe families petitioning for privilege to live in fort and soldiers engaging in food-related activities, including husbanding livestock and tending gardens.
10. Israel Williams Papers, Letter from Daniel, John, and Thomas Sargents, 10 May 1756.
11. Massachusetts Archives, 1749; John Carter Brown Library, Brown University. Maps showing gardens includes Plan of Fort Miller and the Environs on the West Side of Hudsons River, 1759; Plan of Fort Ontario and its Environs, 1760; Plan of the Fort of Annapolis Royal, 1755; Plan of Fort Edward with Environs, 1758.
12. Bowen 1975b; 1975a.
13. Bowen 1975a; Reitz and Honerkamp 1983; Miller 1988; Bowen 1996.
14. Cleland 1970; Martin 1991.
15. Pargellis 1969:162–63.
16. Bergstrom 1939:686; Malone 1971:117.
17. Bergstrom 1939; Malone 1971:114.
18. Malone 1971:121–24.
19. Deetz 1972:116; Bowen 1975a and b.
20. Wood 1967:29.
21. Malone 1971:130–32; Bridenbaugh 1974:17.
22. Deetz 1972:116; Bowen 1975b.
23. Comparability is always an issue. During the 1970s there were three relative dietary estimates available, including NISP, MNIs, and Useable Meat estimates. Grayson 1979; 1984. Because Paul Parmalee did not compute MNIs, and because methods used to compute MNIs are so idiosyncratic and therefore difficult to compare, the only comparable data is NISP. Additionally, today consideration of the effects of recovery techniques, fragmentation, and differential preservation are an essential step in analysis. As this information is not reported in any of the reports or publications, I have opted to compare frequencies of identifiable fragments. For the two sites that have Useable Meat Estimates available, they are included.

24. This figure for the minimum weight, however, should be taken only as a very rough estimate; the weights were computed using the method where the number of individuals were multiplied by the average amount of useable flesh on an individual (White 1953). It was designed to determine the relative importance of different animals, but the accuracy is questionable for useable weights given for the same species; and the accuracy of the minimum number of individuals has also been questioned (Grayson 1979; 1984). The computation of the useable pounds of meat does, however, demonstrate the relative amount of useable flesh from different animals, especially when there is a high percentage of fish and other small fauna present in the site.

25. Gary Shapiro's more recent data was not available for analysis, hence I have used Cleland's data, including his estimates of the Useable Pounds of Meat, an estimate that at least in part corrects for the disproportionate amount of flesh on the larger mammals.

26. Cleland 1970:16–17.

27. Guilday 1970:179.

28. Guilday 1970:179.

29. Cleland 1970:18.

30. Parmalee 1960:29.

31. Bent 1961:361.

32. Wilson 1974:117–19; Bowen and Andrews 2000.

33. Bent 1963:155.

34. Schorger 1955:130.

35. See notes 23 and 24. Figures given by different faunal analysts for the amount of useable flesh varies for some species. Figures have therefore been recomputed to make site figures more compatible.

36. Cruickshank 1966:76–90.

37. Pargellis 1969:34.

38. Pargellis 1969:58–61.

39. Pargellis 1969:85.

40. Guilday 1970:179.

41. Pargellis 1969:82.

42. Guilday 1970:178.

43. Ibid.

44. Parmalee 1960:26.

45. Guilday 1970:179.

46. Cleland 1970:17.

47. Guilday 1970:177.

48. Ibid.

49. Bowen 1988; 1990.

50. Guilday 1970:178.

51. Meat can be cured both on and off the bone. Eighteenth- and nineteenth-century cookbooks refer to both methods, with the boneless method mostly referring to beef (Rundell 1805; Gardiner 1763). Bridenbaugh cites instructions given in 1672 to slay and salt down fat hogs "heades and all, only cutting of[f] the feet and snoughts, and pack them for shipping" (Bridenbaugh 1974:41).

52. Cleland 1970:22.

53. Fletcher ibid.

54. Bidwell and Falconer 1925; Bowen 1975a; Russell 1976; Garrison 1991; Innes 1983; Cronon 1983.

55. Cronon 1983; Bowen 2002; Fletcher 1950.

56. Walsh, Martin, & Bowen 1997; Bowen 2002.

57. Bowen 1975b; Bowen 1975a; Bridenbaugh 1974.

WORKS CITED

Primary Sources

Massachusetts Archives, 1749. John Carter Brown Library, Brown University.
Israel Williams Papers, Massachusetts Historical Society.

Secondary Sources

Anderson, Fred. 1983. A people's army: provincial military service in Massachusetts during the Seven Years' War. *William and Mary Quarterly,* 3rd ser., 40, no. 4:499–527.

Bent, Arthur Cleveland. 1932. *Life Histories of North American Gallinaceous Birds.* New York: Dover Publications.

———. 1961. *Life Histories of North American Birds of Prey.* Part 2. New York: Dover Publications.

———. 1963. *Life Histories of North American Gallinaceous Birds.* New York: Dover Publications.

Bergstrom, E. Alexander. 1939. English game laws and colonial food shortages. *New England Quarterly* 12:681–90.

Bidwell, Percy Wells, and John I. Falconer. 1925. *History of Agriculture in the Northern United States, 1620–1860.* Washington, D.C.: Carnegie Institution of Washington.

Bowen, Joanne. 1975a. *Colonial New England Foodways: The Mott Farm.* Master's thesis, Brown University.

———. 1975b. Probate inventories: An evaluation from the perspective of zooarchaeology and agricultural history at the Mott Farm. *Historical Archaeology* 9:11–25.

———. 1976. "Zooarchaeology and Military Foodways: An Example from Fort Pelham." Paper presented to the Society for American Archaeology, St. Louis, Missouri.

————. 1977. "Zooarchaeology and the Study of Foodways." Paper presented to the Society for Historical Archaeology, Ottawa, Canada.

————. 1988. Seasonality: An agricultural construct. In *Documentary Archaeology in the New World*, edited by Mary C. Beaudry, 161–70. Cambridge: Cambridge University Press.

————. 1990. "A Study of Seasonality and Subsistence: Eighteenth-Century Suffield, Connecticut." Ph.D. diss., Brown University.

————. 1996. "Foodways in the 18th-Century Chesapeake." In *The Archaeology of 18th-Century Virginia*, edited by Theodore R. Reinhart, 87–130. Special Publication no. 35 of the Archaeological Society of Virginia. Richmond, The Archeological Society of Virginia.

————. 2002. "Historical Ecology and the British Landscape." Plenary talk presented to the Society for Historical Archaeology, Mobile, Alabama.

Bowen, Joanne, and Susan Trevarthen Andrews. 2000. "The Starving Time at Jamestown: Faunal Analysis of Pit 1, Pit 3, the Bulwark Ditch, Ditch 6, Ditch 7, and Midden 1." Manuscript report submitted to Jamestown Rediscovery, Association for the Preservation of Virginia Antiquities.

Bridenbaugh, Carl. 1974. *Fat Mutton and Liberty of Conscience*. Providence: Brown University Press.

Chang, K. C. 1967. *Rethinking Archaeology*, New York: Random House.

Cleland, Charles. 1970. Comparison of the faunal remains from French and British refuse pits at Fort Michilimackinac: A study in changing subsistence patterns. *Canadian Historic Sites: Occasional Papers in Archaeology and History* 3:7–23.

Cronon, William. 1983. *Changes in the Land: Indians, Colonists, and the Ecology of New England*. New York: Hill and Wang.

Cruikshank, C. G. 1966. *Elizabeth's Army*. 2nd ed. Oxford: Clarendon Press.

Deetz, James. 1972. Archaeology as a social science. In *Contemporary Archaeology*, edited by Mark P. Leone, 108–17. Carbondale: Southern Illinois University Press.

Fletcher, Steveson W. 1950. *Pennsylvania Agriculture and Country Life, 1640–1840*. Harrisburg, Pa.: Historical and Museum Commission.

Gardiner, R. H. 1938. *Mrs. Gardiner's Receipts from 1763*. Hallowell, Maine: White and Horne.

Garrison, Ritchie. 1991. *Landscape and Material Life in Franklin County, Massachusetts, 1770–1860*. Knoxville: University of Tennessee Press.

Grayson, Donald. 1979. On the quantification of vertebrate archaeofaunas. In *Advances in Archaeolgoical Method and Theory*, edited by M. B. Schiffer, 2:199–237. New York: Academic Press.

————. 1984. *Quantifying Zooarchaeology: Topics in the Analysis of Archaeological Faunals*. Orlando, Fl.: Academic Press.

Guilday, John. 1970. Appendix to *Archaeological Investigation of Fort Ligonier, 1960–1965*, by Jacob L. Grimm. Pittsburgh, Pa.: Carnegie Museum.

Hall, E. Raymond, and Keith R. Kelson. 1959. *The Mammals of North America*. 2 vols. New York: Ronald Press.

Innes, Stephen. 1983. *Labor in a New Land*. Princeton: Princeton University Press.

Jelks, Edward B., Carl J. Ekberg, and Terrance J. Martin. 1989. *Excavations at the*

Laurens Site: Probable Location of Fort de Chartres I. In Studies in Illinois Archaeology 5, Illinois Historic Preservation Agency, Springfield, Illinois.

Malone, Patrick. 1971. *Indians & English Military Systems in New England in the 17th Century.* Ph.D. diss., Brown University.

Martin, Terrance J. 1991. "Modified Animal Remains, Subsistence, and Cultural Interaction at French Colonial Sites in the Midwestern United States." In *Beamers, Bobwhites, and Blue-Points: Tributes to the Career of Paul W. Parmalee*, edited by James R. Purdue, Walter E. Klippel, and Bonnie W. Styles, 409–419. Springfield: Illinois State Museum Scientific Papers, no. 23 (also The University of Tennessee, Department of Anthropology, Report of Investigations no. 52, Knoxville).

Miller, Henry. 1988. "An Archaeological Perspective on the Evolution of Diet in the Colonial Chesapeake." In *Chesapeake Society,* edited by Lois Green Carr, Philip D. Morgan, and Jean B. Russo. Chapel Hill: University of North Carolina Press.

Olsen, Stanley J. 1964. Food animals of the Continental Army at Valley Forge & Morris Town. *American Antiquity* 29:506–509.

Pargellis, Stanley. 1969. *Military Affairs in North America 1748–1755.* North Haven, Conn.: Archon Books.

Parmalee, Paul. 1960. Vertebrate remains from Loudon. *Tennessee Archaeological Society* 6:26–29.

Reitz, Elizabeth J., and Nicholas Honerkamp. 1983. "British colonial subsistence strategy on the southeastern coastal plain." *Historical Archaeology* 17, no. 2:4–26.

Rundell, Maria E. K. 1808. *New System of Domestic Cookery Formed upon Principles of Economy.* Exeter, U.K.: Norris & Sawyer.

Russell, Howard S. 1976. *A Long Deep Furrow: Three Centuries of Farming in New England.* Hanover, N.H.: University Press of New England.

Schorger, A. W. 1955. *The Passenger Pigeon.* Madison: University of Wisconsin Press.

Scott, Elizabeth. 1985. "French Subsistence at Fort Michilimackinac, 1715–1781: The Clergy and the Traders." In *Archaeological Completion Report Series*, no. 9. Mackinac Island State Park Commission, Mackinac City, Michigan.

———. 1996. "Who Ate What? Archaeological Food Remains and Cultural Diversity." In *Case Studies in Environmental Science*, edited by Elizabeth J. Reitz, Lee A. Newsom, and Sylvia J. Scudder, 339–58. New York: Plenum.

Shapiro, Gary. 1979. Early British subsistence strategy at Michilimackinac: A case study in historical particularism. *Conference on Historic Sites Archaeology Papers* 13:315–356.

Shy, John W. 1963. A new look at colonial militia. *William and Mary Quarterly,* 3rd ser., 20, no. 2:175–85.

Trigger, Bruce. 1967. Settlement archaeology—its goals and promise. *American Antiquity* 32:149.

Tringham, Ruth. 1972. "Territorial Demarcation of Prehistoric Settlements." In *Man, Settlement, and Urbanism*, edited by Peter J. Ucko and Ruth Tringham. London: G. W. Dimbleby, Gerald Duckworth; and Cambridge, Mass.: Schenkman.

Walsh, Lorena, Ann Smart Martin, and Joanne Bowen. 1997. *Provisioning Early American Towns. The Chesapeake: A Multidisciplinary Case Study.* Colonial Williamsburg Foundation. Final Performance Report, National Endowment for the Humanities.

White, Theodore. 1953. A method for calculating the dietary percentage of various food animals utilized by aboriginal peoples. *American Antiquity* 18:396–99.

Wilson, C. Anne. 1974. *Food and Drink in Britain.* Great Britain: Harper & Row.

Wood, William. 1967. *Wood's New England Prospect. Printed for the Society, by J. Wilson, 1865.* New York: Burt Franklin.

Appendix 2

Paleobotanical Remains

Wood and wood charcoal identifications

Fort Shirley

Wood from plank in excavated well - - - -   Ash (*Fraxinus* sp.)

Wood from brace, north wall of well - - -   Red Maple (*Acer rubrum*)

Wood from post, south wall of well - - - -   Red Maple

Charcoal from hearth (?) in SW
   corner of N3E1-D-I - - - - - - - - - - - -   Ash

Charcoal from log extending across
   quadrant N4E9-C-I-47 - - - - - - - - - -   Ash

Charcoal from large concentration
   in N3E1-AI - - - - - - - - - - - - - - - - - -   Ash

Charcoal from concentration in
   N6E3-D-II - - - - - - - - - - - - - - - - - -   Ash

Charcoal from concentration in
   N6E3-D-I - - - - - - - - - - - - - - - - - -   Ash

Charcoal from large concentration in
   N3Ei-C-I - - - - - - - - - - - - - - - - - -   Ash

Charcoal in S3E7-C-I - - - - - - - - - - - - -   Red Maple

Fort Pelham

Wood from S12W16-A-IB - - - - - -   Spruce (*Picea sp.*) or Tamarack
                                                       (*Larix americana*)

Charcoal from S4W16-B-II - - - - -   Hemlock (*Tsuga Canadensis*)

Charcoal from concentration in
     S4W16-D-II - - - - - - - - - - - - - -   Hemlock

Charcoal from S6W5-D-upper
     level 4 - - - - - - - - - - - - - - - - - -   Red Maple

Charcoal from soil sample of roof fall,
     Quad B of "powder magazine" - - -   Ash

Charcoal from S6W5-D-lower
     level 4 - - - - - - - - - - - - - - - - - -   Red Maple, Birch (*Betula* sp.)

Charcoal from log in bottom of
     S1W11-A ("powder magazine") - - -   probably Spruce

Report on seeds recovered by flotation (David Starbuck):
Identifications

Fort Shirley

Rubus sp. (raspberry/blackberry)- - - - - - - - - - - - - -   common

Prunus virginianus (chokecherry) - - - - - - - - - - - - -   very common

Aralia sp. (ginseng) -   rare

Galium sp. (bedstraw) - - - - - - - - - - - - - - - - - - -   rare

Sambucus sp. (elderberry) - - - - - - - - - - - - - - - - -   common

Acer sp. (maple) -   rare

Ranunculus sp. (crowfoot/buttercup) - - - - - - - - - - -   rare

Panicum sp. (panic grass) - - - - - - - - - - - - - - - - -   rare

Polygonum sp.-   rare

Fort Pelham

Rubus sp. (raspberry/blackberry)- - - - - - - - - - - - - -   very common

Prunus virginianus (chokecherry) - - - - - - - - - - - - -   very common

Aralia sp. (ginseng) -   very common

Atriplex patula (saltbush) - - - - - - - - - - - - - - - - - -   uncommon

Galium sp. (bedstraw) - - - - - - - - - - - - - - - - - - -   very common

Sambucus sp. (elderberry) - - - - - - - - - - - - - - - - -   very common

The seeds recovered by flotation from the sites of Fort Shirley and Fort Pelham appear to represent only a small portion of the total ground cover that must currently typify the two sites. The samples are heavily biased towards a very few species—*Rubus* sp., *Prunus virginianus*, *Aralia* sp., *Sambucus* sp., *Atriplex patula*, *Galium* sp.—whereas all other species are represented by no more than a couple of specimens each. None of the common species show any signs of charring (although it would be difficult to tell in the case of *Galium*), and it appears probable that none of these have any significant antiquity. There are a few specimens of unidentifiable seeds or fragments that *do* appear to be charred and that *could* be of considerable age; however, these number no more than a half-dozen each.

The lack of seeds clearly pertaining to the occupation of the two forts can probably be explained by any combination of the following conditions:

1. High soil acidity has prevented the preservation of plant remains

2. Few seeds were originally charred (thus reducing the chances of any being preserved).

3. Sampling of the site has not located any areas where charred plant remains were originally dumped.

4. The slow covering-over of the refuse from the forts and the ultimate burial of all deposits to only a very shallow depth ensured the rapid decay of most plant material while later making it possible for modern seeds to filter into the occupational layer from above (this process would be accelerated by the presence of numerous roots from trees and shrubs). I tend to prefer a combination of the first and fourth variables.

Although the seeds that were identified presumably represent modern species, all of these probably would have been available in the general vicinity of the two forts, even though the sites are now covered by forest. However, the seed record is sufficiently incomplete such that it should be heavily supplemented by recording of the plant species now growing on the two sites. This supplementing is necessary in order to round out the plant spectrum with those species that either do not produce seeds or do not produce them in sufficient numbers to be represented in the flotation samples.

NOTES ON THE SPECIES:
1. *Rubus* sp., Family Rosaceae. *Rubus occidentalis* L. appears to be represented, and probably other species as well. Common throughout Massachusetts.

2. *Prunus virginiana* L., Family Rosaceae. Roadside thickets, fencerows, borders of woods and mountaintops. Common throughout Massachusetts.

3. *Aralia* sp. Family Aralacieae (ginseng family). This appears to be either *A. hispida* Vent. (bristly sarsaparilla) or *A. nudicaulis* L. (wild sarsaparilla), both of which are common throughout Massachusetts. Roadsides, dry soil, thickets (*A. hispida*) or dry woods. Thickets (*A. nudicaulis*).

4. *Atriplex patula* L., Family Chenopodiaceae (goosefoot family). Waste ground, roadsides, not especially common. Only at Fort Pelham.

5. *Galium* sp., Family Rubiaceae (madder family). More than one species may be represented (there is a considerable size variation). Common: the habitat varies greatly with the species, and there are many possible species in Massachusetts.

6. *Sambucus* sp. Family Caprifoliaceae (honeysuckle family). More than one species may be represented, and it is possible that this is *not* the common Canadian Elderberry, *Sambucus canadensis*.

7. *Acer* sp.. Family Aceraceae (maple family). Only a single seed is represented (Fort Shirley). There are many possible species in Massachusetts.

8. *Ranunculus* sp., Family Ranunculaceae (crowfoot/buttercup family). Only a single seed is represented (Fort Shirley). There are many possible species in Massachusetts.

9. *Panicum* sp., Family Gramineae (grass family). One seed only, from Fort Shirley. Many possible species in the state.

10. *Polygonum* sp., Family Polygonaceae (smartweeds, knotweeds). The only examples (4) came from Fort Shirley, and these were definitely one of the smartweeds (as opposed to a knotweed). There are a great many species of both smartweeds and knotweeds in Massachusetts.

Identifications of pollen and spores from bottom
of Fort Shirley well (Dr. Margaret B. Davis)

Species	*No. of pollen grains (sample of 40)*
Pine	3
Hemlock	11
Oak	3
Birch	6
Ash	2
Beech	1
Sugar maple	2
Chestnut	2
Elm	1
Tulip-tree	2
Compositaceae	1
Cruciferaceae	1
Unidentified	5

Species	*No. of spores (sample of 18)*
Ferns	6
Club moss (*Lycopodium* spp)	11
Unidentified	1

Appendix 3

Forts in the Line and Related Forts

An asterisk (*) denotes principal forts, usually garrisoned by the Province of Massachusetts. The following are included, from east to west:

1. Northfield
   Shattuck's Fort (built ca. 1736–37; two houses surrounded by palisade)
   Deacon Alexander's Fort (built 1744, rebuilt 1753; mount)
   Mr. Doolittle's Fort (same)
   Capt. Zechariah Field's Fort (same)
   Nathaniel Dickinson's Fort (same)

2. Fall Town (= Bernardston)
   *Burk's Fort (attacked 1747, dismantled after war; 8 houses, surrounded by palisade)
   Samuel Connable's Fort (fortified house)
   Lt. Ebenezer Sheldon's Fort (fortified house)
   Deacon Sheldon's Fort (fortified house, attacked 1746)

3. Colrain
   *Hugh Morrison's Fort (built after 1739; fortified house)
   The Rev. McDowell's Fort (fortified house, palisaded and garrisoned in 1755)
   Fort Lucas (probably blockhouse and palisade)
   South Fort (also known as Fort Morris; blockhouse and palisade)

4. Heath (founded 1785)
   *Fort Shirley (built 1744, abandoned 1754; blockhouse, probably with palisade)

5. Rowe (incorporated 1785)
   *Fort Pelham (built 1744–45, abandoned 1754; single barracks with palisade)

6. East Hoosuck (= North Adams)

    *Fort Massachusetts (built 1745, abandoned by 1759; large
        barracks with palisade)

7. West Hoosuck (= Williamstown)

    *West Hoosuck Fort (built 1756; blockhouse and houses, with
        palisade)

Related forts in Massachusetts include:

1. Deerfield

    Five garrisons built in town itself, one in Wapping

2. Charlemont

    Taylor's Fort (built 1742 or shortly thereafter; two houses,
        connected by palisade walls in 1754)
    Hawks' Fort (two houses, connected by palisade walls in 1754)
    Rice's Fort (built 1742, palisaded house; in 1756, palisade moved
        to son's house)

3. Huntstown (= Ashfield)
    Palisaded fort, built c. 1753
    Second fort built 1759

4. Pontoosuck (= Pittsfield)
    *Fort Anson (built 1754; fortified barracks, with second-story
        walk going around it)
    Two other forts built 1756

Related forts in upper Connecticut Valley include:

1. Brattleboro (Vermont)
    *Fort Dummer (built 1724; houses around parade, connected by
        palisade)
    Sartwell's Fort (blockhouse)
    The Rev. Ebenezer Hinsdale's Fort (opposite Bartwell's on
        other side of river)
    Fort Bridgman

2. Charlestown (New Hampshire)
    *Fort No. 4 (built 1743; a number of houses around parade,
        enclosed by walls of horizontally laid timbers; palisade
        outside)

Appendix 4

Biographical Sketches

Note: These sketches are based in part on local town histories, especially Sheldon 1972, Perry 1904, Patrie 1974, and Brown 1960, and in part on documents such as muster rolls and correspondence between participants in the wars.

Alexander, Ebenezer (1684–1768). Came to Northfield from Wethersfield, Connecticut. Deacon of church for 40 years. Father-in-law of Sergeant Samuel Taylor. Married Mehitable Buck of Wethersfield, 5 children. Saw much service in Father Rasle's War, serving as ensign, then lieutenant. 1744, built fort in Northfield. 9 March 1744 or 1745, commissioned lieutenant in expedition to Louisbourg, was at capture of same, where commissioned captain. In 1748, at age 64, leader of company ranging woods in search of Indians.

Allen (Allin), Joseph (1701–1785). Born Suffield, Connecticut. Married Hannah, daughter of Captain Joseph Clesson, 24 April 1727; 8 children, including Zebulon Allen. At some point, removed to Deerfield. Stationed at Fort Massachusetts as sergeant, 1745, June 1746. Sergeant at Fort Pelham, 11 December 1749–3 June 1750. Sergeant in charge of Northfield garrison, 11 December 1755–22 March 1756. Removed to Fall Town (Bernardston) from Deerfield in 1757 or 1759; became prominent man in town, holding a number of offices.

Allen, Zebulon (1727–1786). Born at Deerfield, son of Sergeant Joseph Allen. Was at Hobbs' Fight, 1748; Chief Sackett knew him, Allen claimed he had killed him. Sentinel at Fort Massachusetts, June 1746, but not there when it was captured. Corporal at Fall Town under Ensign John Burke, 6 September 1754, and again March 1755. Settled in Fall Town about 1756. Married Freedom Cooley of Sunderland, 1751; 8 children. On John Burk's enlistment roll ending 30 November 1758, at which time held rank of sergeant.

Ashley, the Reverend Jonathan (1712–1780). Born Westfield, sixth son and ninth child of Lieutenant Jonathan Ashley and Abigail (Stebbins). Graduated Yale College, class of 1730; ranked no. 12 in a class of 18. Taught in Suffield for a while. Settled in ministry at Deerfield, 8 November 1732, when ordained; the Reverend William Williams of Hatfield delivered sermon. In 1736, married Dorothy, daughter of the Reverend William Williams. On 30 November 1748, preached ordination sermon of the Reverend John

Norton of Fall Town. Active opponent of cousin, the Reverend Jonathan Edwards; accused by Edwards of Arminianism. Prominent loyalist; for this and other reasons found himself at variance with his people. For some years, they refused to fulfill their obligations to him. In May 1780, an ecclesiastical council convened to arrange their differences, but adjourned after ten days without arriving at any conclusion. Widow died 1808 at age 95; one of their daughters married William Williams, Yale College 1754.

Barnard, Joseph (1717–1785). Born Deerfield, son of Ebenezer and Elizabeth (Foster). In 1740, married Thankful, daughter of Ebenezer Sheldon of Deerfield and Fall Town; 7 children. Served in several campaigns in French and Indian Wars. In 1755, ensign in Fort Massachusetts under Captain Isaac Wyman. Commissioned captain in 1759, but generally known as "Ensign Barnard." In 1763, received large estate from uncle Samuel. Engaged in trade for rest of life, prominent in town affairs; a Whig in politics.

Barnard, Salah. Born Deerfield, son of Ebenezer and Elizabeth (Foster), brother of Joseph. Private under Captains Phinehas Stevens and John Hawks in the "old" French war; in the "last" French war was lieutenant of rangers under Captain John Burk, in the regiment of Colonel Joseph Frey; also lieutenant under Captain John Catlin, in Colonel William Williams' regiment, succeeded Catlin on latter's death 24 September 1758. In 1759, had company in regiment of Colonel Timothy Ruggles, served to close of war, coming home with commission of major. Narrowly escaped massacre and built south part of house now standing there. In 1765, married Elizabeth, daughter of Jeremiah Nims; 10 children. Wife died 1827.

Billing (Billings), the Reverend Edward (1707–1760). Born Hatfield, sixth child of Ebenezer and Hannah (Church). In 1713, family moved to that part of Hatfield that is now Sunderland. Graduated Harvard, A.B. 1731; ranked no. 30 out of class of 37. Harvard M.A. 1734. Spent next few years surveying and preaching on western frontiers. In 1739, supply for First Church in Hadley; in latter half of year served province as chaplain at Fort Dummer. That winter returned to Cold Spring (Belchertown). Ordained minister of Cold Spring church in May 1740. In 1751, married Lucy, daughter of the Reverend David Parsons. For a time, he was well liked, but as he was a "New Light," his ministry, like that of Jonathan Edwards, was wrecked on the Half-Way Covenant. In June 1750, against the wishes of his parishioners, he attended the council sitting to try Edwards. In April 1752, dismissed by the eccleciastical council after he had printed an attack on Timothy Woodbridge and Chester Williams, who had tried to dissuade him from abolishing Half-Way Covenant. From spring 1753, preached occasionally at Greenfield; called by residents same year, but bitterly opposed by Jonathan Ashley. Installed 1754, sermon preached by Jonathan Edwards. 1755, prayed in streets of Greenfield before companies on their way to Crown Point.

Bull, John P. (1731–1813). Settled in Deerfield as gunsmith and locksmith. Armorer in regiment of Colonel Ephraim Williams, Jr., in campaign of 1755; same in regiment of Colonel Israel Williams in 1756. Married 1758, Mary, daughter of Captain John Catlin and Mary (Munn); 7 children. Had shop in Deerfield. Died in son's house in Shelburne.

Burk (Burke), John (1717–1784). Born Hatfield, son of John and Mehitabel (Hastings). In 1740, married Sarah Hoyt, daughter of Lieutenant Jonathan and Mary (Field) Hoyt of Deerfield; 5 children. Father-in-law was old Indian fighter in Queen Anne's War, had been taken to Canada as Indian captive when boy, following sack of Deerfield in 1704, and spoke Indian tongue for rest of life. At start of Governor Shirley's War, Burk built own fort in Fall Town, held office of sergeant in command of fort and soldiers. In 1747, Burk's Fort attacked by Indians, he and two others held them off, helped by women; same year, commissioned as ensign in company of volunteers under Captain Phineas Stevens at Fort No. 4 by Governor Shirley. In 1748, participated in Hobbs' Fight. By 1754, held commission as ensign in company of the Fort at Fall Town. By 1755, captain lieutenant of company of fort under Colonel Ephraim Williams, Jr., at Battle of Lake George (Crown Point). In 1757, escaped from the capture of Fort William Henry and subsequent massacre. By 1758, lieutenant of forces "posted at Fall Town, Colrain, Charlemont, Northfield, Greenfield, Hunts Town, Pontoosuck, and Stockbridge" under Israel Williams. By 1759, captain of company of foot under Brigadier General Timothy Ruggles. In 1760, commissioned major in Ruggles's regiment. After 1763, led active civilian life in Bernardston (formerly Fall Town), including career as tavernkeeper. During Revolution, was active Whig, on Committee of Correspondence and Safety.

Catlin, John (1704–1758). Born Deerfield, son of Joseph, who fell in Meadow Fight at Deerfield (1704); mother Hannah wounded at same time in attack on Benoni Stebbins house. Entered military service early, attaining rank of captain; served under Captain Kellogg in Father Rasle's War. Married 1727 to Mary Munn, daughter of a Deerfield carpenter, 9 children. Lieutenant of a company of snowshoe men in 1743. From 10 December 1747 to 3 April 1749, in command of Fort Shirley. Summer 1749, in command of a company above Northfield. By 20 July 1756, captain at West Hoosuck. On 15 September 1757, led company of 52 men from Deerfield to Fort Massachusetts. By 1758, in command of cordon of 12 forts extending from Northfield to Pontoosuck, with headquarters at Burk's Fort, but in Colrain in May of that year. Died in Burk's Fort on 24 September 1758.

Chapin, Caleb (1701–1755). Born in Springfield. In 1726, married Catherine Dickinson of Hatfield, 10 children. Removed c. 1746 from Springfield to Fall Town. Sergeant with regiment of Ephraim Williams, Jr., at Battle of Lake George, 1755. Mortally wounded when Williams killed, told sons Joel and Hezekiah to leave him, thus saving them from certain death; they returned next day to find him dead and scalped.

Chapin, Elisha (d. 1756). Said to have been of "Chickobee," that is, Springfield. Married to Miriam (last name unknown). Succeeded Ephraim Williams, Jr., as captain in command of Fort Massachusetts in spring of 1752; at same time, bought (in conjunction with Moses Graves of Hatfield) Williams's land grant around fort (for £350 in bonds). Held command until Ephraim Jr. returned to post in September 1754. In January 1753, was original owner of house lot in West Hoosuck, and became leader of discontents there; considered by Williamses as bold and imprudent. By 1755, clerk in Fort Massachusetts. Made leader of fort in West Hoosuck and main opponent of Isaac Wyman at Fort Massachusetts, but killed and scalped by large force of French and Indians on 11 July 1756. Had been left legacy to pay off his bond by Ephraim Williams, Jr.

Chidester, William (d. 1756). From Cornwall, Connecticut. Partisan of Elisha Chapin and leader of Connecticut faction in West Hoosuck. Dring February and March 1756, responsible for building of West Hoosuck fort. April 1756, went to Boston and obtained commission as sergeant in command of new fort from Governor Shirley. Killed along with Chapin on 11 July 1756, near West Hoosuck Fort.

Childs, Samuel (1712–1786). Born Deerfield. Trained as tailor. In 1739, married Sarah, daughter of Judah Wright, 6 children (she died 1797); first three children born 1740, 1742, 1745. June 1746, lieutenant on muster of Ephraim Williams, Jr., company. In 1748, lieutenant in charge of Fort Pelham with 30 men. By 1764, deacon in Deerfield.

Childs, Timothy, Sr. (1686–1776). Resident of Deerfield. In 1719, married Hannah Chapin; children included Timothy Jr. (captain in last French war and captain of militia in 1776) and Anna, who married Dr. Thomas Williams in 1740). Active as scout on Canadian frontiers in latter part of Queen Anne's War; lieutenant under Captain Joseph Kellogg in Father Rasle's War; later captain stationed at Deerfield with part of his company at Sunderland. In 1724, appointed commissary for Hampshire County.

Clesson, Matthew (1713–1756). Born Deerfield, son of Joseph and Hannah (Arms). 1743, married Abigail, daughter of Jonathan Hoyt; 6 children. Was in frontier service under Captain Kellogg at age 19; was one of party under Sergeant John Hawks in 1746 that escorted Lieutenant Pierre Raimbault St. Blein to Canada to redeem captives. June 1747, lieutenant at Fort Massachusetts. 8 August 1755, had scout of 15 men at Hugh Morrison's Fort. On 18 October 1756, died on expedition to Lake George.

Connable, Samuel (1717–1796). Born Boston. Married Mary English c. 1740 in New Haven. Removed to new house in Fall Town; 7 children. This was fortified house that he had built in 1739. During 1775, served as private in Continental Army.

Denio (Denyo, Denieur, Denayon), Aaron (1704–1780). Son of James, a French Canadian who had married Abigail, daughter of John Stebbins of Deerfield; the father and daughter had been carried off to Canada as captives in 1704; while they were returned, the boy stayed there. When the boy was about ten years old, the Indians brought him to visit Deerfield; the Indians had to return without him, as Aaron wished to stay with his grandfather Stebbins. He inherited his grandfather's property. In 1730, married Anna Combs, 12 children. Served under Captain Samuel Barnard in Father Rasle's War. 1748, corporal at Fort Massachusetts. By 1756, ensign in Canada campaign. In civilian life, was shoemaker; became tavernkeeper in Greenfield. A notable hunter on the frontier.

Dwight, Joseph H. (1703–1765). Born Dedham, Massachusetts, son of Henry and Lydia Dwight. Graduated Harvard College, class of 1722; ranked no. 29 out of a class of 32. In 1726, married Mary, daughter of Colonel John and Bathsheba (Pynchon) of Springfield; 9 children. From 1723 to 1731, lived in Cambridge, then moved to Brookfield, where he practiced law for 22 years. Represented Brookfield in General Court many times from 1731 to 1747; councillor from 1742 to 1746; Speaker of the House in 1749. Judgeships: Worcester County 1739, Hampshire County 1753, Berkshire County 1751–65. In 1752, removed to Stockbridge as trustee of Indian schools. In 1751, his wife died; in 1752, he married Abigail (Williams) Sergeant, 3 children. In 1758, became resident of Upper Sheffield (Great Barrington). Long military career. In 1734, became member of Ancient and Honorable Artillery Company, was its captain in 1734. In 1745, commissioned colonel of train of artillery from Massachusetts at Louisbourg, and also brigadier general. In 1756, led brigade of Massachusetts militia to Lake Champlain.

Dwight, Timothy (1694–1771). Son of Justice Nathaniel and Mehitabel (Partridge) of Northampton. Born Hatfield, but lived and died at Northampton. In 1716, married Experience King of Northampton. Judge of probate and judge (1737–41 and 1748–57) in Hampshire County Court. Colonel of regiment, surveyor, lawyer, landowner. In 1724, Fort Dummer built under his direction, following orders from Colonel John Stoddard; same year, supervised construction of another fort in Northfield. By 1727, seems to have moved from Fort Dummer to home in Northampton; surveyed territory of Cold Spring (later Northampton). Open and active friend of Jonathan Edwards. In 1739, part of committee (with Ephraim Williams, Sr., and Thomas Wells of Deerfield) that surveyed and laid out three townships in northwestern Massachusetts, on Hoosac and Maynoosuck Rivers (west of Housatonic).

Dwight, Timothy, Jr. (1726–1777). Born at Fort Dummer, only surviving son of Timothy Sr. and Experience (King). Became merchant in Northampton. In 1748, succeeded father as registrar of probate for Hampshire County, at which time Timothy Sr. advanced to judge of court; 1758, father resigned judgeship of County Court of Common Pleas, Timothy Jr. succeeds to post, which he kept until end of provincial government. In 1750, married Mary, fourth daughter of Jonathan Edwards, just as latter leaving Northampton for Stockbridge; 9 sons and 4 daughters. Eldest child was Timothy Dwight, the future Yale president. Wife Mary died 1807. Loyalist during Revolution, migrated to Natchez to start new colony, where he died.

Edwards, the Reverend Jonathan (1703–1758). Greatest American theologian. Born East (now South) Windsor, Connecticut. Father was the Reverend Timothy (1669–1758), graduate of Harvard. In 1716, he entered Yale College at age of 12, graduated 1720 as valedictorian and head of class. Spent next two years in New Haven studying theology. From 1722 to 1723, at small Presbyterian church in New York City. From 1724 to 1726, tutor at Yale. In 1727, ordained assistant minister at Northampton to grandfather, the Reverend Solomon Stoddard; same year, married Sarah Pierrepont of New Haven. In 1729, Solomon Stoddard died, leaving grandson in sole charge of Northampton church. In 1733, revival began in Northampton, reaching peak of intensity in winter 1734 and the following spring; by 1735, the movement began to subside, as a reaction set in. During 1739–40, the Great Awakening, led by Edwards, took place; it proposed conduct as sole test of conversion rather than public profession. By 1748, the Northampton congregation was in uproar. In 1750, Edwards was dismissed; he became pastor of the church in Stockbridge and missionary to Housatonic Indians; defended Indian interests against Ephraim Williams, Sr. In 1757, on death of President Burr, who had married Edwards's daughter Esther, he accepted presidency of Princeton; installed 1758, but soon died as result of smallpox inoculation.

Foster, John (b. 1702). Born Ipswich. In 1724, married Hannah Thorp of Lebanon, Connecticut, where he resided for a while. By 1741, living in Deerfield.

By 1744, was carpenter in construction of Fort Shirley. In June 1746, sergeant on muster roll of Ephraim Williams, Jr., company. From 15 December 1747 to 10 March 1748, sergeant at Fort Massachusetts. In 1748, sergeant at Fort Pelham (muster roll of Elisha Hawley). From October 1756 to January 1757, stationed at Colrain in Ephraim Williams, Jr., company. By 30 November 1758, name on John Burk's enlistment roll; died in Burk's Fort. Children: Isaac (b. 1725), Ezekiel (b. 1727), John (date of birth unknown).

Graves, Moses (dates unknown). Lieutenant at Fort Massachusetts. By January 1753, original house lot owner, West Hoosuck Township. In November 1768, named as "merchant" in deed, and described as having, along with Oliver Partridge and Elijah Williams, divided and set off Green and Walker tract (in Heath) to Joseph Green in December 1764.

Green, Joseph (1701–1765). Son of the Reverend Joseph Green (Harvard A.B., 1695). Distinguished merchant, wholesaler (with Isaac Walker) to Elijah Williams. Often confused with Joseph Green (Harvard A.B., 1726), who was convivial merchant, distiller, writer of humorous verse. Known as public spirit, "patriot" in Boston. In 1734, bought a Hanover Street mansion from Governor Belcher. With Isaac Walker, built brick warehouse in Brattle Street. With James Bowdoin, Sr., speculated in western lands, and with Walker bought the Green and Walker Tract in what was to be Heath. Appointed justice of the peace in 1755. An active man and a Whig, left many descendants.

Hall, George (dates unknown). Alone with family at Fort Pelham some time up to 1754; letter of Israel Williams to Ephraim Williams, Jr., of 16 December 1754, says Hall has already been dismissed from Pelham, but that he has been mustered. Nothing further known of him.

Hawks, Eleazor (Eliezer) Jr. (1693–1774). Son of Eliezer Hawks of Deerfield, a sergeant in King Philip's War. Settled at Wapping (Deerfield). In 1743, bought land in Charlemont from speculator, the Reverend John Chickley; lived there for a period of time during which traded with Fort Massachusetts. Probably moved in 1762, was living in Charlemont, but perhaps left; returned to die in Charlemont. In 1714, married Abigail Wells; 13 children, including Gershom, Eleazor III, and Joshua, who all lived with their father in Charlemont during the 1740s.

Hawks, Gershom (1716–1799). Son of Eleazor Jr. Served as sergeant through French Wars. In 1744, married Thankful Corse of Deerfield, 11 Children. On 11 June 1746 wounded in ambush near Fort Massachusetts. Settled at Charlemont, where his house and that of brother Seth were placed near each other and connected by palisade walls; put in command of Hawks' Fort as sergeant in 1755. From December 1749 to June 1750, soldier at Fort Shirley. Died Charlemont.

Hawks, John (1707–1784). Born Deerfield, son of Eliezer Sr. and Judith (Snead); brother of Eliezer Jr., uncle of Gershom, Joshua, and Seth Hawks. Entered military service early. Sergeant at Fort Massachusetts under Captain Ephraim Williams Jr., where wounded 9 May 1746. By August 1746, sergeant in command when Fort Massachusetts taken, captive in Canada for one year. In 1748, sent to Canada with French prisoner of war to be exchanged for English captives. Served throughout last French War. From 1754 to 1757, in charge of eastern part of Line of Forts as sergeant and lieutenant, headquarters at Hugh Morrison's fort in Colrain. In 1758, company commander in attack on Fort Ticonderoga. By 1759, major under General Amherst. By 1760, lieutenant colonel in army of conquest in Canada. After hostilities ceased, returned to Deerfield, where he lived out the rest of his days as honored hero and successful civilian.

Hawks, Joshua (1722–1761). Son of Eleazar Jr. From 1747 to 1748, at Fort Pelham. In 1750, settled at Charlemont. Married, 7 children.

Hawley, Elisha (d. 1755). Born Northampton, son of Lieutenant Joseph and Rebekah (Stoddard); father committed suicide in 1735 during early phase of Great Awakening. Only sibling of Joseph Hawley, Jr. By December 1747, lieutenant in command of company at Fort Massachusetts, until March 1748, when Ephraim Williams, Jr., returned. By January 1753, original owner of house lot in West Hoosuck. In 1755, a captain under Ephraim Williams, Jr., on Crown Point expedition; 8 September of that year, badly wounded at "Bloody Morning Scout" during battle of Lake George; died of wounds.

Hawley, Joseph (1723–1788). Born Northampton, son of Lieutenant Joseph Sr. and Rebekah (Stoddard), brother of Elisha. Graduated Yale College in 1739, ranked no. 4 in a class of 17. On leaving Yale, studied theology with first cousin Jonathan Edwards. In 1746, served as chaplain with provincial forces at Louisburg; planned to be ordained, but converted to Arminianism, and changed to law. Became violent opposer of Jonathan Edwards, active in effecting his removal from Northampton; later, however, recanted his actions. In 1752, married Mercy Wyman of Northampton, no children; she died 1806. Subsequently member Massachusetts House of Representatives; October 1754, opposed to Williams' family schemes at Pontoosuck and Hoosuck, promised to block them in House. Commissioned major by Governor Shirley in September 1754; 2nd major in Colonel Israel Williams's regiment, 1759. Most influential member of House from 1746 to 1776, where he opposed Stamp Act. Went insane in 1766, but subsequently recovered. Became "patriot" in the Revolution, active in war on American side. From Stamp Act on, played same role in western Massachusetts that Samuel Adams played in eastern Massachusetts.

Hudson (Hutson), Seth (1728–1814?). Born Marlboro. Probably received medical education in youth. In 1749, married Rebecca Smead of Deerfield. Listed on Fort Massachusetts muster rolls as follows: March to June 1749, centinel, then surgeon; December 1749 to June 1750, surgeon; January 1750 to June 1751, centinel. January 1753, owned two house lots in West Hoosuck, where removed; became active malcontent against Williamses. Helped build and maintain blockhouse in West Hoosuck. In 1756, on death of Sergeant William Chidester, became commanding officer of West Hoosuck with rank of captain; continued to act as surgeon in that fort and Fort Massachusetts. In 1762, pilloried in Boston (his supposed speech from the pillory was published, and begins: "What mean these Crowds, this Noise and Roar! / Did ye ne'er see a *Rogue* before?"). Said to have played active part in Revolution.

Lucas (McLucas, Lukes), Andrew (c. 1710–1789). Scotch-Irish, came with family to America between 1728 and 1732. In 1742, bought land in East Colrain, lived in Fort Lucas. Listed as centinel on Colrain muster roll of 1746. About 1740 married Agnes; in 1758, married Esther (McCrellis), widow of Archibald Pannell.

Lyman, William (b. 1715). Born Northampton (?), ninth child of Lieutenant Benjamin and Medad (Pomroy); two younger brothers went to Yale, but he did not. In 1748, in command of Fort Massachusetts. From December 1749 to June 1750, lieutenant on Fort Shirley muster roll. From September to December 1756, in command of company that included Northfield men.

Marsh, Perez (1729–1784). Born Hadley, son of Captain Job and Mehitable (Porter). Graduated Harvard, class of 1748. April 1751, appointed college librarian but afterward considered negligent by Harvard Corporation. In 1751, began to study theology. In 1754, took an *ad eundem* degree in theology at Yale, but soon abandoned theology. Read medicine with Dr. Thomas Williams. In spring 1755, enlisted as surgeon's mate to Dr. Williams in regiment of Ephraim Williams, Jr. Latter was then infatuated with Sarah, daughter of Israel Williams; Ephraim Jr. offered to draw his will to leave his fortune to her; she declined, saying she preferred Marsh; Ephraim Jr. then changed will. On return from 1755 campaign, Marsh married Sarah, settled in Ashuelot Equivalent (later Dalton). During the rest of the French War, he spent his summers in field as army surgeon; at Fort Massachusetts in

1758, on General Amherst expedition of 1759. In 1761, appointed justice of the peace; in 1765, appointed to Court of Common Pleas on death of Joseph H. Dwight. A Tory, his loyalist views closed the doors of many patriots to him and brought him to bankruptcy.

McDowell, the Reverend Alexander (d. 1768?). Scotch-Irish. At end of 1752, congregation of Presbyterian church at Colrain sent him a call, but this call was not made formal until vote of March 1751. Settled as minister in September 1753, duly ordained; remained as pastor for eight years. Dismissed, supposedly for intemperance. Continued to live at Colrain, where he died.

Morrison, Hugh (d. 1765). Scotch-Irish. Born Londonderry, Ireland. Came to America about 1725 with brothers William and David. About 1723, married, in Ireland, Martha McCrellis, 5 children: first child David, born Ireland, captured by Indians in 1746. In 1725–26 bought land in Londonderry, New Hampshire, lived there several years. In 1739 and 1744 bought 600 acres of undivided land in Colrain, came to live there, built fort. Prominent citizen of Colrain, farmer, and extensive dealer in land.

Norton, the Reverend John (1715–1778). Born in parish of Kensington, then part of Farmington, Connecticut (now in Berlin). Fourth son of John and Anna Norton. Graduated Yale College, 1737; ranked no. 19 in a class of 24. Probably studied theology at Springfield. On 25 November 1741, settled as pastor in Fall Town; Jonathan Ashley gave long ordination sermon. Dismissed in February 1746 because of duties as chaplain of Line of Forts. Had married Eunice, daughter of Luke and Elizabeth (Walker) Hitchcock of Springfield, 9 children. First four were Asenath, born Springfield 1738; Elizabeth, born Springfield 1740; John Jr. probably born Fall Town 1743; Anna, born Fall Town 1745. However, according to Dexter (1885:587–88), Norton had a previous wife who died after the birth of their first child in 1738. He then married Eunice in 1742, and she bore him five children; furthermore, when Anna died at Fort Shirley in 1747, her gravestone says she was in the seventh year of life. August 1746, taken captive at Fort Massachusetts, spent year in Canada, during which wife and children remained at post, Fort Shirley. October 1747, presented petition to Connecticut General Assembly regarding his sufferings and losses in captivity, voted £100 Old Tenor, but only received £37 10s. November 1748, installed as first pastor of Congregational Church in East Hampton, Connecticut; remained as such until death, with the exception of a few months in 1755–56, when he acted as chaplain of Crown Point forces from Connecticut. In 1760, was chaplain of third regiment, raised for expedition against Canada. Died of smallpox.

Pannell (Pennel, Pennill), Archibald (Archer) (c. 1724–1754). Son of John Sr., born in England and came with father to New England in 1728. Settled in Westboro, then migrated to Colrain. In 1748, married in Deerfield, Esther McCrellis, daughter of John and Margaret (Harvey). Four children: Sarah, b. 1748; Isaac, b. 1750; Esther, b. 1752; Archibald Jr., b. posthumously 1754. Owned lot on North River and island west of it, as well as two neighboring lots in Colrain. December 1745 to June 1746, on muster roll for Fort Shirley; June 1748 to October 1748, on muster roll for Hugh Morrison's Fort. Had been in Seth Pomroy's Louisbourg company in 1745. From some time until 1754, alone with family at Fort Shirley, where he probably died.

Partridge, Oliver (1712–1792). Born Hatfield, third child and only son of Colonel Edward, grandson of Colonel Samuel Partridge. Graduated Yale College in 1730, where he studied surveying; ranked no. 2 in a class of 18. In 1734 married Anna, daughter of the Reverend William Williams of Weston; 13 children. Same year appointed joint Clerk of Court of Common Pleas of Hampshire County (with Israel Williams); selectman of Hatfield almost every year from 1731 to 1774, again in 1780 and 1781; representative in General Court 1741, 1747, 1761, and 1765–67. From 1741 to 1743, high sheriff of Hampshire County. Conducted many surveys of new towns. June 1744, substituted for Ephraim Williams, Sr., on Committee for Defense of Province, along with John Stoddard and John Leonard, planning line of Forts. January 1753, original owner of house lot, West Hoosuck. In 1754, represented Massachusetts at Albany Congress; returned to Massachusetts, commissioned colonel 1757, succeeded Israel Williams in command of western forces. By 1759, lieutenant colonel in Colonel Israel Williams's regiment. In 1765, represented Massachusetts at Stamp Act Congress. A Tory during the Revolution, but was said to have accepted the situation. Died in Hadley.

Phips, Spencer (1685–1757). Born Rowley, as Spencer Bannett. Adopted by Governor Sir William Phips, became his heir. Graduated Harvard College, 1703. In 1707, married Elizabeth Hutchinson, 6 children. Settled on farm in Middlesex County, became colonel in cavalry organization. In 1721, elected to Massachusetts House of Representatives, took active interest in Indian education. In 1730, chosen by the Crown as lieutenant governor to Governor Belcher. Became commissioner of Society for Propagating the Gospel among the Indians. By 1741, on resignation of Belcher, incoming Governor Shirley used him much more than had his predecessor. Summer 1745, when Shirley went to Louisbourg, he was left as acting governor and commander-in-chief; proved honest but incompetent in face of various crises, including Indian attacks, but tried to get northern colonies to cooperate to counter enemy. Same situation in summer of 1748, when Shirley went to Albany. September 1749, Shirley on leave of absence in England; until

Shirley's return in August 1753, again was acting governor. Worked hard to make peace with eastern Indians and redeem captives in Canada, but usually blocked or impeded by General Court; continued efforts to get New York and Connecticut to cooperate with Massachusetts. Early in 1755, Shirley off to Niagara expedition; Phips spent summer aiding William Johnson in raising and dispatching troops. In 1756, Shirley returned to England; Governor Phips died that year in his Cambridge house.

Pomroy (Pomeroy, Ponroy), Seth (1706–1777). Born Northampton, son of Major Ebenezer and Sarah (King); member of family of blacksmiths and gunsmiths. Was most widely known in his time as gunsmith, but also acted as blacksmith throughout life. In 1732, married Mary Hunt of Deerfield, 9 children. In 1743, commissioned by Governor Shirley as captain of Third Company of "Snow Shoe Men" in Hampshire County (Colonel John Stoddard, commander); later commissioned ensign of first "Foot Company in town of Northampton" under Stoddard. In 1745, major in Colonel Samuel Willard's regiment against Louisbourg; kept diary of trip and siege. June 1746, captain in Colonel Joseph Dwight's regiment for abortive expedition against Canada; not liked by Dwight. That November, Colonel Israel Williams orders him to send 27 of his men to Colrain to relieve troops there, and another 35 to Northfield. June 1947, ordered by Stoddard to take charge of men raised for special service and proceed from Deerfield to Fort Massachusetts; still at fort following August, apparently in command and doing all blacksmith and gunsmith work. July 1750 to July 1751, presented bills to Captain Ephraim Williams, Jr., for mending "your soldiers' guns and locks." In 1755, commissioned lieutenant colonel on Crown Point expedition, at Battle of Lake George; in September, commissioned colonel in place of Ephraim Williams, Jr., who had been killed. In 1757, with volunteers under Colonel Israel Williams, defended Fort William Henry. From October 1759 to June 1750, in command of Line of Forts. During the Revolution, played active role on American side in spite of age; commissioned brigadier general; killed in action.

Rice, Moses (1694–1755). Born Sudbury, son of John and Tabitha (Stone). In 1719, married Sarah King of Sudbury, 7 children. Moved to Worcester, where he kept a tavern and was captain in a cavalry company; then moved to Rutland (north of Worcester) with garrison. In 1741, bought 2,200 acres of land in Charlemont to settle there; in 1742, arrived there as first settler, probably with older sons. In 1744, contracted to build Fort Pelham, which he probably finished by summer of 1745. Had grist mill by 1745. From May to June 1746, on Pelham muster roll as centinel. August 1746, fled with family to Deerfield just before fall of Fort Massachusetts, vacant house burned and crops destroyed by enemy. In 1749, returned to Charlemont with family, rebuilt house. In 1752, built another house further east for eldest son and family of three children who had come to Charlemont. On 11 June 1755, died of wounds after being shot and scalped by Indians; grandson Asa taken captive to Canada.

Rigaud de Vaudreuil, François-Pierre (1703–1779). Born Montreal, son of the former governor of Canada, the marquis Philippe de Rigaud de Vaudreuil (1643–1725); younger brother of the last French governor, the marquis Pierre de Riguad de Vaudreuil de Cavagnial (1698–1778). Headed French and Indian forces against New England colonies. August 1746, led attack on Fort Massachusetts, wounded. July 1756, field commander of French and Indians in taking of Oswego. Named governor of Trois-Rivières in 1748 and of Montreal in 1757. Montcalm thought he had "meager talents."

Sergeant, the Reverend John (1710–1749). Born Newark, N.J., of Connecticut parents. Accident to left hand made manual labor impossible, prepared way for college education. In 1729, graduated Yale College with outstanding record, became tutor at Yale. In 1734, accepted position as missionary to Housatonic Indians offered by Society for Propagating the Gospel among the Indians in New England. July 1735, settled at Great Barrington; ordained at Deerfield that August, during Belcher's conference with Indians. In 1736, moved residence and Indian school from Great Barrington to Stockbridge. In 1739, married Abigail, eldest daughter of Ephraim Williams, Sr., and half-sister of Ephraim Williams, Jr.; 3 children. May 1747, chaplain at Fort Massachusetts. After his death in 1749, Abigail married Joseph H. Dwight, by whom she had three children; she was a great friend of Yale President Ezra Stiles, and died in 1791.

Severance (Siverance, Siverans), Daniel (1702–1748). Son of Ebenezer Severance, who was killed in Northfield by Indians in 1723. From 1723 to 1730, soldier under Captain Joseph Kellogg at Fort Dummer; letter of Colonel Partridge to governor in June 1727 describes him as particularly disorderly and spirited, and that he "declares openly, that he will kill the Indian that scalped his father"; warned by Partridge that if he did so in time of peace he would stand trial for his life. In 1733, married Rebekah Jones of Springfield; 3 children, born at Northfield. June 1746, in Line of Forts; in early March of that year, one of 6 men taken by Captain Stevens to Fort No. 4, then returned. From January 1747 to his death in December was lieutenant in Line of Forts.

Shattuck, Daniel (1692–1760). lived in Groton; in Worcester from 1719 to 1724; then removed to Northfield. Built fort in 1736 that was assaulted by Indians in 1746. Held rank of captain 1753, became selectman of Hinsdale, New Hampshire.

Sheldon, Ebenezer, Sr. (1691–1774). Born Deerfield. Taken captive to Canada in attack of 1704, but later "redeemed." In 1714, married Thankful Barnard, daughter of Joseph and Sarah (Strong), 10 children; later lived in old Indian House in Deerfield, kept a tavern. In 1744, sold house, moved to Fall Town, where he built Lieutenant Sheldon's Fort. In 1756, petitioned governor for funds to repair fort; said his son killed in previous year.

Sheldon, Ebenezer, Jr. (b. 1715?). Eldest son of Ebenezer Sr. In 1740, married Mary, daughter of Jonathan Hoyt of Deerfield; therefore brother-in-law of John Burk; 9 children. In 1749, listed on rolls as centinel and sergeant. From December 1755 to October 1756, sergeant on muster roll of Israel Williams's Company, scouting to westward; was a winter scout. October 1756 to January 1757, stationed at Colrain in same company. Built fort on Buckle Hill, Fall Town, known as Deacon Sheldon Fort. After war, held many town offices.

Shirley, William (1694–1771). Born Preston, Sussex, England. Attended Pembroke College, Cambridge. Married c. 1717, Frances Barker; 8 children. Studied law at Inner Temple, entered Middle Bar. 1731, emigrated to Massachusetts where practiced law. Had come under patronage of Duke of Newcastle. Appointed advocate general for all of New England except Connecticut. In 1741, appointed governor of Massachusetts. In 1745, planned successful invasion of Louisbourg. September 1749, English coin brought to Boston to cover outlay of Massachusetts in venture reestablished finances of province. In 1747, wife died. From 1749 to 1753, in England on leave of absence; remarried beneath his station in 1751, but did not bring wife to America. In 1755, led unsuccessful expedition to Fort Niagara; after death of Braddock, commander-in-chief of all the British forces in America until 1756. September 1756, enemies forced his recall to England, succeeded by Spencer Phips. Regained lost patronage, made governor of Bahamas in 1758, which post he occupied until 1770; given rank of lieutenant general in early 1759. In 1770, returned to home in Roxbury, where he died the following year.

Stevens, Phinehas (Phineas) (1706–1756). Born Sudbury, son of Joseph and Prudence (Rice). On 14 August 1723, captured by Indians along with younger brother, taken to Canada; "redeemed" by father. In 1734, married cousin Elizabeth Stevens of Petersham. Early settler of Charlestown, New Hampshire (Fort No. 4). In 1743, commissioned lieutenant; captain by 1745. In 1746, captain of company in intended expedition to Canada. Sent twice to Canada to negotiate release of captives. After active military life, died of fever.

Stoddard, John (1682–1748). Born Northampton, tenth child of the Reverend Solomon Stoddard. Graduated Harvard College, 1701; ranked no. 3 in a class of 19. In 1704, enlisted in Hampshire County militia, soldier in house of the Reverend John Williams. Commissioned captain in 1706, major in 1712, colonel in 1721. In 1731, married Prudence Chester of Wethersfield, Connecticut; 10 children. From late 1720s until death, the chief personage of Hampshire County: judge in Court of Common Pleas; member of General Court, member of Governor's Council, colonel of Hampshire County militia. In 1744, chairman of committee that drew up plan for Line of Forts; in July, sent specifications for Fort Shirley to Captain William Williams. In 1745, delegate at Albany Conference. From 1746 to 1747, friction with Colonel Joseph Dwight over Canada soldiers posted to guarding frontiers. Died June 1748. Staunch royalist; friend and loyal supporter of Jonathan Edwards, who wrote of him: "He was probably one of the ablest politicians that ever New England bred: He had a very uncommon insight into human nature, and a marvelous ability to penetrate into the particular tempers and dispositions of such as he had to deal with, and to discern the fittest way of treating them, so as most effectually to influence them to any good and wise purpose."

Taylor, John (dates unknown). Brother of Othniel and Jonathan. In 1757, sergeant at Colrain.

Taylor, Jonathan (1724–1800). Son of Samuel and Mary (Hitchcock); father was Deerfield settler and store and tavernkeeper. Brother of Samuel, Othniel, and John. In 1742, bought land with Othniel in East Charlemont and began to clear it. In 1745, bought half-interest in Othniel's 1,000-acre tract. In 1750, two children baptized in Deerfield; he and wife Lucy joined church same day; 4 more children. About 1760, removed to Heath, where he died.

Taylor, Othniel (1719–1788). Son of Samuel and Mary (Hitchcock) of Springfield. From 1742 to 1743, clearing land in East Charlemont with brother Jonathan. In 1743, married stepsister Martha Arms when she was fourteen; 13 children. In 1746, joined with David Field and Joseph Barnard in trading furs and deer leather from New England. Manufacturer of snowshoes and user of them on his winter scouts from Taylor's Fort. After death of Moses Rice in 1754, became the leading citizen of Charlemont. Active Whig and captain in Continental Army.

Taylor, Samuel (b. 1716?). Son of Samuel and Mary (Hitchcock), elder brother of Othniel, Jonathan, and John. Resided Northfield. From 1746 to 1757, in service at Fort Massachusetts and West Hoosuck; sergeant in 1755. Wife Anne (daughter of Ebenezer Alexander) with him much of time; daughter Susanna born at Fort Massachusetts in June 1754, son Elias two years later at West Hoosuck Fort; had 9 children. By 3 October 1756 sergeant at West Hoosuck, but requested that he be dismissed from this post, which was granted because he was greatly imposed upon by men. March 1757, in service at Charlemont. In 1758, returned home to Northfield. March 1780, removed to Hartford, Vermont.

Williams, Elijah (1712–1771). Born Deerfield, youngest son of the Reverend John and Abigail (Allen). Graduated Harvard College, 1732; ranked no. 6 in class of 29. Harvard A.M., 1758. In 1735, married Lydia Dwight of Hatfield, 6 children. Active member of militia at Deerfield. In 1744, captain of Snow Shoe Men. In 1745, obtained grant for fortification of Deerfield. Lived on father's homestead and kept store at the corner, better known as the "Ware Store" in later years; this served as depot for military supplies. From 1748 to 1752, in trade in Enfield, Connecticut (having inherited proprietorship there in 1745). In 1749, wife died in Enfield. On 1 January 1750 married Margaret, daughter of Colonel William Pynchon of Springfield (she died 1772). May 1750, justice of the peace for Hartford County; from October to November in Connecticut General Assembly as deputy of Enfield. March 1752, moved back to Deerfield, again kept store; returned to General Court, where he served for 12 of the next 17 years. January 1753, justice of the peace and quorum. August 1754, rebuilding old fortifications under direction of Israel Williams. On 27 September 1754 commissioned commissary and major, with particular charge of Connecticut soldiers who were garrisoning at Greenfield and other exposed points. In 1756, questions raised in Province Council regarding his accounts as commissary. August 1757, reached Kinderhook by march to relieve Fort William Henry. December 1757, he and Captain Isaac Wyman tried before House of Representatives; Wyman found guilty of withholding provisions from soldiers in West Hoosuck. Williams cleared, but then sharply attacked Seth Hudson before House; was forced to own publicly that he was mistaken in part, and had his case dismissed. In 1770, lost seat in House to man with less of a Tory record.

Williams, Ephraim, Sr. (1691–1754). Born Newton, youngest child of Isaac and second wife Judith (Cooper). Isaac left greater part of estate to Ephraim Sr., but children of first wife successfully contested will. In 1714, married Elizabeth Jackson of Newton; in 1719, married Abigail Jones. Province had bought from Mohican Indians two townships of land; in 1734 it settled Indians at Stockbridge, with the Reverend John Sergeant named as missionary to them. In 1737, Ephraim Sr. was head of one of four families chosen to settle among and "civilize" these Indians, which he did in 1738. Exploited Indians there for rest of life. May 1744, represented Stockbridge in General Court, and in following June was the captain appointed to committee to defend province in time of war and to check on military stores. June 1747, in charge of Fort Massachusetts; oversaw rebuilding of barracks. Died in

Deerfield, having left Stockbridge under odium of selfish and unchristian conduct toward Indians; funeral sermon preached by Jonathan Ashley.

Williams, Ephraim, Jr. (1715–1755). Born Newton, son of Ephraim Sr. and Elizabeth (Jackson). Mother died 1718, he and younger brother Thomas raised and educated by Jackson grandparents in Newton; father remarried. Possibly went to sea in period before 1740, said to have been persuaded by father to give it up; supposedly made several voyages to Europe, including England, Spain, and Holland, perhaps representing business interests of cousin William Williams. In 1738, persuaded by father to move to Stockbridge to aid in settlement; actually moved there in 1742. In 1745, in command of Line of Forts at Fort Shirley, with rank of captain; June 1746, moved headquarters to Fort Massachusetts, which remained under his command, with a few interruptions, until 1755. In August 1748, led defense of Fort Massachusetts against French and Indian attack. From 1749 to 1753, often in Boston on real estate business. In 1750, began work on West Hoosuck development; town laid out by 1752. January 1753, original owner of two house lots in West Hoosuck. September 1754, returned to active command of Fort Massachusetts. Commissioned colonel for Crown Point expedition; on 8 August 1755, killed in "Bloody Morning Scout." Never married; according to tradition, he was turned down by Sarah Williams, daughter of Israel, just before leaving for Crown Point. In will, left sum of money for school in West Hoosuck, with proviso that latter town was to be renamed "Williamstown"; school eventually became Williams College.

Williams, Israel (1709–1789). Born Hatfield, son of the Reverend William Williams. Graduated Harvard, 1727, ranked no. 10 in a class of 37; same class as his lifelong friend, Thomas Hutchinson, the future governor. Married Sarah Chester, of important family in Wethersfield, Connecticut. Later became richest man in Hatfield. With passing of uncles, became the "monarch" of the Connecticut Valley and greatest of the River Gods. Selectman in Hatfield for 32 consecutive years, beginning in 1732. In 1733, elected member of General Court. From opening of war in 1744, colonel in command of northern regiment of militia in Hampshire County; commissary for western frontiers. In September 1754, submitted plans to Governor Shirley for defense of western frontiers, resulting in abandonment of Forts Shirley and Pelham. Most prominent Tory in western Massachusetts, persecuted by "patriots" during the Revolution; refused to recant.

Williams, Dr. Thomas (1718–1775). Born Newton, second child of Ephraim Sr. and Elizabeth (Jackson). Mother died two weeks later. Raised by Jackson grandparents along with Ephraim Jr. Studied medicine with a Dr. Wheat in Boston. About 1739, settled as doctor in Boston; later that year, settled as doctor in Deerfield. In 1740, left £140 by grandfather Jackson. In 1741, awarded M.A. degree by Yale, but seems never to have attended college; paid fee of £9, covering three years of tuition charges. From 1746 onward, acted as surgeon for Line of Forts; also in 1746, surgeon in abortive Canadian expedition. In 1746, married Anna Childs of Deerfield, three children; in 1748, married Esther, daughter of the Reverend William Williams of Weston; 11 children. In May 1747, surgeon at Fort Massachusetts. In 1755, surgeon in regiment of brother Ephraim Jr. at Battle of Lake George; treated Baron Dieskau's wounds. Lieutenant colonel in campaign of 1756. Continued until death as doctor and apothecary in Deerfield, where he held many civilian posts; representative, selectman, town clerk, judge of probate and justice of Court of Common Pleas.

Williams, William (1713–1784). Born Weston, son of the Reverend William and Hannah (Stoddard). Graduated Harvard College, 1729, ranked no. 11 in a class of 28; established himself in business in Boston. In 1733, married Miriam, daughter of Andrew Tyler and Miriam (Pepperrell) and niece of Sir William Pepperrell. In 1739, served as surgeon in Oglethorpe's expedition (had left business to go into medicine). In 1741, ensign in expedition under Admiral Vernon against Havana and Cartagena. About 1743, came to Deerfield, became lieutenant colonel in Northern Hampshire regiment. In 1744, in charge of building Fort Shirley; he became its first commander and also oversaw construction of Fort Pelham. In 1745, raised company in Hampshire County, sailed for Louisbourg, but arrived after it had been taken; was of the garrison that held it until spring. In 1747, in charge of rebuilding Fort Massachusetts; refused Governor Shirley's request to remain as commander, but made commissary for Line of Forts; he resigned this November 1748, because of difficulty in getting provisions. Remained at Deerfield. In 1748, justice of the peace in Deerfield. From 1750 to 1753, kept store in place of Elijah Williams. In 1751, selectman. About 1754 moved to Pontoosuck, built house that became Fort Anson. From 1755 to 1758, served as captain in regiment commanded by Sir William Pepperrell, uncle of his first wife (she died after 1748). In 1752, married Sarah, the 16-year-old daughter of Thomas Wells of Deerfield. In 1758, colonel under General Abercrombie; at end of campaign of that year, retired on half-pay. In 1761, judge of Court of Common Pleas in Pittsfield (formerly Pontoosuck), after judge of probate; almost continually in town office in Pittsfield until the Revolution, during which he was a Tory. Wife Sarah had died; in 1765 married Hannah, daughter of Samuel Dickinson of Deerfield.

Woodbridge, the Reverend Timothy (1713–1770). Oldest child of the Reverend Timothy Woodbridge, Sr. (Yale, 1706) and Dorothy (Lamb) of Simsbury, Connecticut. Graduated Yale College, 1732. Studied theology, probably with father. In 1735, licensed to preach, started in Harwinton, Connecticut. In 1737, chosen tutor at Yale; during latter part of two-year tutorship, began to preach in Hatfield. Ordained in Hatfield as colleague pastor to the Reverend William Williams (1665–1741); succeeded Williams upon his death as sole pastor in Hatfield, which he was until his own death. In 1750, member of the council that dismissed Jonathan Edwards; voted with majority. January 1753, original house lot owner, West Hoosuck. In 1757, chaplain in Colonel Israel Williams's regiment. Married to Sarah (probably daughter of Gideon) Welles of Deerfield; she died in 1781 at age 57.

Wright, William (1702–1763). Son of Benjamin and Mary (Baker). Married Sarah; 8 children. June 1746, lieutenant on muster roll of Ephraim Williams, Jr., company. In 1748, lieutenant in company raised at Northfield, commanded by Captain Josiah Willard, Jr., to find bodies of persons killed north of Fort Dummer. Served again as lieutenant in another relief party. Acted as scout for Northfield. In 1750, selectman in Northfield; in 1751, on Northfield list of proprietors.

Wyman, Isaac (dates unknown). From Auburn. Married Sarah, daughter of John Wells. At Fort Massachusetts from 1747 until its final abandonment in 1760. From December 1747 to March 1748, centinel at Fort Massachusetts. In 1755, in charge as lieutenant during preparations for Crown Point; captain in 1756. By January 1753, original owner of two house lots in West Hoosuck. Target of West Hoosuck proprietors, especially Seth Hudson; December 1757, tried before House of Representatives with Elijah Williams, found guilty of withholding provisions from West Hoosuck soldiers, with implications of graft. After 1759–60, continued to cultivate farm within and without palisade of Fort Massachusetts. Then removed to Keene, New Hampshire. During the Revolution, appointed lieutenant colonel of First New Hampshire Regiment, commanded by Colonel John Stark; did not hold position long, after which "passes out of sight."

Appendix 5

John Hawks's Journal

Introduction

THIS JOURNAL was kept by Lieutenant John Hawks when he was commanding officer of Hugh Morrison's Fort in Colrain, and the eastern forts in the Line of Forts, from Northfield in the east to Taylor's Fort in the west.[1] It covers the period from 23 March 1756 through 1 July 1757. By this time both Shirley and Pelham had been abandoned. In this period, Hawks and the forts that he supervised were under the overall command of Colonel Israel Williams of Hatfield, and Hawks was frequently instructed to ride there to receive his orders, which often concerned the recruitment and impressing of men for the forts and for the campaigns in New York.

The day-to-day events of the journal took place against the background of the military campaign in New York, which was then going badly for the provincial militia and the British regular army (see chapter 3). Among Hawks's duties were the recruitment of volunteers for the campaign there, or the impressment of men if not enough volunteers were available.

The journal gives a very good idea of the mind-numbing routine of the soldiers in the Line of Forts, of the dangers typical of this frontier zone, and of the long and difficult winters faced by those manning these outposts. The main task of these men was to maintain a regular scout (patrol) between the forts, on snowshoes in the winter, and with moccasins in the other months of the year. Hawks was also an accomplished woodsman, and occasionally went "ranging" through the forests looking for signs of Indians.

It will be noted that in those days there was no celebration of Christmas, Thanksgiving, or any other holiday; the only days noted were those of the Sabbath, with obligatory attendance at a sermon by one of the local ministers. A wedding, though, was occasion for a party.

Hawks, although a first-class military man and the sharpshooting hero of Fort Massachusetts, was not a member of the River God gentry, and probably had little formal schooling. His spelling is highly erratic, yet its quasi-phoneticism affords a hint of how frontiersmen in northwestern

Massachusetts spoke in the mid–eighteenth century. Hawks's dialect is closer to what we would today consider an Irish brogue (for example, "Cornel" for "Colonel") than to the New England "twang" so typical even today of the northern Berkshires. The published journal that he kept in 1759–60, when he was a major serving under General Jeffrey Amherst on the Ticonderoga–Crown Point campaign, has far better spelling; this is surely due to the hand of his twentieth-century editor, Hugh Hastings, who tells us, "The original spelling has not been molested, except in instances where flagrant eccentricity might bewilder the mind not acquainted with it."[2]

I have made no attempt to correct his English, but have added in brackets the true spelling of many persons and places (most of these can be found in chapter 3 and appendix 4).[3] The journal proceeds consecutively from one numbered day to the next, without any indication of the month; I have added this before each entry. It should be noted that in the journal, the year began on 25 March. Thus the journal begins on New Year's Day 1756, even though the changeover to the Gregorian calendar and its January 1 date for New Year's Day took place in British America in 1751–52.

During all of the time covered by this journal, his wife Elizabeth and eight children were living in his house in Deerfield, which explains his many visits to that village.

The Journal

An a Count from March ye 23 1756 wha I have Don.

March 23. ye Recruts that was raised Cam to Derfield I had not Reseved orders.

March 24. wated til noon for orders and reseved orders from Cor Williams [probably Israel Williams] and how to post ye men sent ye 5 men to Greenfield and 5 to Colrain

March 25. set out with ye men for fooltoun [Fall Town] Got their about noon tock our Dinnr with Cp Borck [John Burk] left ye men that ware stasened thare with ye Cornels orders went to Sheldans [Sheldon's] fort left ye men stacined thare and orders went to north field [Northfield] a Plied to ye Commisnors how tha wold have ye men stacined

March 26. By ye Desier of ye inhabitens ordered the to ye soth [South] fort after Dinnor set out and Cam to Derfield

March 27. set out for Colrain left ye Corl orders at Greenfield
Cam to Colrain went to 3 of ye forts

March 28. was Saboth went to Church

March 29. foul wether stad at Cp Morsons [Capt. Morrison's]

March 30. went to Talors [Taylor's] toock a Dinnor and went to Hawks fort soon after Cam Mr Billens [the Reverend Edward Billings] that evening Prech a sermn to them

March 31. left orders Cam to rics [Rice's] and toock Brexfast thay Preveld with mr Bilens to Prech a sermn to them after serves Cam to Talors and heard another sermon la their night on this Day met 4 sogers a goin to Rics

April 1. stormy weather Gave the Corl orders to ye sogers at Talors

April 2. Cam to Cp Morsons

April 3. went to the south fort in Colrain have the Corl orders and mr mc Donel [Rev. Alexander McDowell] and ——— to Cp Morsons whar I was Post ———

April 4. Saboth went to church ———

April 5. stad at my Post

April 6. went to Derfield

April 7. went to Reseved orders from Corl Williams Cam to Derfield sam Da

April 8. went to Colrain

April 9. stad at Colrain.

April 10.

April 11. was Saboth Cept fort

April 12. went to Deirfield after those tha had Inlistted with lieut Roggers [probably Richard Rogers, brother of Robert and officer of Rogers's Rangers]

April 13. stad at Derfield

April 15. Cept fort

April 16. rany day Cept fort no scout went out

April 17. went to hear sermon no scout went out

April 18. Rany Day it was sacrament at Colrain.

April 19. went to hear a sermon after sacrament Day is a rev Daniel Nims was taken with the fevr and ago [ague]

April 20. Dannel Nims went to Dcr [Deerfield?] I went to mr mc Dowels to help John Tomson to Cover his house.

April 21. Cept fort.

April 22. went to Derfield to yᵉ Muster to Raes men for Crounpoint [Crown Point, New York]

April 23. Cept fort

April 25. Saboth Da went to meten thi Da had yᵉ nyes lieut Chesson [Matthew Clesson] brout in of ue tracks and Guns

April 26 and 27. Cept fort

April 28. went to Corl William Willams [William Williams] at yᵉ Carring Place [Carrying Place, in New York]

April 29. Saboth Cept fort

April 30. went to Derfield

May 1. wet wather stad at Derfield

May 2. Saboth it aws sacrament Da at Derfield

May 3. went to hatfield and Reseved orders returned to Derfield yᵉ sam Da

May 4. ent to Colrain at Derfield admitted ———— Alle in to yᵉ servs

May 5. Cept fort

May 6. Cept fort

May 7. ———

May 8. likewise

May 9. Saboth Day Cept fort

May 10 and 11. Cept fort

May 12. went a scout to Talors

May 13. wet wather ye foornoon in ye afternoon Cam to Colrain

May 14. went to Derfield

May 15. rany wather

May 16. Saboth went to Church heard mr Ashley Prech

May 17. went to foltond [Fall Town] lay thar that night

May 18. Cam to Derfield

May 19. went to Colrain

May 20, 21, 22. Cept fort

May 23. Saboth Cept fort

May 24. went to Derfield to a sist Cp Morson to settle a Counts with majr Williams a Bout ye Billilling [billeting] ye sogers

May 25. went to Colrain

May 26. went a scout to Talors and tock a Dinnor and went to Hawks es fort

May 27. Rany wether ye foornoon Clerd up in ye afternoon went to Pellam fort lay ther

May 28. Cam to Colrain

May 29, 30. Cept fort

May 31. went to Derfield

June 1. went to Cherlymont [Charlemont] to help lieut Cheson [Clesson] with the recruts that war a going to Crounpint [Crown Point]

June 2. rany weather stad at Talors foort

June 3. went to Colrain

June 4 and 5. Cept fort

June 6. Saboth Day Cept foort ther Cam 2 sogers to tack shad [Benjamin Shed?] and Dickson [Joshua Dickinson?] Plac ye name Elenezer Bartlitt [Ebenezer Bartlett] Crofoot [Crawford?] went to Hawks fort I Cept fort ye afternoon in ye foornoon ———— a Brig over ye river

June 7. help to ———— lor in ye mount

June 8. I had an Expres from major Wellams that yesterday Josiah Foster of Winchester was Taken and family; also Benjn King and Willam meach was killed a bout half a mil from Fort masiaChwit [Massachusetts]; yes Day sarg Talor Cam to so me

June 9. Corp Peck Cam to Reccon sile som Difficeltis at Lucks [Lucas] Fort in ye afternoon worck at ye fort a little Before night Sama morson [Samuel Morrison] went up the river saw som indons tracks and heard them Chop twris I sent 10 men out who brout a Confermation I sent 2 men wi ye nus to Derfield

June 11. worked at ye foort. 120 of Colrin men Cam who had Ben a ranging after ye Indians

June 12. our scout Cam in Brout nus of descovern tracks of our Enemis and herd a Gon, went in ye afternoon to ye severl forts at Colrain to setl ye Difrancs a mong ye sogers

June 13. Saboth Da went to metan

June 14. wnt to Derfield

June 15. went to Hatfield Reseved orders Cam to Derfield

June 16. stad at Derfield it was muster Da to tri arms

June 17. went to Colrain

June 18. went a scout with 13 men Round the tound mad no Decovry

June 19. went a scout with 15 men up to North river and a Crost to Green river till we Cam to morsons

June 20. Saboth Da Cept fort an scout brout me ye a count of the Indons Cilling lieut major Willard [Moses Willard] and wonding his son on ———— Days of June at Nomber 4

June 21. I Cept fort admitted Ammasi Sheldan [Amasa Sheldon] in ye serves

June 22 wasa Rany Da Cept fort

June 23. went a scout to Talors thar Came 2 sogers to Colrain to tack Gats [Amos Gates's?] and Sandsons [Samuel Sanderson's] Places I tack Sandson went to Talors

June 24. Cam from Taoors to Cp Morsons

June 25. Cept fort Elijah Sherdan [Sheldon] went to Cherlymont to Seply Harpers Plac ye scout went to tach Dc Bolten to Dannel Dannelson [Damiel Dannelson]

June 26. Cept fort had a letter from Talors Bye the scout that gave an account of one French man sean at howluck [Hoosuck] and heard mor Ben a mong ye Bruch and of 2 men being tacken at Gren Bush and a scout of 160 men that Cam from our army from stilwater who saw one frnch man and 3 Indons tha had ye misforten to Cill one of thar men by Pistel being shot accidentally

June 27. Saboth Da I stad at hom and Cept fort

June 28. Cept fort nothing remar a bel this Da

June 29. Cept fort had no nus.

June 30. Cept fort hear ye nus of ye scout being kild and tackken at huck Cok [Hoosuck] ye scout was Coming from our army to fech som of ther sick that was left I hear that 14 was in the scout and but one a scapt it was on June 23 1756 tha this mischief was Don

July 1. Cept fort nothing remerkebl

July 2. whent to Derfield

July 3. stad at Derfield

July 4. Saboth Day ye Sacriment was adminstrd at Derfield

July 5. went to Colran

July 6. Cept fort nothing Remarkeble

July 7. Cept fort had no nus this Da

July 8. Cept fort had nus of tracls of injons at fooltoun [Fall Town]

July 9. Cept fort

July 10. Cept fort our scout Can and Brout ye a Count that John Stuerd [Stewart] on yᵉ 9 of July Shot an ingon yᵉ west of Talors feld and Wonded him or Cilled him By yᵉ line thar was Blod Plenty after Stuerd had Shot and yᵉ men had Gon out and Loock whar Stuerd had Shot thar was too Gons heard over yᵉ river as tha thought to a larrom yᵉ Rest

July 11. went to meten this Da Cept Chapns [Elisha Chapin] and Chisster [William Chidester] and his son went a little wa from yᵉ west fort at hook-suck [Hoosuck] tond ship thar was shot upon Chapns and Chidder son was killed and Chidder was tackken By yᵉ French

July 12. went a scout to Talors

July 13. Cam hom in yᵉ Ran

July 14. went to Der field marck around Doon by yᵉ mash Ponds Doon to Greenfield and to Derfield

July 15. set out for Colrain Cam on a Havishour lay at Greenfield

July 16. Cam to Colrain

July 17. Cept fort Ezekel [Ezekiel] Foster had a son born yᵉ scout Cam from Talors Brout nus that Chiddester was kild which we soPosed was tackken

July 18. Saboth Day Cept fort Iccobord worner [Ichabod Warner] Cam from fooltond [Fall Town] to go to Rices

July 19. Cept fort Pool Ric [Paul Rice?] I Dismist

July 20. Cept fort Jerry Cock [Cook?] admitted in ye serves a gan Iccobord worner went from Cp morsons to Go to Rices

July 21. Cept fort

July 22. was fast Day went to metten heard mr mc Donel Preech from Jms 4-9 latter part of ye vers thos words let your Joy be turned into morning and your lafter in to hevenes

July 23 Cept fort

July 24. Cept fort Deck Cohrens [Deacon John Cochran's] wife sent for the wimen was in trevl

July 25. Saboth Day ye Deckn wif Remed Bad I and Jon morison [John Morrison] and Ezekel Foster went for ye Dockter Mather [Samuel Mather] and Granny King brought Gr King a bout 2 a clock ye women remaned Bad

July 26. Dot mather Cam a bout 9 a clock ye Deck wife Remaned Bad about 6 a clock in ye afternoon shee was Delivered of a Child it was Deed I set out with ye Dc and Granny with a gard of 8 men about 10 a Clock Gat to Greenriver about yessam ye woman Died I gat to Deerfield at 12 a clock

July 27. stad at Deerfield

July 28. stad at Deerfield

July 29. stad and Rept at night had orders to tack 15 men from Cherlymont and gard ye Povenc Stors to fort maschitshet ye next Day

July 30. Rany Day we did not set out

July 31. set out for masachuset with 16 men and 13 horses loded with stors Gat to Cherlymont at Talors had 2 men to ajin from Colrain 5 from Talors loged at Rices

August 1. had 3 for Rices 5men from Hawkses set out with out loding and 32 men it was Saboth Day Gat saf to ye fort

August 2. Cam back to Talors

August 3. Cam to Deerfield

August 4. went to Hatfield and back to Deefield

August 5. went to Colrain

August 6. Cept fort had a larram one of Kerruns Darters saw one indon west of Kerruns hous We hear from yᵉ south fort of a larram bine Shot at Talors and a Grat mani Guns sent a scout to Talors

August 7. in yᵉ morning sar Talor Cam to our fort with yᵉ nus of Derfield bing a larrmed and mer 50 men gon to ther sistenc a bout 9 a clock our scout Cam informed that yᵉ a larom began at Hawkses by 3 men shutting at Ducks and Derfield men gong hom

August 8. Saboth Day went to meten

August 9. went to yᵉ south fort la ther

August 10. went to Deerfield

August 11 went to Hatfield Cam back to Deerfield

August 12. Cam to Colrain

August 13 Cept fort

August 14 Rept for Cp morison

August 16 went a scout acroust to Foultound [Fall Town] and from there to Northfield By orders of yᵉ Corl Willams

August 17 stad at Northfield

August 18. Came to Colraine

August 19. Cept fort

August 20. Cept fort

August 21. Cept fort had orders from Corl Willams to Com Doun forthwith

August 22. Saboth Day went to meten after Excies went to Deerfield

August 23. fornon Preparred our a jornels ye afternoon had ye nus of ye mischel [mischief] at Greendield went in hast to Coring farms [Country Farms] whar the mischief was Don found Shubet arllen [Shubal Atherton] Ded and scelpd and Birooke [Nathaniel Brooks] and Grany [Daniel Graves] tacken as we seposed by ye 6 inDons

August 24. went to Hatfield and Gave a Count of what I nue of ye Rood Doun Blackriver and ford to it and Returned to Derfield

August 25. went to Colrain

August 26. Cept fort

August 27. Cept fort

August 28. Cept fort had the nus of oswago [Oswego] being tacken

August 29. Saboth Day went to meting

August 30. Cept fort Rany Day

August 31. Cept fort it Remaned Cloudy Dul Wether Clerd of in ye afternoon Sarg Talor Cam from Cherlymont at night Dannel Dannelson and Ickkabod worner Cam to Colrain to Call Sarg Talor to his Child he fell out of ye mount and hurt himself sad Talor went to git ye Dockter to go to his Child Sarg Jon Talor [John Taylor] went a Gard

September 1. Cept fort ye fornoon Garded ye afternoon

September 2. Went a scout to Hawkses

September 3. Cam from Hawkses Doun to Talors fort

September 4. Cam to morsons fort

September 5. Saboth Day Cept fort mr mc Donel was gon to Pellam [Pelham, Massachusetts]

September 6. Cept fort

September 7. went to ye south fort

September 8. went to Derfield

September 9. stad at Derfield Cpt Mc Lieen and Cpt Pick went out of Derfield with thar men to go to ye Camp

September 10. had ye nus of ye fort Willams [Fort William Henry] ye Caring Plac [Carrying Place] being blon up I cam from Derfield to Colrain

September 11. Cept fort

September 12. Saboth Day Cept fort

September 13. Cept fort

September 14. Cept fort

September 15. Cept fort

Septmeber 16. went a Ranging in ye fournoon Cept fort ye afternoon

September 17. Cept fort

September 18. Went to Luckes [Lucas] fort

September 19. Saboth Day Cept fort

September 20. Cept fort

September 21. Ranged ye woods

September 22. Range ye woods

September 24. went to Derfield Stad at Derfield til ye 30

September 30. ten Came to Colrain

October 1. Cept fort

October 2. Cept fort

October 3. Saboth Day went to meten

October 4. Cept fort

October 5. went to Derfield

October 6. stad at Derfield and ye 7

October 7. our men that ware Imprest went to Hatfield in order to go to ye army

October 8. I cam to Colrain

October 9. Cept fort

October 10. Saboth Day Stad at home

October 11. went out in to ye woods a hnting

October 12. Capt fort

October 13. went to Derfield Egain

October 14. went to Hatfield

October 15. Came to Derfield

October 16. Cam to Colrain

October 17. was Sabbath Day Cept fort

October 18. Cept fort

October 19. Cept fort

October 20. Cept fort

October 21. we went to Derfield in order to get Reddy to go to messer ye Distance from ye Grat river [Great River; that is, the Connecticut] to other Crik [Otter Creek]

October 22. Stad at Derfield til ye 26

October 27. to hindel [Hinsdale]

October 28. foul wether ye fornon ye afternoon went to N 2 [Fort No. 2]

October 29. went to N 4 [Fort No. 4]

October 30. set out ———— 9 mils up yᵉ River

November 4. Returned to N 4.

November 5. Cam to majr Bellesses [Major Bellows]

November 6. Cam to hindels [Hinsdale]

November 7. to Northfield

November 8. to Derfield

November 9. stad at Derfield

November 10. went to Hatfield and Hampton [Northampton]

November 11. stad at Northamton

November 12. Cam to Derfield

November 13. Cam to Colrain

November 14. Saboth Day

November 15. Cept fort

November 16. storny day

November 17. went a hunting

November 18. work at my seller

November 19. work at my house

November 20. a gitting timber

November 21. Saboth Day Cept fort

November 22. workws at gitting timber for my house

November 23. Cept fort

November 24. went to Derfield

November 27. went to hatfield

November 28. Saboth Day

November 29. stad at Derfield

November 30. setout for Colran Came to Grenfield

December 1. Cam to Colran

December 2. Cept fort

December 3. went to Luckes fort to settle ye Bilten [billeting] a Count Lay ther

December 4. Cam to Cpt morisson

December 5. Saboth Day went to meting

December 6. went to Cherlymont setle ye Billeting with Taylor

December 7. went to Hawkses and settle with ye Hawkses and Rices

December 8. Cam to Taylors

December 9. Cam to Colrain and Dun out my a Counts

December 10. went to Derfield

December 11. settled ye Billting a Count with majr Willams [Elijah Williams]

December 12. Saboth Da went to meting stormy wether Clerd up in ye night

December 13. Plesent wether I set our focks a Picking up appels to mack sider

December 14. mad 5 barrels of sider

December 15. Cam to Colran

December 16. went to Deck Cohrens wedden saw him marred to widow jenna had a jolly weddan[4]

December 17. stormy Day of snoo

December 18. Cept fort

December 19. Saboth Day

December 20. a tedas Day of snow and wind

December 21. Cept fort

December 22. Cept fort

December 23. Cept fort

December 24. went to Derfield

December 25. had orders to stay till wensday for Cor Willams stad at Deerfield till Jenuary ye 3

January 3. then Cam to Colrain to Luckes fort

January 4. Cam to Capt mors fort

January 5. medded snoshus

January 6. Cept fort

January 7. Cept fort

January 8. stomy Day

January 9. Saboth Day stormy Da stad at homand Cept fort

January 10. Cept fort

January 11. went to ye south fort

January 12. Cept fort

January 15. Went to Derfield

January 16. Saboth Day went to metan at Deerfield

January 17. had orders to Dismis ye sigers at Norfield and Greenfield and at Each fort in ye line forts I went to Northfield and Greenfield I Cam ye sam Day to Colrain and Dismist ye sogers at ye south fort

January 18. I went to ye other forts and Dismist ye Rest and Don a list if ye men and went to Derfield stad at Derfield till 21

January 21. then set out Cam to Greenfield it was a reniwl Day

January 22. Cam to Colrain

January 23. Saboth Day Cept fort

January 24. Q Cept fort at Capt morsons

January 25. went to widen at Mc Crilles [John McCrellis] when Dc Luckes [Andrew Lucas] was marred lay at Dc Geas

January 26. went to wat on the groom and went to ye grooms and tuck a Dinner and rturned to morsons

January 27. went a scout to Taylors

January 28. went to Hawkes

January 29. Cam to Talylors

January 30. Cam to Cpt morsons Sabboth Day stormy of rain

January 31. stormy I Cept fort

February 1. Cept fort

February 2. Snowey Day and Hawl of a very stormy Day Cept fort at night had ye nues of a mischief Don on Rogers men [Rogers's Rangers] Ner ye narrows 20 men ware missing Capt spickman is one and 2 Hugh morson and William morris and Jearry Henrey

February 3. Cept fort

February 4. went to Deirfield

February 5. stad at Dearfield til ye 8

February 8. and then set out for Colrain ye lay at En Stuerds

February 9. Cam to Cpt morsons

February 10. Rany Day I help to Dres 4 hogs

February 11. Cept fort

February 12. Got Wood

February 13. Sabbath Day Cept fort

February 14. Cept fort

February 15. Cept fort and mended ye snoshus

February 16. Cept fort

February 17. Reiny Day Cept fort

February 18, 19. Rany days Cept fort

February 20. Saboth Day Cept fort

February 21. went a scout to Taylors

February 22. Cam to Cpt morsons

February 23. Cept fort

February 25. I went to Deefield stad at Derfield till ye 1 0 march

March 1. then Cam to Colran

March 2. Cept fort

March 3, 4. went a Diging up trofs in order to shuger

March 5. Cept fort

March 6. Sabath Day Cept fort

March 7. went a shugering

March 8. went to Derfield

March 9. stad at Derfield

March 10. went to Hatfield and Cam Back to Deerfield

March 11. Cam to Colran

March 12. Cept fort

March 13. Sabath Day went to meten

March 14. went to Taylors

March 15. went to Hawkses

March 16. Back to Taylors

March 17. went to Derfield

March 18. sta at Derfield ye 1 gard

March 20. stad at Derfield

March 21. went to Hatfield

March 22. Cam back to Derfield ye stormy of snow

March 23. snow Day

March 24. Cam to Colrain

March 25. Cept fort

March 26. Cept fort foul wether

March 27. Sabouth Day Cept fort

March 28. went a sugeren

March 29. a shugern

March 30. foul wethe ran and snoo

March 31. went a shugern

April 1. went a shugern

April 2. Cept fort wentto ye fot of ye montten and mesyerd ye Depth of the snoo foor fet and 8 inches as Jacob Abbet and Peter Kerred can a test

April 3. went a giting Plank

April 4. snoey Day

April 5. Cept fort

April 6. Rany and Hal Cept fort

April 8. Cept fort

April 9. went to Derfield stad at Derfield til ye 13 April

April 13. Cam to Colran

April 14. went a Gitting Plank

April 15. Cept fort

April 17. Saboth Day went to meten

April 18. went to Grenfield mad fenc

April 19. mad fence at ammos alen [Amos Allen] y^e for non ye afternoon in listed solgrs for ye front ters and stad at Derfield ainlis and stacionin 14 for Norfield 14 for Greenfield 14 for Colran for Fooltown 4 for Cherlymont 3 for hunts tound [Huntstown]

May 13. went to hunts tound to settle ye plac Whar the foort shod Be

May 17. Cam to Colran

May 18. Gave ye sogers orders and Plact them 6 at Luckes 6 at ye south fort 6 at rev Mc Donels and Cam to Cptn morssons

May 19. Cept fort

May 20. Cept fort

May 21. Went to Luck [Lucas] fort and mc mr donels

May 22. Saboth Day Cept fort

May 23. [?] ye befor Went to Pellam loged ther

May 24. went to Hakses and Rices

May 25, 26. Cam to Capt morissons

May 27. Cept fort

May 28. Cept fort

May 29. Saboth Day went to meten Cept fort

May 30. Cept fort

May 31. Cept fort in ye fornon and in ye afternoon had too men Com from Derfield Which had Ben after ye Dockter to go to Wellon Was wond

June 1. I toock 8 men and went to Taylors 3 went from ther I hired Dc Morrison to go with us When we got thear found Whellon not Badly wnoded

June 2. setout and Came to Derfield With a gard of 12 men

June 3. stad at Derfield

June 4. stad at Derfield

June 5. had nus of Inggons and mar Cilled I ordered a scout of 13 to go to Pellam whar my mar was cilled and to Derfield River and mack a thorer serch.

June 6. ye scout went I stad at Derfield

June 7. set out and Cam to Colrain

June 8. ye scout Cam in Gave an Count of tracks of a small Party of ingens ner Pellam fort

June 9. Cept fort nothing Remarckedl

June 10. and Cept fort nothing Remarckedl

June 11. Cept fort

June 12. Sabath Day mr mc Donel was gone to Pellam

June 13. went a scout to Taylors

June 14. Cam to Colrain

June 15. Cept fort

June 16. Cept fort

June 17. Cept fort

June 18. went to Derfield sad at Derfield till ye 23 in that time went to Hatfield once on Cornels orders

June 24. Cept fort

June 25. Cept fort

June 26. Sabth Day Cept fort

June 27. went a scout to foultound [Fall Town] Lay at Sheldons foort

June 28. went to Northdield Lay thar

June 29. Cam to Borcks foert Lay thar

June 30. Cam to Colrain

July 1. Cept fort

NOTES

1. The typescript of the John Hawks journal is owned by the Greenfield Historical Society, Greenfield, Massachusetts. The original is in a Vermont private collection.
2. Hawks 1911:vii.

3. For an account of the forts under Hawks's command and a general history of Colrain during the French and Indian Wars, see Patrie 1974:23–59.
4. Deacon Cochran's first wife had died in childbirth on 26 July. Speedy remarriage was the norm for both widows and widowers, as long as they were not too old in years.

Bibliography

Adams, James Truslow. 1970. Provincial society, 1690–1763. In *Class and Society in Early America*, edited by Gary B. Nash, 27–48. Englewood Cliffs, N.J.: Prentice-Hall.

Aiken, John A. 1912. The Mohawk Trail. *History and Proceedings, Pocumtuck Valley Memorial Association* 5:33–35.

Anderson, Fred. 1984. *A People's Army. Massachusetts Soldiers and Society in the Seven Years' War*. Chapel Hill: University of North Carolina Press.

———. 2000. *Crucible of War: The Seven Years' War and the Fate of Empire in British North America, 1754–1766*. New York: Knopf.

Atkinson, D. R. 1972. A brief guide for the identification of Dutch clay tobacco pipes found in England. *Post-Medieval Archaeology* 6:175–82.

Bailyn, Bernard. 1974. *The Ordeal of Thomas Hutchinson*. Cambridge, Mass.: Belknap Press of Harvard University Press.

Baugher, Sherene, and Robert W. Venables. 1987. Ceramics as indicators of class and status in eighteenth-century New York. In *Socio-Economic Status and Consumer Choices in Historical Archaeology*, edited by Suzanne Spencer Wood, 31–53. New York: Plenum.

Bent, Arthur Cleveland. 1932. *Life Histories of North American Gallinaceous Birds*. New York: Dover Publications.

———. 1961. *Life Histories of North American Birds of Prey*. Part 2. New York: Dover Publications.

Bergstrom, E. Alexander. 1939. English game laws and colonial food shortages. *New England Quarterly* 12:681–90.

Bidwell, Percy Wells, and John I. Falconer. 1925. *History of Agriculture in the Northern United States, 1620–1860*. Washington, D.C.: Carnegie Institution of Washington.

Blades, Brooke S. N.d. Cultural behavior and material culture in eighteenth-century Deerfield, Massachusetts. Unpublished December 1976.

Bowen, Joanne. 1975. Colonial New England foodways: The Mott Farm. Master's thesis, Brown University.

Breen, T. H. 2004. *The Marketplace of Revolution: How Consumer Politics Shaped American Independence*. Oxford: Oxford University Press.

Bridenbaugh, Carl. 1974. *Fat Mutton and Liberty of Conscience*. Providence: Brown University Press.

Brown, Margaret Kimball. 1971. Glass from Fort Michilimackinac: A classification for eighteenth-century glass. *Michigan Archaeologist* 17, nos. 3–4.

Brown, Percy W. 1921. *History of Rowe, Massachusetts*. Boston: privately printed.

———. 1960. *History of Rowe, Massachusetts*, 3rd edition. Rowe, Mass.: Town of Rowe.

Bump, Gardiner, et al. 1974. *The Ruffed Grouse*. Buffalo, N.Y.: Holling Press.

Carson, Cary. 1978. Doing history with material culture. In *Material Culture and the Study of American Life*, edited by Ian Quimby, 41–74. New York: Norton.

Chaplin, Raymond E. 1971. *The Study of Animal Bones from Archaeological Sites*. New York: Seminar Press.

Chappell, Edward. 1973. A study of horseshoes in the Department of Archaeology, Colonial Williamsburg. In *Five Artifact Studies*, edited by Ivor Noël Hume. Williamsburg, Va.: Colonial Williamsburg Foundation.

Chet, Guy. 2003. *Conquering the American Wilderness: The Triumph of European Warfare in the Colonial Northeast*. Amherst: University of Massachusetts Press.

Cleland, Charles. 1970. *Comparison of the Faunal Remains from French and British Refuse Pits at Ft. Michilimackinac: A Study in Changing Subsistence Patterns*. Canadian Historic Sites, Occasional Papers in Archaeology and History, no. 3.

Coe, Michael D. 1977. The Line of Forts: Archeology of the mid-eighteenth century on the Massachusetts frontier. In *New England Historical Archeology*, edited by Peter Benes, 44–55. Boston: Boston University, The Dublin Seminar for New England Folklife.

Coe, Michael D., and Sophie D. Coe. 1984. Mid-eighteenth century food and drink on the Massachusetts frontier. In *Foodways in the Northeast*, edited by Peter Benes and Jane Montague Benes, 39–46. Boston: Boston University, The Dublin Seminar for New England Folklife.

Cooke, Edward S. N.d. Pewter and ceramics in Deerfield, Massachusetts. Unpublished paper for Anthropology 47-2a [course], Yale University, 1976.

Costello, David L. 1975. *The Mohawk Trail, Showing Old Roads and Other Points of Interest*. Greenfield, Mass.: privately printed.

Cruikshank, C. G. 1966. *Elizabeth's Army*. 2nd ed. Oxford: Clarendon Press.

De Forest, Louis Effingham. 1926. *The Journals and Papers of Seth Pomeroy, Sometime General in the Colonial Service*. New Haven, Conn.: Tuttle, Morehouse & Taylor.

Deetz, James. 1972. Archaeology as a social science. In *Contemporary Archaeology*, edited by Mark P. Leone, 108–17. Carbondale: Southern Illinois University Press.

———. 1973. Ceramics from Plymouth, 1620–1835: the archaeological evidence. In *Ceramics in America*, edited by Ian M. G. Quimby, 15–74. Charlottesville, Va.: Henry Francis du Pont Winterthur Museum.

Dexter, Franklin Bowditch. 1885. *Biographical Sketches of the Graduates of Yale College with Annals of the College History* 1 (October 1701–May 1745). New York: Henry Holt and Company.

Dow, George Francis. 1927. *The Arts and Crafts in New England, 1704–1775*. Topsfield, Mass.: Wayside Press.

Feister, Lois M., and Paul R. Huey. 1985. Archaeological testing at Fort Gage, a Provincial redoubt of 1758 at Lake George, New York. *Bulletin and Journal of Archaeology for New York* 90:40–59.

Fisher, Charles L., ed. 2004. *"The Most Advantageous Situation in the Highlands": An Archaeological Study of Fort Montgomery State Historic Site*. Albany: New York State Museum.

Fletcher, Stevenson W. 1950. *Pennsylvania Agriculture and Country Life, 1640–1840*. Harrisburg, Pa.: Historical and Museum Commission.

Fry, Bruce W. 1984. *"An Appearance of Strength": The Fortifications of Louisbourg.* 2 vols. Ottawa: Parks Canada.

Gardiner, R. H. 1938. *Mrs. Gardiner's Receipts from 1763.* Hallowell, Maine: White & Horne.

Gipson, Lawrence Henry. 1967. *The British Isles and the American Colonies: The Northern Plantations, 1748–1754.* New York: Knopf.

Grimm, Jacob L. 1970. *Archaeological Investigation of Fort Ligonier, 1960–1965.* Pittsburgh, Pa.: Carnegie Museum.

Grubb, F. W. 1990. Growth of literacy in colonial America: Longitudinal patterns, economic models, and the direction of future research. *Social Science History* 14, no. 4:451–82.

Haefeli, Evan, and Kevin Sweeney. 2003. *Captors and Captives: The 1704 French and Indian raid on Deerfield.* Amherst: University of Massachusetts Press.

Hall, E. Raymond, and Keith R. Kelson. 1959. *The Mammals of North America.* 2 vols. New York: Ronald Press.

Hamilton, T. M., and K. O. Emery. 1988. *Eighteenth-Century Gunflints from Fort Michilimackinac and Other Colonial Sites.* Mackinac Island, Mich.: Mackinac Island State Park Commission.

Hamilton, T. M., and Bruce W. Fry. 1975. A survey of Louisbourg gunflints. *Occasional Papers in Archaeology and History* 12:101–28. Ottawa, Canada.

Hanson, Lee. 1969. Kaolin pipestems—boring in on a fallacy. *Historical Site Archaeology* 4:2–15.

Hatch, Norman L., Jr., and Joseph H. Hartshorn. 1968. *Geologic Map of the Heath Quadrangle, Massachusetts and Vermont.* Washington, D.C.: U.S. Geological Survey.

Hawks, John. 1911. *Orderly Book and Journal of Major John Hawks on the Ticonderoga–Crown Point Campaign, under General Jeffrey Amherst, 1759–1760.* New York: Society of Colonial Wars.

Hazzen, Richard. 1879. The boundary line of New Hampshire and Massachusetts. Journal of Richard Hazzen, surveyor, 1741. In *Hazen Family. Four American Generations*, by Richard Allen Hazen. Boston: n.p.

Healy, Allan. 1965. *Charlemont, Massachusetts: Frontier Village and Hill Town.* Charlemont, Mass.: Town of Charlemont.

Henretta, James A. 1973. *The Evolution of American Society, 1700–1815.* Lexington, Mass.: Heath.

Hoyt, Epaphras. 1824. *Antiquarian Researches.* Greenfield, Mass.: A. Phelps.

Hudson, J. Paul. 1962. English glass wine bottles of the 17th and 18th centuries. *Southeastern Archaeological Conference Newsletter* 9, no. 1:6–9.

Jackson, R. G., and R. H. Price. 1974. *Bristol Clay Pipes. A study of Their Marks.* Bristol, U.K.: Bristol City Museum.

James, Alfred Proctor, and Charles Morse Stotz. 1958. *Drums in the Forest: Decision at the Forks, Defense in the Wilderness.* Pittsburgh: Historical Society of Western Pennsylvania.

Jorgensen, Neil. 1971. *A Guide to New England's Landscape.* Barre, Mass.: Barre Publishers.

Kaplan, Reid W., and Michael D. Coe. 1976. Pictures of the past: Artifact density and computer graphics. *Historical Archaeology* 10:54–67.

Kendrick, Fannie S. S. 1937. *History of Buckland, 1779–1935*. Rutland, Vt.: Tuttle Publishing.

Kenmotsu, Nancy. 1990. Gunflints: A study. *Historical Archaeology* 24, no. 2:92–124.

Lindsay, Merrill. 1972. *The Kentucky Rifle*. New York: Arma Press.

Malone, Patrick. *Indians and English Military Systems in New England in the 17th Century*. Ph.D. diss., Brown University.

Mankowitz, Wolf, and Reginald G. Haggar. 1957. *The Concise Encyclopedia of English Pottery and Porcelain*. New York: Praeger.

———. 1968. *The Concise Encylopedia of English Pottery and Porcelain*. London: André Deutsch.

Mauncy, Albert C. 1962. *The Fort at Frederica*. Florida State University Notes in Anthropology, no. 5. Tallahassee, Fla.

Maxwell, Moreau S., and Lewis R. Binford. 1961. *Excavation at Fort Michilimackinac, Mackinac Island, Michigan*. East Lansing: Michigan State University.

McClellan, Bruce. 1954. Two shepherds contending. *New England Quarterly* 27, no. 4:455–71.

McDermott, Gerald R. 1999. Jonathan Edwards and American Indians: The Devil sucks their blood. *New England Quarterly* 72, no. 4:539–57.

McManis, Douglas R. 1975. *Colonial New England: A Historical Geography*. New York: Oxford University Press.

Melvoin, Richard I. 1989. *New England Outpost: War and Society in Colonial Deerfield*. New York: Norton.

Millar, David R. 1967. *The Militia, the Army, and Independency in Colonial Massachusetts*. Ann Arbor: University Microfilms.

Miller, J. Jefferson, and Lyle M. Stone. 1970. *Eighteenth-Century Ceramics from Fort Michilimackinac: A Study in Historical Archaeology*. Washington, D.C.: Smithsonian Institution Press.

Moorhouse, Stephen A. 1971. Finds from Basing House, Hampshire (c. 1540–1645), Part Two. *Post-Medieval Archaeology* 5:35–70.

Mott, John R., and Donald C. Fuller. 1967. *Soil Survey of Franklin County, Massachusetts*. Washington, D.C.: Natural Resources Conservation Service (USDA).

Mountford, Arnold R. 1971. *The Illustrated History of Staffordshire Salt-Glazed Stoneware*. London: Barrie & Jenkins.

———. 1973. Staffordshire salt-glazed stoneware. In *Ceramics in America*, edited by Ian M. G. Quimby, 197–215. Charlottesville, Va.: Henry Francis du Pont Winterthur Museum.

Noël Hume, Ivor. 1963. Excavations at Rosewell in Gloucester County, Virginia, 1957–1958. *Contributions from the Museum of History and Technology*, Paper 18. Washington, D.C.: Smithsonian Institution.

———. 1969. *Historical Archaeology*. New York: Knopf.

———. 1970. *A Guide to Artifacts of Colonial America*. New York: Knopf.

Norton, John. 1870. *Narrative of the Capture and Burning of Fort Massachusetts by the French and Indians, in the Time of the War of 1744–1749*. Albany, N.Y.: S. G. Drake.

Olsen, Stanley J. 1964. Food animals of the Continental Army at Valley Forge & Morris Town. *American Antiquity* 29:506–509.

Pargellis, Stanley. 1969. *Military Affairs in North America, 1748–1755*. North Haven, Conn.: Archon Books.

Parkman, Francis. 1892. *A Half-Century of Conflict*. 2 vols. Boston: Little, Brown.

Parmalee, Paul. 1960. Vertebrate remains from Loudon. *Tennessee Archaeological Society* 6:26–29.

Patrie, Lois McClellan. 1974. *A History of Colrain, Massachusetts*. Privately printed.

Perry, Arthur Latham. 1885. Address by Prof. A. L. Perry of Williams College. In *Centennial Anniversary of the Town of Heath, Mass.*, edited by Edward P. Guild. Boston: Published for the Committee.

———. 1904. *Origins in Williamstown: A History*. 3rd ed. Published by the author.

Peterson, Harold L. 1956. *Arms and Armor in Colonial America*. New York: Bramhall.

———. 1968. *The Book of the Continental Soldier*. Harrisburg, Pa.: Stackpole Books.

Phillips, Hugh. 1964. *Mid-Georgian London: A Topographical and Social Survey of Central and Western London about 1750*. London: Collins.

Phillips, Paul C. 1961. *The Fur Trade*. 2 vols. Norman: University of Oklahoma Press.

Plumb, J. H. 1950. *England in the Eighteenth Century*. Harmondsworth, U.K.: Penguin Books.

Purvis, Thomas L. 1999. *Colonial America to 1763*. New York: Facts on File.

Rundell, Maria E. K. 1808. *New System of Domestic Cookery Formed upon Principles of Economy*. Exeter, U.K.: Norris & Sawyer.

Schorger, A. W. 1955. *The Passenger Pigeon*. Madison: University of Wisconsin Press.

Schutz, John A. 1961. *William Shirley*. Chapel Hill: University of North Carolina Press.

Sheldon, George. 1893. Negro slavery in Old Deerfield. *New England Magazine*, n.s., 8:49–60.

———. 1904. The Pocumtuck Confederacy. *Papers and Proceeedings of the Pocumtuck Valley Historical Society, 1882–1903*, 2:78–99.

———. 1972. *A History of Deerfield, Massachusetts*. 2 vols., facsimile ed. Somersworth, N.H.: New Hampshire Publishing.

Silver, Helenette. 1957. *A History of New Hampshire Game and Furbearers*. New Hampshire Fish and Game Department, Survey Report No. 6.

Silver, I. A. 1970. The aging of domestic animals. In *Science in Archaeology*, edited by Don Brothwell and Eric Higgs. New York: Praeger.

Sloane, Eric. 1974. *A Museum of Early American Tools*. New York: Ballantine Books.

Snowman, A. Kenneth. 1990. *Eighteenth-Century Gold Boxes of Europe*. Woodbridge, U.K.: Antique Collectors' Club.

South, Stanley. 1962. The ceramic types at Brunswick Town, North Carolina. *Southeastern Archaeological Conference Newsletter* 9, 1:1–15.

———. 1964. Analysis of the buttons from Brunswick Town and Fort Fisher. *Florida Anthropologist* 17, no. 2:113–33.

Starbuck, David R. 1997. Military hospitals on the frontier of colonial America. *Expedition* 39, no. 1:45.

———. 1999. *The Great Warpath: British Military Sites from Albany to Crown Point*. Hanover, N.H.: University Press of New England.

———. 2004. *Rangers and Redcoats on the Hudson: Exploring the Past on Rogers Island, the Birthplace of the U.S. Army Rangers*. Lebanon, N.H.: University Press of New England.

Stone, Garry Wheeler, J. Glenn Little III, and Stephen Krael. 1973. Ceramics from the John Hicks Site, 1723–1743: The material culture. In *Ceramics in America*, edited by I. M. G. Quimby, 103–39.

Stone, Lyle M. 1974. *Fort Michilimackinac, 1715–1781: An Archaeological Perspective on the Revolutionary Frontier.* Publications of the Museum, Michigan State University, East Lansing, in cooperation with the Mackinac Island State Park Commission, Mackinac Island, Michigan.

Sullivan, Catherine. 1986. *Legacy of the Machault: A Collection of 18th-Century Artifacts.* Ottawa: Parks Canada.

Swedlund, Alan C. 1975. Population growth and settlement pattern in Franklin and Hampshire Counties, Massachusetts, 1650–1850. *American Antiquity* 40, no. 2, part 2:22–33.

Sweeney, Kevin M. 1982. River Gods in the making: The Williamses of western Massachusetts. In *The Bay and the River: 1600–1900*, edited by Peter Benes, 101–116. Boston: Boston University (The Dublin Seminar for New England Folklife, *Annual Proceedings*, 1981).

Tanner, Pearle. 1935. Heath and its families. In *Sesquicentennial Anniversary of the Town of Heath, Massachusetts*, edited by Howard Chandler Robbins, 53–137. Heath, Mass.: Heath Historical Society.

Thompson, Zadock. 1853. *Appendix to the History of Vermont, Natural, Civil and Statistical.* Burlington, Vt.: Stacy & Jameson.

Turnbull, George A., and Anthony G. Herron. 1970. *The Price Guide to English 18th Century Drinking Glasses.* Woodbridge, U.K.: Antique Collectors' Club.

Walker, Iain C. 1971a. An archaeological study of clay pipes from the King's Bastion, Fortress of Louisbourg. *Canadian Historic Sites, Occasional Papers in Archaeology* 2:55–122. Ottawa.

———. 1971b. *The Bristol Clay Tobacco-Pipe Industry.* Bristol, U.K.: City Museum.

———. 1974. Binford, science, and history: The probabilistic variability of explicated epistemology and nomothetic paradigms in historical archaeology. *Conference on Historic Site Archaeology Papers* 7:159–201.

Watkins, Laura W. 1950. *Early New England Potters and Their Wares.* Cambridge, Mass.: Harvard University Press.

Whisker, James Biser. 1997. *The American Colonial Militia: Introduction to the American Colonial Militia.* Vol. 1. Lewiston, N.Y.: Edwin Mellen Press.

White, Theodore. 1953. A method for calculating the dietary percentage of various food animals utilized by aboriginal peoples. *American Antiquity* 18:396–99.

Wildung, Frank H. 1957. *Woodworking Tools at Shelburne Museum.* Shelburne, Vt.: Shelburne Museum.

Williams, John. 1969. *The Redeemed Captive Returning to Zion; or, The Captivity and Deliverance of Rev. John Williams of Deerfield.* New York: Kraus Reprint.

Witthoft, John. 1966. A history of gunflints. *Pennsylvania Archaeologist* 26, nos. 1–2:12–49.

Wood, William. 1967. *Wood's New England Prospect. Printed for the Society, by J. Wilson, 1865.* New York: Burt Franklin.

Woodward, Carl. 1941. *Ploughs and Politics, 1715–1774.* New Brunswick, N.J.: Rutgers University Press.

Wrangham, Richard. 2005. Planet of the apes. *Harper's Magazine* 310:15–19.

Wright, Wyllis E. 1970. *Colonel Ephraim Williams: A Documentary Life*. Pittsfield, Mass.: Berkshire County Historical Society.

Yellen, John. 1974. Cultural patterning in faunal remains, evidence from the !Kung Bushman. Unpublished manuscript.

Zemsky, Robert. 1969. Power, influence, and status: Leadership patterns in the Massachusetts Assembly, 1740–1755. *William and Mary Quarterly*, 3rd series, 4:502–520.

———. 1971. *Merchants, Farmers, and River Gods: An Essay on Eighteenth-Century American Politics*. Boston: Gambit.

Ziegler, Alan C. 1973. *Inference from Prehistoric Faunal Remains*. Modules in Anthropology 43. Boston: Addison-Wesley.

Index

Page references given in *italics* indicate maps, illustrations, or captions.